MW00340532

What the Private Saw *is definitely one of the very best of the many published collections of Civil War letters and diaries. Pvt. O. F. Sweet of the 1st Pennsylvania Light Artillery wrote prolifically to members of his family and kept a diary from 1863 until just after the close of the war. . . .*

Numerous period photographs supplement the account. What the Private Saw *does just that — provide a very clear picture of the Civil War as seen and experienced by a private soldier of the Union.*

—Gene C. Armistead, author
Horse: and Mules in the Civil War

I enjoyed every bit of it. Private Sweet's account of his service in the First Pennsylvania Reserve Light Artillery is another missing puzzle piece back in its proper place.

—August J. Marchetti
Penn. Reserve Volunteer
Corps Historical Society

What the
Private Saw

The Civil War Letters *&* Diaries
of Oney Foster Sweet

1st Pennsylvania Light Artillery
43rd Volunteers (14th Reserves)
Battery F
(Ricketts' Battery)
1861-1865

Edited and annotated by Larry M. Edwards

Wigeon
Publishing
San Diego

Copyright © 2015 by Larry M. Edwards

All rights reserved. No part of this book shall be reproduced or transmitted in any form or by any means, electronic, mechanical, magnetic, photographic including photocopying, recording or by any information storage and retrieval system, without prior written permission of the publisher.

Wigeon Publishing
San Diego, California
www.WigeonPublishing.com

April 9, 2015

ISBN-10: 0989691349
ISBN-13: 978-0-9896913-4-5

Library of Congress Control Number: 2015932623

BIO008000: BIOGRAPHY & AUTOBIOGRAPHY/Military
HIS036050: HISTORY/United States/Civil War Period

Oney F. Sweet letters and diaries used with permission
from great-grandson William J. Ketchum.
Cover images courtesy of William J. Ketchum and Joan Ketchum Reamer.
Back cover images courtesy of Library of Congress.
Cover layout by Tim Brittain.

Printed in the United States of America

The generals did not see what the privates saw.

—Oney Foster Sweet
1st Pennsylvania Light Artillery
43rd Volunteers, Battery F

Contents

Illustrations

Foreword

This material was written by our grandfather, Oney F. Sweet, during his service as an enlisted volunteer in the Union Army. He enlisted on September 4, 1861, when he was nineteen (born December 13, 1841). The earliest diary is for 1863. We do not know whether he kept one for 1861 or 1862, but his letters were more frequent and informative in that period.

The three diaries are small. Each different but all leather bound and from two and one-half inches wide to three or four inches high, with a page for each day. Most entries are in ink and in many instances faded, so some words are illegible (when a key word did not come up with a magnifying glass, I made a guess or used a blank).

Many abbreviations appear throughout and have been as written where possible. However, some military terms, such as the abbreviation for regiment, is quite stylized and not suitable for duplication on a printer. Also there are some interesting spellings and a bit of transition or evaluation from start to finish. For example, "crosst" appears in the diary for over a year before coming out "crossed"; "Sara" and "Sarah" are both used in reference to his sister. The objective has been to reproduce what he wrote as he wrote it.

Nearly every diary entry begins with an observation of the prevailing weather conditions. That was very important, since heat and cold, rain, snow, and humidity dictated the way each day might turn out. The conditions in the field, where most of the entries were written, are difficult to imagine today.

The feeding of thousands of men in the 1860s was, at best, primitive. On some occasions regular hot meals were dished out from a cook tent. But much of the time field rations requiring preparation were issued in bulk for several days' meals. This encouraged soldiers to forage for what they could find to supplement their provisions. It also brought small groups together to prepare their food over open fires.

Even water supplies were limited, so the streams and rivers were used for drinking as well as bathing and washing clothes. Often toilet facilities consisted of a designated area behind a tree! During cold or wet weather the men would make a shelter of stacked logs for walls with lighter limbs supporting tent parts overhead. Two to four men would share these huts when they were not moving camp for a few days. On a march they slept where they stopped, off the line of march, by a tree or shrub out of the mud.

On marches, each man carried his pack containing extra clothing, such as a coat, underwear, socks, food, and personal gear, such as a diary, plus his weapon and ammunition. While a march might cover only five or six miles, some were thirty or more. The roads or trails were unpaved and in wet weather the mud was deep and sometimes very cold.

Yet, with all these hardships, Oney Foster Sweet seems to have greeted most days with a remarkable zeal. He was smaller than most men, weighing about 130 pounds and standing five foot three. He had spunk, a good attitude, was loyal and he was a survivor. That is why we are here!

Credit should be given to Ruth Sweet Carmichael for copying the letters. To Mildred Sweet Johnston Ketchum and Phyllis Atkinson Mieldazies for locating and sending along the additional material. To Welesley "Duke" "Tommy" Atkinson for preserving the diaries and trusting them to me. And to my sister, Mary Virginia Sweet Wagner, for transcribing the tapes from my puzzling, sporadic dictation as I tried to decipher the faded entries.

Now to the letters and diaries. They often seem as interesting for what is *not* said as for what *is* said.

George Olney Sweet (1912-2010)
Grandson of Oney F. Sweet

Introduction

After attending the 25th anniversary of the Battle of Gettysburg in 1888, Oney Foster Sweet wrote:

> *The unwritten part of our war is greater than all that has been written. Two soldiers side by side in a hot place in our battles did not see the same things. The generals did not see what the privates saw.*

He knew whereof he spoke—he had a front-row seat as one of those privates. His personal account promises to be a distinct addition to the many existing volumes on the U.S. Civil War.

Oney F. Sweet, along with tens of thousands of other young men of the time, answered President Abraham Lincoln's Call to Arms and volunteered to join in the War of the Rebellion. Perhaps he gained inspiration from his great-grandfather Amos Sweet, who fought in the American Revolutionary War with a number of Massachusetts regiments and later moved to Pennsylvania.

Oney enlisted as a private in the 1st Pennsylvania Light Artillery, 43rd Volunteers, Battery F, and began service as a cannoneer. His regiment joined the Army of the Potomac to protect the nation's capital, and he fought in most of the major battles in Virginia, Maryland, and Pennsylvania.

His words paint a decidedly human portrait of an often faceless conflagration, leaving one to ponder why such a horror—in which some 620,000 Union and Confederate soldiers sacrificed their lives and millions of others mourned their loss—had to occur in the first place.

He reflects an attitude prevalent on both sides of the line at the onset of hostilities in 1861, when many soldiers believed they would be home for Christmas:

> *I think I shall like a soldier's life first rate.*

A year later, however, following the Battle of Antietam, he revealed a different mindset in a letter to his mother, Caroline Foster Sweet:

*I went over the field after the fight and the dead and wounded
lay so thick you could hardly step. Some had legs, arms, and heads
torn off. Some groaning and breathing their last. . . . I never want
to see such a sight again. . . . I have seen enough of war.*

At the time, he did not know the war would last another two and a
half years, and that he would see more, much more.

Family members transcribed the letters and diaries as the pencil lead
and ink began to fade. Perhaps their efforts, which made this book
possible, will inspire modern-day readers and military personnel to put pen
to paper and write letters—their personal stories—that their descendants
may enjoy the narratives decades or even centuries later.

To provide context for some of the terms and events Oney mentions,
I supplemented his correspondence and diary entries with annotations in
footnotes or sidebars. For instances where I found discrepancies in
historical records and resources, I placed amendments in brackets and
provided explanations in footnotes.

Oney names scores of people—those with whom he served and
corresponded. Frequent correspondents included friends as well as his
mother, sister Sarah, brother William ("Willie"), and Uncle Joseph Foster,
the brother of Oney's mother. Some names appear dozens of times, so I
limited the index to the first mention, unless the name is associated with an
event of some kind.

I have included explanatory notes on many of these people; however,
I could not identify them all. If readers have more information, or can
identify those individuals for whom I could not find reliable information,
please let me know. If I inadvertently made an error in identification, I
apologize in advance. I may be contacted at: info@whattheprivatesaw.com.

I hope you enjoy reading Oney F. Sweet's words as much as I have.

Larry M. Edwards, editor

Larry M. Edwards is an award-winning author, editor, and investigative
journalist—and a historical reenactor. He lives in San Diego, California.

Letters, 1861

The boys are all sitting around the room writing letters on chairs and I am writing on the window sill.

—Oney F. Sweet

Harrisburgh, Sept. 12 [1861]

Dear Mother:

We are all in here safe and sound in a big room and we have all got to sleep on the hard floor tonight in a hotel. While we stay here we will get two meals a day. We don't know how long we shall stay here, perhaps two or three days. We are going to get our equipment tomorrow.

We stayed Scranton last night at Geo Perigas's, he keeps a hotel there. We arrived here about 1 o'clock today, and this afternoon went up to Camp Curtin this afternoon and saw about five thousand soldiers there. There is 14 of us altogether. About a hundred other soldiers came down in the [train] cars today with us. True [Case] was here just now; he says we will leave day after tomorrow for Washington.*

The boys are all sitting around the room writing letters on chairs and I am writing on the window sill. Harrisburgh is a nice place. Today has been quite pleasant. I have enjoyed myself first rate so far.

I will write tomorrow perhaps. True Case just told me I could sleep with him tonight so I will not have to lay on the hard floor. We did not have any dinner today only cake and cheese.

I saw Henry Tarbox this morning and Simon Reynolds.

I will write again soon. Give my love to all.

Oney F. Sweet.

---

* Lt. Truman L. Case, appears to have been a close friend, if not a relative, of Oney F. Sweet. He served as a recruiting officer as well as with the battery. References to his being away on "business" may be indicative of his continued involvement in recruiting, as the army needed a constant supply of men to replace those lost to death, severe wounds, disease, and desertion. Case enlisted on July 8, 1861, and was discharged on February 4, 1863, following prolonged illness.

Harrisburgh, Sept. 25, 1861

Dear Mother:

I have written two letters to you and have not heard from home since I left. I like it here first rate. We live tip top, have peaches and cream and peach pie, etc. etc. Since I have been here we have equipped and sent on to Washington 56 men. I may stay here two or three weeks before I go on to Washington.*

We arrested a deserter here last week and he broke away from the guards and run and we searched half of one night for him and could not find him, but we found him last Sunday afternoon hid in a house in a bed and we had to draw our revolvers on him to make him come. It took 6 men to hold him. I watched him one night with a revolver in my hand kept him safe till morning when we had him tied and sent on to Washington. He was a powerful man. He came near shooting one of the men that helped catch him. He was an officer.

I have no expenses except my washing. I shall send all of my clothes home that I don't want when I leave here. Write me all the news. We have had pretty warm weather but it is cooler now.

I expect there will be some fighting near Washington soon and I want to be down there when they fight.

I have written a letter to Gill and one to Gus and have not had any answer. Do not worry about me, I will take care of myself. I think I shall like a soldier's life first rate.

I saw a horse sold here for three dollars which was sound every way, but he was grey and the government rejected him.

Give my love to all

Your ever true and most affectionate

Son O. F. Sweet

---

* Sweet served at the recruiting center in Harrisburg before joining his unit in Virginia.

Casualties of War

*There is only two or three cases of small pox in camp now.
. . . I was vaccinated when I lived in Newark. . . . I am more
afraid of disease than the bullet. It is more fatal in this army.*
—Oney F. Sweet

The specific number of deaths during the U.S. Civil War varies, depending on who does the counting, but historians agree that more casualties (dead, wounded, missing in action) resulted from disease than combat. Although the death toll for the war has been estimated at 620,000—more than all other U.S. wars combined—for every three soldiers killed in battle, five more died of disease.

The 16th New Hampshire Infantry had no dead or wounded on the battlefield in the first nine months of service, but it lost 221 men from disease. The 8th New Hampshire Infantry had 102 killed in battle while 258 succumbed to disease. On the Confederate side, almost one third of the 15th Alabama regiment died before it ever saw combat due to a measles outbreak. (Lord, 1960; LaFantasie, 2006)

Besides measles, other maladies also afflicted combatants, including cholera, typhoid fever, mumps, dysentery, small pox, and malaria.

The modern conception of casualties includes those who have been psychologically damaged by warfare. This distinction did not exist during the Civil War. Soldiers suffering from what would be classified today as post-traumatic stress disorder (PTSD) went uncared for. (Civil War Trust)

Some numbers:
- Average death rate for all Civil War soldiers   1 in 5
- Ratio of Confederate deaths to Union deaths   3 to 1
- Battle w/highest number of casualties: Gettysburg   23,049
- Battles w/highest % of casualties: Wilderness/Spotsylvania   29%
- Percentage of casualties, Civil War vs. WWI and WWII   29/7/6%
- Battle victories for the Union vs. the Confederacy   34/29
- Estimated number of horses killed at Gettysburg   3,000-5,000

(Lord, 1960; Armistead, 2013)

Harrisburgh, Dec. 4th, 1861

Dear Mother, Sister and Brother and all the rest of Gibson folks,

I received your letter about 5 minutes ago. I had a letter from Uncle Joseph yesterday and I answered it. Did not write only a few lines and nothing of any importance. Case has gone to Washington today.

It is quite warm here today. We have had some quite cold days. There is only two or three cases of small pox in camp now and they are getting better, and there is not so much sickness now. When it is wet weather they take cold. I was vaccinated when I lived in Newark. There is 5 or 6 regiments here now in camp.

Leuit [Lieutenant] Case is here superintending the recruiting, the same as he has been doing for the past 3 months and the prospect is he will be here for some time but he belongs to the regiment and is subject to the Col. orders and I suppose of course there is all kind of stories about him. But he is not to blame because he is lucky and smart enough to have a bed instead of the ground. If people would mind their own business and not trouble themselves with other's business they would get along better. Ask Guss Roper what we are doing and he will tell you.* Tell people not to worry about True Case's business.

There is not much news to write.

I expect to get my money soon. $13 a month is all the soldiers get.

Write soon all of you and let me know all the news and oblige.

O. F. Sweet

---

* Augustus J. Roper, corporal, promoted to sergeant, 141st Regiment, Pennsylvania Infantry, born July 20, 1839, Gibson, Pennsylvania.

In our deatachment there is fourteen. Seargt Stradford, he rides on a horse, in an action he dismounts and looks to the men and sees that the men do their right duty. Corporal Smith L. French, he is gunner and sights the gun. No. 1 David Maynard, he rams the loads. No. 2 Eastman he is from Jackson, he puts the charge in the gun. No. 3 Patrick Curry he holds his thumb over the vent while loading. No. 4 is Maynard Gates, he used to work for George Perry, at command "ready" he puts a primer in the vent, and at the command "fire" he pulls the string and off she goes. No. 5 is Henry Tiffany, he carrys ammunition to No. 2. No. 6 is Simon Flory, he takes the ammunition out of the chest and prepares it ready for firing. No. 7 Oney F. I carry the ammunition from No. 6 to No. 5. We can fire very fast. We fire mostly shells. If a person stands solid on his feet when the gun goes off it will almost stun him, but if he stands on his toes it will not.

We have six horses on the gun and six horses on the caisson. Fred Mosel drives the lead team on the gun. The lead horses when we are firing stand 15 yards from the gun right behind it. The drivers ride the near horse and lead the off one. Velasco Lake, he is from Jackson, he rides the middle team. Jo Strong he rides the wheel team. Forrest Simpson rides the lead team on the caisson, his horses are directly behind the other ones. Oscar G. Larrabee drives the middle team and J. Watts drives the wheel team.

We have a caisson for carrying ammunition to every gun. When I joined the Battery Oscar Larrabee was sgt. on our gun, then he was corporal and now he drives team. Alf. Larrabee he is a private now. He used to be sgt.

Sgt. Scott is quartermaster seargt. He has charge of the commissary department. He draws the rations and deals them out. We have a saddler, two blacksmiths, a carpenter, and a horse doctor. The horses have to be drilled as well as the men. I have drilled at every post so that I can act anywhere I am needed.

Our horses have just gone down to water. They water them in Bull Run.

You can not say but what this is a long letter enough and I want a long one from you and Sarah.

If a person stands solid on his feet when the gun goes off it will almost stun him, but if he stands on his toes it will not.

We have six horses on the gun and six horses on the caisson. . . . The horses have to be drilled as well as the men.

—Oney F. Sweet

The gun crew serving with Oney F. Sweet:

"Seargt Stradford" possibly Richard S. Stratford, although the military record lists him as mustering in and out as a private.

Smith L. French, corporal, mustered in July 8, 1861; promoted to sergeant; mustered out with Battery, June 10, 1865.

David P. Manard, private, mustered in September 11, 1861; discharged on Surgeon's Certificate, February 26, 1862.

Patrick Curry, private, mustered in July 8, 1861, mustered out with battery, June 10, 1865.

Eli F. Eastman, private, transferred to Battery G, March 26, 1864.

Maynard Gates, private, mustered in July 8, 1861; transferred to Battery G, March 26, 1864.

Henry Tiffany, private, mustered in December 11, 1861; died while at home on furlough, January 16, 1864.

Simon Floray, private, mustered in July 8, 1861; mustered out August 31, 1864, expiration of term.

Frederick Mosil, private, mustered in July 8, 1861, mustered out with battery, June 10, 1865.

Velasco Lake, private, mustered in July 8, 1861; mustered out with battery, June 10, 1865.

Joseph Strong, private, mustered in July 8, 1861; mustered out with battery, June 10, 1865.

Forrest Simpson, private, mustered in July 8, 1861; mustered out with battery, June 10, 1865.

Oscar G. Larabee, private, mustered in July 8, 1861; prisoner at Gettysburg; mustered out with battery, June 10, 1865.

Alfred W. Larabee, private, mustered in July 8, 1861; discharged on Surgeon's Certificate, March 5, 1863.

"Sgt. Scott" possibly Raymond T. Scott, although the military record lists him as a private, mustered out July 16, 1864, expiration of term.

Shot, Shell & Canister
Light Artillery of the Civil War

The standard Civil War-era light (or field) artillery battery was commanded by a captain and consisted of six cannons: four guns and two howitzers. Howitzers had shorter barrels than guns because they were designed to shoot projectiles in a higher trajectory over a shorter distance, such as when targeting enemy personnel and equipment behind breastworks or fortifications.

A battery had three sections, each with two cannons and commanded by a lieutenant. Each cannon—or artillery piece, as it was called—required twelve men and twelve horses to mobilize and operate. It took about 100 soldiers to engage a full battery. A battery's makeup could change according to circumstance, depending on casualties—men and horses—as well as weapons out of action or captured.

A field artillery piece, depending on the model, could fire a projectile one-half mile to two and a half miles. It required six to eight men to fire it, and four more men to handle the equipment and the teams of horses needed to pull the cannon, caisson, and limber into battle.

A limber was a two-wheeled carriage that held an ammunition chest

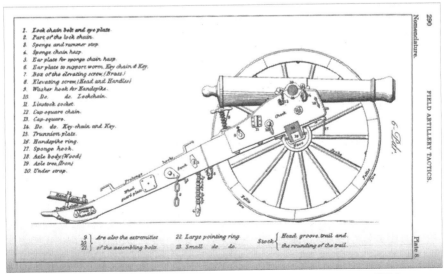

Diagram from the U.S. Army *Instruction for Field Artillery* manual, 1860.

Union army limber and cannon. (Library of Congress)

and had either a cannon or caisson attached to it; a six-horse team pulled the combined unit, which could weigh nearly two tons. When the gun crew set up a cannon for use, they "unlimbered" it; i.e., they disconnected it from the limber.

A caisson was a two-wheeled carriage that hauled ammunition, and when fully loaded it, too, could weigh nearly two tons. When attached to a limber, the caisson looked like a four-wheeled wagon, but it had greater maneuverability than a wagon because it was hinged in the middle.

The muzzle-loaded cannons fired various types of projectiles, depending on the target. A shot or bolt (commonly known as a "cannonball") was a solid, battering projectile, while a spherical shell was hollow. The shell contained an explosive charge, designed to burst either in the air or, in the case of a percussion shell, when it struck the ground or solid object. The shell, or case, could be filled with small iron balls or lead bullets, which became known as shrapnel.*

Shots and shells were typically used against enemy fortifications and artillery batteries, although shot was also used against infantry. It acted like a bowling ball, rolling or bouncing across the battlefield, and it could take off a soldier's limb or head.

---

* Shrapnel: an artillery projectile filled with lead balls, named for its inventor, Englishman Henry Shrapnel, in the 19th century. (Blakely, 1952)

To mow down charging infantry, the cannons also fired grapeshot or canister shot—small iron balls bundled together in a cylindrical device or canister. If the enemy soldiers advanced to within a few hundred yards, the cannoneers often fired double-loaded canister shot.

The field artillery units used guns that fell into two broad categories: smoothbore and rifle. The inside of a rifle barrel had spiral grooves to spin the projectile as it left the barrel, increasing the range and accuracy. The models included the Napoleon (smoothbore), three-inch Ordnance rifle, Parrott rifle, and Whitworth rifle.* The cannons were further classified by the diameter of the bore or the weight of the projectile; for example, a three-inch or a 12-pounder.

The Parrott was a new design introduced by the Union and had greater range and accuracy than its predecessors. It became a prized target of Confederate infantry. The Confederate army, when it could procure them, also deployed the highly accurate Whitworth rifles, which were made in Great Britain.

An efficient gun crew could fire twice per minute, and when under assault they were known to fire at twice that rate, according to the U.S. Army Ordnance Corps:

> *Capable of firing four canister shots per minute, the Napoleon proved to be efficient killers of infantry. Firing canister at massed troops under 400 yards distance had a devastating effect as Union artillery proved on July 3 against Pickett's assault.*

During the Battle of Gettysburg, Union forces fired more than 33,000 artillery rounds and the Confederate forces fired an estimated 22,000.

Attacking infantry targeted artillery batteries to silence and capture the weapons. As the gun crews limbered up to retreat, the assaulting infantry shot the horses, forcing the crew to abandon the cannons. If capture appeared imminent, gun crews shot their own horses to prevent the enemy from moving the pieces. Spiking a cannon by driving a piece of metal into the firing vent also rendered it inoperative, at least for a while.

(U.S. Army Ordnance Corps)

---

* Parrott rifle, developed by U.S. Army officer Robert P. Parrott, was one of the two most common rifled field pieces used by the Union and Confederate armies. It had a characteristic iron band reinforcing the breech. (Johnson & Anderson, 1995)

Whitworth rifle, designed by Sir Joseph Whitworth, a British engineer. (Atkinson, 1996)

Battery F Artillery Pieces

Pennsylvania historian Samuel P. Bates (1869) provided some insight into the weapons used by Battery F:

> On the 8th of October, 1861, the battery was enlarged by the addition of two Parrott rifled, ten-pounder guns.
>
> Early in January, 1862, [Lieutenant] Ricketts, with his section, after a wearysome night march, joined General Lander, near Hancock, in time to participate in the engagement with Jackson in his attack upon the town, and in effecting his complete repulse.* Jackson's column consisted of twenty thousand men, and twenty-six pieces of artillery. To oppose him, General Lander had two thousand infantry, and a battery of four guns.** Jackson's pieces were of smooth bore and short range, whereas Ricketts' section consisted of two rifled, ten-pounder, Parrott guns. He could therefore take position out of range of the enemy, and easily reach him with his missiles. Jackson was consequently forced to withdraw.
>
> On the 20th of February, 1862, the sections were united at Hagerstown, where new equipments were received, and the guns furnished by the State were exchanged for six regulation, three-inch, rifled guns, together with new carriages and Sibley tents.***

---

* Ricketts, Robert Bruce, lieutenant, mustered in as a private on July 8, 1861; promoted to 1st lieutenant August 5, 1861, to captain May 8, 1863, to major December 1, 1864; took command of Battery F after Matthews was promoted to major. Best known for his battery's defense against the assault of the Louisiana Tigers on East Cemetery Hill on the second day of the Battle of Gettysburg.

** Union Brigadier General Frederick W. Lander, died of an infection on March 2, 1862, at Paw Paw, West Virginia.

*** Sibley tent: a cone-shaped tent designed to accommodate twelve men; named for Henry Hopkins Sibley, who patented the design in 1858.

We can fire very fast. We fire mostly shells.

—Oney F. Sweet

Union soldiers preparing cannons on the battlefield. (Library of Congress)

Letters, 1862

I like soldiering first rate. We have beans coffee pork and crackers to live on.

—Oney F. Sweet

Camp near Bell Plains, Va.
Battery F 1st Pa Artillery
Jan 18th 1862

Dear Brother:
I received your letter last night. We have not got the box yet, but we are in hopes we will get it. I suppose it is between here and Washington. Our boys have had a great many boxes sent them but have not reached here.

We have not had any sleighing here. We have not had any snow this winter of any account. Last night was as cold a night as we have had this winter, but I never slept better or warmer than last night at home. We have real comfortable quarters. We have a bed made out of boards and we have six blankets and two heavy overcoats, two of us together in one tent. We have a good fire this morning and have just finished our breakfast of fresh beef, coffee and crackers.

Mr. Ridgeway came here to see his son and brought him some bread, butter and roast chicken.* We lived bully while it lasted. I borrowed some money and yesterday we bought some sugar and corn meal and we live at the top of the heap.

We have marching orders and we expect to leave here tomorrow morning early. We hate to leave this camp. We do not know where we are agoing, but I expect we will have another fight.

Jim Warner was over here and took supper with me one day last week.** He looks well and hearty. I wrote to mother last Sunday.

Direct: Battery F 1st Pa Artillery, P. R. V. C. Washington, D.C.***

P.S. Write soon and all the news. Have you heard anything about the French or Larrabee Boys? They have not come here.

---

* Stephen E. Ridgway, quartermaster sergeant, mustered in December 30, 1861; mustered out with battery, June 10, 1865.

** James M. Warner, artificier, mustered in September 2, 1861; transferred to Battery A; mustered out with battery, July 25, 1865.

*** P.R.V.C.: Pennsylvania Reserve Volunteer Corps.

We have real comfortable quarters. We have a bed made out of boards and we have six blankets and two heavy overcoats, two of us together in one tent.

—Oney F. Sweet

Union encampment, Belle Plain Landing, Virginia. (Library of Congress)

Harrisburg, Feb. 5th, 1862

Dear Mother:

I received your letter this morning. You need not be worried about my pay. I am sure of getting it next pay day. Case draws his pay by going down to Washington. What money I have wanted I have borrowed of Case. If Case stays here I will stay here and if he leaves here I will leave.

I saw Captain Mathews on Monday and he said my pay was all right and I am sure it is all right.

The fellows that are here in the office say they would rather be in Virginia sleeping on the ground than to be here and they want to get to their regiments but Captain Dodge won't let them leave here.*

Don't fret yourself to death about me, I will take care of myself, just as well as you would and better too. I may be here for a month yet.

I will write again soon. From your son O. F. Sweet

I know my pay is all right so don't make the thing worse than there is any need of.

---

* "Captain Dodge" possibly Charles F. Dodge, 52nd Regiment, Pennsylvania Infantry.

Camp near Bell Plains Va.
Feb. 10th, 1862

Dear Sister:

I received a letter from Mother night before last and another one last night, stating that you had sent another box by way of Lieut. Brainard.* We have sent to Washington for the other one.

Guss Roper and Brainard are camped about 8 miles from here, but we can get the box from there. George Bennett and Jim Warner have left this division.** Their battery I believe is going to North Carolina and we will not likely see them again until the war is over. I sent $30.00 home by express and 50 cents to you. I will enclose the receipt and one dollar for postage stamps. I bought some potatoes for 70 cents a bushel, onions for $1.50 a bushel, butter 50¢ a pound, sugar 12 cents.

Write soon.

I think we will get the box now.

I had a letter from Uncle Jo last night.

Two of our boys started for home on a furlough this morning.

I am on guard today. We are having real spring weather.

From O.F.S.

---

* Elisha B. Brainard, 141st Regiment, Pennsylvania Infantry, rank in: second lieutenant, rank out: adjutant.

** George W. Bennett, corporal, mustered in September 7, 1861; transferred to Battery A; mustered out with battery, July 25, 1865.

Camp near Bell Plains, Va.
Battery F 1st Pa Arty.
Feb. 23 1862

Dear Mother:

I received your letter day before yesterday and was glad to hear that you got the money safe. Use the money for anything you have a mind to. Pay your debts or buy cattle, but do not keep any money on hand unless gold or silver. Gold and silver is very scarce here, we do not see any at all. We had a big snow storm yesterday and today is cold as blazes. I began to build a new log house but this snow storm has put a stop to it for the present.

Dear Sister:

I will answer your letter on this paper. I must not waste any paper it is too scarce. The boys that went on a furlough have come back and you do not know them. Last night we drew for furloughs again and I was not lucky enough to get one. We will draw again in ten days. The boys that go this time are Charley Silby and Myron French.* Myron French lives in Jackson and is a brother to the other French boys. He will start for home in a day or two and you can send some little things to me by him, but do not send a very large package as it will load him down. Send me a dollars worth of stamps by mail.

Write soon.
From your ever true Brother
Oney F. Sweet

When I left home I left some pennies and old letters in a trunk up stairs. If you have not destroyed them I wish you would lay them away and keep them. I will send you in this letter a piece of Rebel money and I want you to keep it for me.

I will close.

---

* Charles H. Sibley, private, mustered in July 15, 1861; transferred to Battery G, March 26, 1864.

Myron French, sergeant, mustered in July 8, 1861; killed at Gettysburg, July 2, 1863.

Harrisburg, Pa.
February 25th, 1862

Dear Father:

Enclosed please find five ($5) dollars. We are going to leave here on next Thursday the 27th for Hagerstown Md. to join our company. I will write soon after I get there. Tell Mother that I am well provided for in clothes. I have bought all the little necessary things that I need. I had a letter from Willie last Monday (yesterday) and I will write to him as soon as I get down to the company. I sent home my ambrotype yesterday.* We have very pleasant weather here and I do not think we will have much more cold weather this winter.

From O. F. Sweet

---

* ambrotype: an early type of photograph (collodion positive) made by placing a glass negative against a dark background; less expensive than daguerreotypes. (National Media Museum)

Oney F. Sweet (left) and comrades.* (Courtesy of Joan Ketchum Reamer)

---

* This type of photograph is known as a "carte de visite" or calling card, which was popular at the time. It measures 4" x 2½" and is credited to Chas. G. Crane, No. 532 Arch Street, Philadelphia. A note on the reverse reads: "O. F. Sweet and his comrades in the Gettysburg battle." The hats worn by Oney and two of the seated men are not army issue. The man seated in the middle is wearing pants with sergeant's stripes. The photograph was probably taken in early 1864 while the men were on furlough after reenlisting.

Martinsburg, Va.
March 4th 1862

Dear Mother:

I wrote to Willie when we were in Hagerstown. We left Hagerstown day before yesterday about 10 o'clock in the morning and arrived here at 10 o'clock at night. We marched 18 miles and it snowed part of the time. We are now in the rebels country and there is lots of sesesh here.* There is not many men here, only women. Stores and houses are shut up, the people all gone with the rebels.

The town is about as large as Montrose and there is not but two or three stores in town that is open and they charge very large prices for everything they have. There is no salt in town only what we brought with us. Coffee is worth 50¢ a pound, butter 50¢ and everything is scarce. Calicos worth 1 shilling in Gibson is worth 4 shillings here.

The people that are here say they are Union, but they do not dare to say anything else. We have a plenty of provisions we brought with us. We are quartered in a church and some of the regiments are in houses. We have two stoves in the church.

There is a good many soldiers here now and they are coming in every day. I saw two of Jeff Davis soldiers yesterday.** They deserted from the rebel army.

Bryant is sick.*** We took him yesterday to a private house. We left Scott in Hagerstown sick. We do not expect to stay here long as we expect to march on to Winchester in a day or two.

I like soldiering first rate. We have beans coffee pork and crackers to live on. Direct your letters to Martinsburg VA in care of Capt. E. W. Mathews, Battery F 1st Pa. Artillery.**** I believe I have written all the news at present. I will write again soon.

From Oney

---

* sesesh (more commonly spelled secesh): a supporter of the Confederacy during the U.S. Civil War.

** Jefferson Davis, president of the Confederate States of America.

*** Delos D. Bryant, corporal, mustered in July 8, 1861; discharged on Surgeon's Certificate, May 19, 1862.

**** Ezra W. Matthews, captain, mustered in July 8, 1861; promoted to major, April 11, 1863.

Bunker Hill, Va.
March 6th, 1862

Dear Mother:

I wrote a letter home on last Monday. Since then we have marched 11 miles farther into Virginia. We are now at a little town called Bunker Hill. We do not expect to stay here long. We expect to march on to Winchester. We had a little skirmish yesterday and caught 7 rebels.

Enclosed you will find a Virginia shin plaster* that is the only kind of money they have seen here for six months till we come here.

We have six thousand troops here and General Banks is within 6 miles of here with 30 or 40 thousand men, and you may expect a big battle in a few days.** We had a drill this morning.

I have been hearty since I have been in camp. Bryant is sick. We left him in Martinsburg in a private house. We left Scott in Hagerstown, Md. This country is a very fine country, but a great many people have run away and left their farms with the women and niggers to take care of them. When we stop to camp we put our horses in the barn and feed them all the hay and grain we can find. I had a letter from Louisa Foster. She said Aunt Julia DeWitt was in New York but had not come to see them. Henry Tiffany is here in our tent and he is about sick. He fell and hurt himself when he was in Hancock. Dave, Larrabee, Tiffany and myself are all writing home today. I will have to close and go to roll call and then go and wash myself and get ready for supper of coffee, crackers and pork. Direct to Martinsburg, Va. Care of Capt. E. W. Mathews, Battery F, 1st Pa Artillery.

From Your son.

---

* shinplaster, a piece of privately issued paper currency, especially one poorly secured and depreciated in value; a piece of fractional currency. (*Merriam-Webster*)

** Major General Nathaniel P. Banks, commander, Department of the Shenandoah.

Winchester, Virginia, March 14th, 1862

Dear Mother:

I have not heard from home since I left Harrisburg. I have written several letters home since I left Harrisburg. We have marched 33 miles into Virginia and we have had several little skirmishes with the rebels and we have killed some of them, but I believe we have not lost but two of our men and they were taken prisoners. We had two or three wounded but our company has not lost a man, and we were ahead of the army when we marched.

We fired several shells and killed some of their men and some of their horses. We expected to have a hard fight before we got into Winchester but they all run away the night before we arrived here they took away all of their large guns. If they had stayed here we would have had a hard fight, but we were ready for them. We had about 30 thousand men and they only had 7 or 8 thousand.

4 of our guns have just been ordered out to have a fight, and they are getting ready as fast as possible to go, but the gun that I belong to is not ordered out, so I have not got to go, but we may have orders at any minute to go.

If they had given us a fight when we came here they would have given us a mighty hard fight and our boys may have a hard fight today for they have attacked us three miles from here and I do not know how large their force is. When we came here we caught 13 prisoneers.

This place is about as large as Binghampton and it is a very pretty place, but the people are all secesh, what there is left here but most of the people have gone to fight in the rebel army. But there is a good many women and niggers here. The niggers are as thick as flies in the summer time.

I believe I have heard you speak of Sally Ann Madison. Her son is here in our tent. His name is Lake. I have not heard from Scott since we left Hagerstown, but I heard his wife had gone to see him. I like camp life first rate and I am healthy except for a little cold. They have not had any snow here of any account this winter and it seems like the month of May here now. I shall not mail this letter until I hear how the fight goes.

Direct your letters plain.
Oney F. Sweet
Winchester, Virginia
care of Capt. E. W. Mathews
Battery F, 1st Pa Artillery

Virginia, Warrington Junction, April 4th 1862.

Dear Mother:

I wrote a few lines some time ago but I have not had a chance to mail it since I wrote it. I will write you few more lines today but we have no way of sending our letters from here at present but I expect there will be in a day or two. I have not had but one letter from Gibson since I left Harrisburg. I suppose I have several letters laying some where and I think I will get them after a while. Since I wrote to you we have travelled over a hundred miles. Last Saturday night we camped on the battle field of Bull Run and it was a hard looking place and it was the toughest road I ever travelled. We are now about 20 miles from Bull Run. There is lots of rebels near here. They have burned bridges and destroyed everything they could. It is just like summer here. I have never heard whether you received my daguerrotype or not.*

April 9th, 1862

Last Sunday we marched 1½ miles and camped here. It commenced raining last Monday and it has rained nearly all the time since. We have not seen anything of the rest of the regiment yet and I do not know where they are. I am going to mail this letter as soon as possible. We expect to get our mail soon. I will write again soon. O.F. Sweet

---

* daguerreotype, an early type of photograph (with a reversed image) made on a piece of silver or a piece of copper covered in silver. (National Media Museum)

Warrington Junction, April 24th, 1862

Dear Mother:

I was yesterday up to see the Belcher boys and Jim Warner. They were all well and in good spirits. They are camped about 3 miles from here.

We have had a good deal of wet weather here. We heard that Scott was on his way here and we are looking for him every day. We cannot tell how long we will stay here, but I do not think we will stay here long.

Dave's business is to ram in the balls my business is to carry the ammunition to the gun.

I have not had but two letters from you since I left Harrisburg, but we will get our letters more punctual after this. I will write as often as I can.

I like soldier's life full as well as I expected I would. The names of the men in our tent: Seargeant Stradford, Oscar Larrabee, D. Bryant, Galloway, Gates, Eastman, Maynard, Tiffany, Lake, Simpson, Curry, Mosel, Tabas, Flora, Kenny.* Most all of the boys in this tent are from Susquehanna County. Bryant is unwell and has been ever since I joined the Company.

---

* Aaron B. Galloway, private, mustered in September 7, 1861; discharged on Surgeon's Certificate, August 8, 1862.

"Tabas," possibly Gordon Tabor, private, mustered in July 8, 1861; mustered out with battery, June 10, 1865.

"Kenny" possibly William T. Kinney, private, mustered in July 8, 1861; mustered out with battery, June 10, 1865.

Fredericksburg, Va. May 24th, 1862

Dear Mother:

We got our pay yesterday and I expressed home thirty dollars. It will come in care of C. P. Hawley. We expect to leave here today or tomorrow. We are going onto Richmond. They do not allow us to have any tents and we were ordered to leave our coats and blankets behind or send them home. Dave and me sent a box and we only kept one blanket apiece. I sent my overcoat, two blankets and a pair of shoulder scales which we have to wear on our shoulders, but we were ordered to leave them or send them home.

I did not pay the expressage on the box or money. You pay Mrs. Maynard half the cost. We have not received your box you sent.

We were reveiwed by President Lincoln yesterday.

Scott has been sick but he is better now. Bryant left here for Washington two weeks ago. He expected to get his discharge and I presume he is home now.

I enclose you the receipts and if the things don't come in 8 or 10 days you can make the express company pay for them. We expect to have some hard marching and all I ask is that I can be as healthy and well as I am now and I can stand it.

Write as soon as you get these things.

Direct as before in my last letter.

From Oney F. Sweet

Front Royal, VA., June 17th 1862

Dear Mother:

I received a letter from you this morning dated May 27th. I have been looking for a letter from you every day for a week. I sent home a box and $30.00 when we was at Fredericksburg and I have been anxious for a letter to hear if you got it safe. I suppose you have got it for Dave has had a letter from home and his money went through safe and the box. We have not got the box that was sent to us and I do not believe we ever will get it. You can settle with Mrs. Maynard as you think right.

We left Fredericksburg soon after I wrote to you and we marched to Manassas and then here. We marched seven days and nights. We had a very hard march. We expected to have a fight here with Jackson but he got the start of us. We expected to cut off his retreat. This is the place where Jackson and Banks had a fight.

We are 30 miles from Winchester. We are not so far south as we was when we was at Fredericksburg. When we was at Fredericksburg we was 60 miles from Richmond, now we are one hundred and thirty miles from Richmond. We have laid here over two weeks and we have expected to leave here every day and I think we will leave here in a very few days. We have come very near being in two or three fights, but just escaped being in them.

We have had very cool weather here for this time of year. The middle of the day is pretty warm but nights are cool and heavy dews.

We have had eight men discharged since we was at Fredericksburg. We had one man kicked by a horse and broke his leg and a seagt. accidentlly shot himself in the leg.

I expect to have a letter from you in a day or two and then I will write the rest of the news.

> Direct Oney F. Sweet
> 1st Pa Artillery, Capt. E. W. Mathews,
> Hartsuffs Brigade*
> Washington, D.C.

I can not tell where we will be a week from now.

---

* George Lucas Hartsuff, a Union general who led brigades at the Second Battle of Bull Run, Antietam, Vicksburg, and Knoxville, among others. (Wright, 2013)

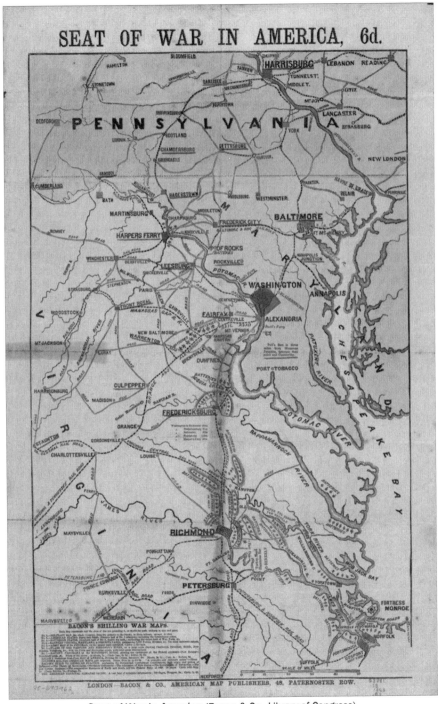

Seat of War in America (Bacon & Co., Library of Congress)

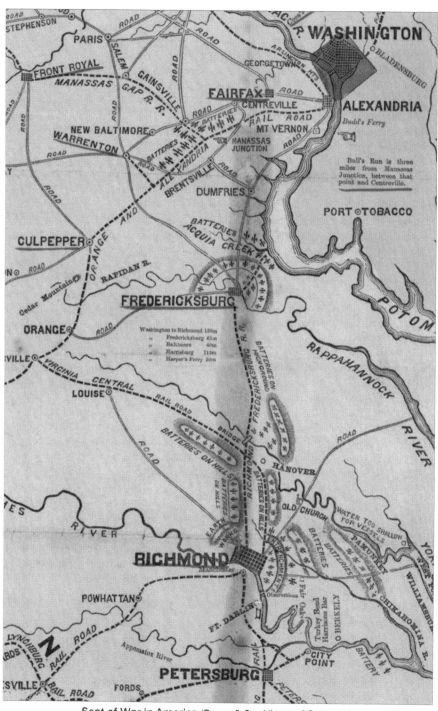

Seat of War in America (Bacon & Co., Library of Congress)

Manassas Junction, VA., July 3rd 1862

Dear Brother:

I received your letter with Sarah's last week and I answered Sarah's as soon as I received it. I think I write two letters to your one. Tomorrow is the fourth of July and I expect it will pass off the same here as all other days do with the soldiers, that is laying around camp doing nothing much but drilling and standing guard. Our guard duty is very light. My turn comes once in about ten days. Perhaps tomorrow we may fire a salute or something of that kind.

One day last week we went out and shot at a target. I acted at post No. 2 on the gun that is to put the ammunition and shells in the gun. We made some very good shots. My regular post is No. 7, that is to carry ammunition from the caisson to No. 5, but as we was short of cannoneers I took the post of No. 2 and when we got through firing my ears rung all day.

We have four roll calls a day, one at five in the morning, one at two o'clock, one at six o'clock and one at nine o'clock. If we miss a roll call we have to stand guard. I will try and give you some description of how a Battery is commanded. We have six guns and they are divided into 3 sections, the right section is commanded by Lieut. Ricketts, he is now sick and Case takes his place, but Case is not here now, he went to Washington on business. The left section is commanded by Lieut. Gadbold [Godbold].* I am in his section. The center section is comanded by Lieut. Brockway** and then the Battery is divided into six detachments, one detachment for each gun, commanded by a seargent.

When we have a full Battery there is 18 men in a detachment, but a Battery can be worked nearly as Well when it is half full. We have not a full Battery now, there has been so many discharged and sick. The first detachment is commanded by Seagt. Hague, the 2nd by Seagt. Lee Greenwood, the 3rd by Seagt. Gillespie, he is a cousin of Sam and Jo Gillespie, 4th by Seagt. Stradford. I am in his detachment, the 5th by Seagt. Campbell, the 6th by Seagt. Harder or Melick. Melick is now in the hospital.***

---

* Henry L. Godbald, captain, mustered in July 8, 1861; died September 22, 1862, of wounds received at Rappahannock Station, Virginia. (See August 13, 1862.)

** Charles B. Brockway, mustered in July 8, 1861; promoted to 2nd lieutenant, February 28, 1862, promoted to 1st lieutenant, March 16, 1863, commissioned captain, November 30, 1864, and brevet captain, March 13, 1865; discharged October 22, 1864.

*** "Seagt. Hague" possibly James J. Hague, although the military record lists him as a private.

continued on page 31

Warrington, Virginia, July 11th, 1862

Dear Mother:

I received your letter about an hour ago. We are all well and in a beautiful healthy country. I will tell you how I spent my fourth. We marched all day and after we camped for the night I spent my time eating cherries. This is a great country for fruit.

We marched here in two days, we are 20 miles from Manassas. We expect to leave here every day. We live tip top here. We have a plenty of milk. The town of Warrington is the prettiest place I ever was in. We are nine miles from Warrington Junction. You recollect we layed there a long time.

Scott was down to the depot this afternoon and brought up the long looked for box. There was nothing in it fit to eat except the sugar and dried apples. Everything was all jammed up and the cakes were moldy. Scott's things kept middling well. Gillespie's cake was almost eatable, it was the best of the lot. We took the box cakes and threw them out of sight. I can tell you I feel mad, but still I can't blame anybody but old Genl. Hartsuff. I think he might of stayed at Warrington Junction until we got it. We could see that there was some nice cakes in the box.

We have had some very warm days here but I have seen just as warm days in the north this time of year. It is now getting near dark and I will have to close for I want to go down to the brook and have a wash. I will write as soon as I get Sarah's letter.

From your son Oney.
Direct as before.

---

continued from page 30

Lee Greenwood, sergeant, mustered in as a private July 8, 1861; discharged on Surgeon's Certificate, January 13, 1863.

Melwood C. Gillespie, sergeant, mustered in as a private July 1, 1861; promoted to 2nd lieutenant, Battery G, June 12, 1863.

John F. Campbell, sergeant, mustered in July 8, 1861; promoted to 2nd lieutenant May 20, 1864, to 1st lieutenant December 6, 1864, to captain, April 17, 1865; mustered out with battery, June 10, 1865.

"Seagt. Harder" possibly Priestley S. Harder, although the military record lists him as a private, mustered in December 31, 1861; mustered out January 23, 1865.

"Melick" possibly William B. Mellick, although the military record lists him as a private, mustered in July 6, 1861; discharged on Surgeon's Certificate, July 18, 1862.

July 24th, 1862

Dear Mother:

We moved from Warrington day before yesterday. We are camped near the river 7 miles from Warrington. We do not know how long we will stay here, we expect to move every day. I received Sarah's letter in due time. When we were camped near Warrington Mrs. S. L. Case came to see her husband. She spent three or four days. She was in camp several times. She stopped in town most of the time. I was up to see her and had a long talk with her. She staid here until we left and then she started for home. She is not coming to Gibson I believe.

We got our pay yesterday and I would like to send some money home but I bought me a good revolver and shirts etc. and I have some left., but while I am where I can buy eggs, butter, milk, etc. I am going to have them, for it is hard living to live on soldier's fare.

It has been very rainy here for two or three days. Tell Sarah to write to me again. I will write as often as I can, but when we are on the march we don't have time to write.

Direct your letters as follows

> Oney F. Sweet
> Washington, D.C.
> Capt. Mathews Battery
> Hartsuffs Brigade
> Ricketts Division

Battle of Cedar Mountain

August 9, 1862

The rebels began shelling us but our battery opened fire on them and soon stopped their work.

—Oney F. Sweet

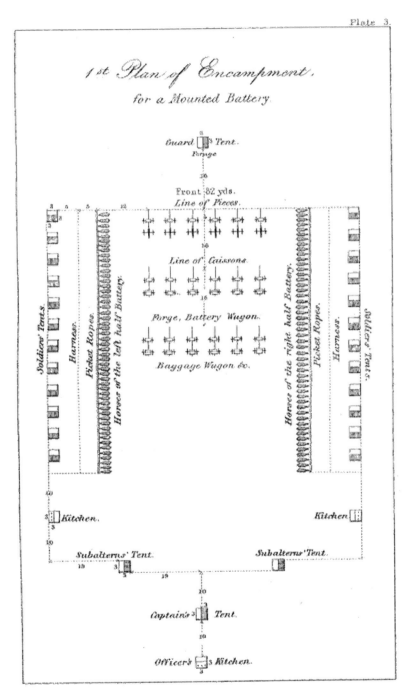

1st Plan of Encampment, U.S. Army *Instruction for Field Artillery*, 1860.

Camp Near Cedar Creek, August 13th, 1862

Dear Mother:

Enclosed you will find a letter for Sarah written on the 8th, the same day that I wrote this letter. We received marching orders and we expected to have a fight. We were ready for marching in 20 minutes after the orders came. We marched about three miles and it came on night and we slept without our tents so as to be ready at a moment's notice.

In the morning we got ready for a fight, but they kept us as a reserve. They put Genl. Banks force in the advance and kept us in the rear. At about noon we could hear the roar of cannon and we waited expecting to be called on at any moment. They fought hard all the afternoon.

At about 5 o'clock we were called on to go in to the fight. We had to march about 3 miles to the battlefield it was dark and both parties stopped fighting. Our division was formed in a line of battle. On the same ground the other division had occupied while we were getting in position the rebels began shelling us but our battery opened fire on them and soon stopped their work.

We layed very near the rebels all night. I went to sleep under the gun and slept about 3 hours. It was a beautiful moonlight night. In the morning we expected to fight them again, but in the morning the rebels did not seem to want to fight us again and we did not move but layed in our position all day and we picked up our wounded.

On Monday the rebels retreated and we buried our dead. I was out on the field and saw hundreds of killed and wounded. I will not say anything about the wounded that I saw and I hope I may never see such a sight again. The rebels have fell back some distance, but I expect we will give them a fight soon. We lost a good many men but I think the rebels got the worst of it. I saw a good many prisoners and talked with them. I will have to close for the present.

Second Battle of Bull Run

August 28–30, 1862

We were in the thickest of the fight. The rebels charged on our battery and we lost two pieces.

—Oney F. Sweet

The first Battle of Bull Run took place on July 16, 1861, prior to the formation of the 1st Pennsylvania Light Artillery. Brig. Gen. Irvin McDowell led Union forces against the Confederate army, which had assembled near Bull Run and Manassas, not far from Centreville, Virginia. Late in the day, Confederates broke through the Union right flank, and the battle turned into a rout of the Federals. Confederate General Thomas J. Jackson earned the nickname "Stonewall." (Hitchcock, 1868)

2nd Bull Run Battle
Camp Near Washington, D.C.
Sept. 3d, 1862

Dear Mother:

This is the first chance I have had to write to you since I last wrote and I may not have time to finish this before we will have to march or fight. I will have to write with a lead pencil for I have no ink and I have nothing but what is on my back. I am thankful to get away with my head.

I will commence and give you an account from the time I last wrote to you. I wrote to you on August 13th.

On August 15th we marched towards Gordonsville 5 miles.

On August 17th marched 4 miles farther on.

On August 18th heard that Jackson was advancing on us. We prepared for a march back. Got ready to march at about noon. We did not march until 12 o'clock at night and then we marched 5 miles and we layed down by the road side and I slept about 2 hours and very nearly froze.

On August 19th we commenced marching or retreating at 7 o'clock and we marched all day until 11 o'clock at night and it was a hot day. On August 20th the rebels followed us up and we got ready to fight them. We never unharnessed our horses all night.

On August 21st the rebels attacked us and we fought them two hours and they withdrew behind the woods. We had one man killed and two wounded and four horses killed. Lieut. Case had his horse killed. On August 22nd only fired a few guns.

On August 23rd the battle commenced early, as soon as it was light. The fight lasted about four hours. Lieut. Gadbold had his leg shot off by a cannon ball and we had one other man wounded.* 3 horses killed. We retreated back. I had nothing to eat all day until night. Marched 8 miles after the fight. In the fight we had two guns disabled.

On August 24th marched 7 miles. Saw the Belcher boys, Jim Warner, Henry Whitmarsh.** Fighting all day but our battery was not engaged.

On August 25th marched 3 miles. There was fighting all day but our battery was not engaged.

---

* Lieutenant Godbald, in command of the left section, was struck by a percussion shell, losing a leg from the effects of the wound, and soon after died. (Bates, 1869)

** William H. Whitmarsh, Battery A, mustered in September 4, 1861; promoted to sergeant, June 16, 1865; mustered out with battery, July 25, 1865.

August 26th marched 6 miles.

August 27th marched 9 miles. Layed by the roadside all night.

August 28th heard hard fighting near Manasses. Marched 13 miles to Thoroughfare Gap. Got there about 3 o'clock and had a fight. Lasted 3 hours. Had nobody hurt in the battery but there was about 100 hundred killed and wounded in our Brigade. We fought until dark and then we retreated 6 miles and layed by the road-side. Our rations run out and we had nothing to eat but what we could find.

August 29th marched all day. Marched 15 miles. Passed through Manasses. Old Jackson had been at Manassas and burnt nearly everything. Thousands of dollars worth of property were destroyed. We did not stop at Manasses but marched on to the battle field where they had been fighting all day. We reached the battlefield at about dark.

August 30th the fighting commenced slow until about 2 p.m. when it raged very hot. We were in the thickest of the fight. The rebels charged on our battery and we lost two pieces and they drove us back about 1 mile and then Lieut. Brockway took the gun that I am on and placed it in position near a hospital where there was hundreds of wounded. We stopped there to cover the retreat and try and check the rebels if we could.

By this time it was getting dark and we fired 6 or 8 shots at them and we were just going to leave when we found that they had surrounded us. I thought I would try and get away if I could. So I run for dear life.

The bullets flew thick around me and how I got out without being shot I don't know. I run about a half mile and then I walked. There was thousands running every way. Everything was strewn over the ground I walked on until I came to Bull Run Creek and then I could not find the bridge. So I plunged in with hundreds of others and waded across. I got wet to my waist, but I did not mind that. I walked on till I could not walk any farther and then I layed down by a fire to try to sleep. But the fire soon went out and I waked up nearly froze, and the rear guard told me I had better walk on or the rebels would overtake me. So I trudged on till morning and it commenced raining.

To make matters worse. I got to Centerville about 6 o'clock and there I found the Captain, Lt. Case and what was left of our old battery. I got some coffee and I felt almost as good as new.

There was 15 of us together when we were surrounded and it was dark and I could not tell whether the rest run or not. Only 7 of us got away and some of them was slightly wounded. I will give you the names of them that are either shot or taken prisoner. Lieut. Brockway, Dave, Henry Tiffany, Simon Flora,

Eastman, Riggins, Orange, Jo Strong, Rake, O. G. Larrabee.* We had some wounded that got away.

The gun, caisson and all the horses were taken. We only brought 1 gun off the field. I was talking to Dave about 1 minute before they charged on us but I didn't see which way he run. Some of the boys say they saw him trying to get away. He is either shot or taken prisoner.

All of our boys fought nobly and stood by the guns as long as they could. Scott was not in the fight. He was with the baggage wagons. Case was through all the fight and come out safe but he is down sick and went to Washington yesterday. We have another battery now. Most all of the boys are nearly sick and it is a wonder I am not sick for I have slept on the ground without any blankets several nights and we have had nothing to eat half of the time.

We are now in sight of Washington and I think the whole army is falling back here to save Washington if we can and I am sure we can. I can hear fighting all day today and it is not a great ways off. I have had two letters from home since I wrote. I will write as often as I have a chance. Write soon.

They say they will not let any letters go out of Washington but I will send them to Washington and I hope you will get it.

From your son Oney

There has been thousands of men killed in the last two weeks.

P.S. Since I wrote this letter I have seen Dave and the rest of the boys. They were taken prisoners and have been paroled.

---

* James H. Riggin, private, mustered in November 1, 1861; killed at Gettysburg, July 2, 1863.

Robert Orange, private, [reenlisted] March 28, 1864; mustered out with battery, June 10, 1865.

John G. Rake, private, [reenlisted] January 1, 1864; mustered out with battery, June 10, 1865.

Battle of Antietam

September 17, 1862

It was the hardest fight I have ever been in yet. I had my stockings pulled over my pants and a bullet went through my stocking.

—Oney F. Sweet

Camp Near Sharpsburg, Md. September 20th, 1862

Dear Mother:

This is the first chance I have had to write to you since we came into Maryland. We have been chasing old Jackson. On Sept. 14th we whipped him. We was not in the fight but we was near by.

On Sept. 17th we was in a fight and we whipped him very bad. Our battery was engaged. We was in the thickest of the fight. We had 3 men killed and 9 wounded. The Captain's horse was shot dead from under him and two of our seagts. had their horses shot. We had 12 horses killed altogether.

It was the hardest fight I have ever been in yet. I had my stockings pulled over my pants and a bullet went through my stocking. A good many of our boys had bullet holes in their pants, blouses and one had a bullet in the sole of his shoe.

The boys that were killed and wounded were all strangers to you. One man by the name of Thomson stood by me when he was shot in the leg.* I tied my handkerchief around his leg to stop the blood and he walked a few steps and layed down and died. One of the other boys was slightly wounded in the foot and on his way off of the field he was struck by a cannon ball in the head and killed. Oh mother it was an awful sight to see thousands of men laying dead and wounded on the field.

I helped bury the boys that was killed in our Battery. I would like to write you more but this is enough to let you know that I came out safe.

Charley Belcher was wounded in the head, not dangerous.* Write soon and let me know how things are getting along in Gibson. Give my love to all.

From Oney.

We only have 30 men fit for duty in our Battery now.

---

* Edward Thompson, private, killed at Antietam, September 17, 1862.

** Charles T. Belcher, sergeant, July 17, 1861, Company K, 6th Pennsylvania Reserves; at Antietam blinded by a shot in the head and left for dead; discharged Nov. 11, 1862. (PRVCHS)

Page 2 of Oney F. Sweet's letter to his mother, dated September 20, 1862.

I helped to bury the boys that were killed in our Battery. I would like to write you more but this is enough to let you know that I came out safe.

- Charley Belcher was wounded in the head, not dangerous. Write soon and let me know how things are getting along in Gibson. Give my love to all.

From Oney.

... only have thirty men fit for ... in our Battery now.

Sharpsburg, Md.
Sept. 21st 1862

Dear Brother:

I received your letter this morning. I wrote a letter to mother yesterday. I had a letter from Sarah and I answered it and directed the letter to Binghampton. We are now laying about a half mile from the battlefield. They say the rebels have all crossed over into Virginia. We are about one mile from the river.

The fight of last Wednesday was one of the hardest battles ever fought in America. Our loss was very heavy but the rebels lost more than us. We lost 3 killed and 9 wounded. We had a good many horses killed. The rebels charged on our Battery and came within a few yards of us when they were driven back. The bullets flew like hail and the shells burst all around us. The battle at Bull Run was nothing compared to this battle. The fight was in a corn field where we fought. The battle field extended 5 miles. The corn field was fought over 5 times but we held the field at last. I went over the field after the fight and the dead and wounded lay so thick you could hardly step.

Some had legs, arms, and heads torn off. Some groaning and breathing their last. It was awful. I never want to see such a sight again and I hope I may never have the bullets fly so close to my head again. I have seen enough of war. We have only 41 men fit for duty now and we cannot do much more fighting until we are recruited up. When I came to the company we had 132 men.

Our Brigadier Genl was wounded. What does the people think about the war in Pennsylvania? I am in hopes it will end soon. I don't blame Dave for going home. If I was in his place I would come home too.

I saw about 1000 rebel prisoners and talked with them. They say they are tired of the war but they are a ragged _____ set of fellows as ever I saw.

I have been nearly sick for the past two or three days. I tell you it is seeing things and lying around on the ground and eating crackers and coffee.

Write soon and all the news. Direct as before.

from Oney.

Oney F. Sweet's letter to his brother, dated September 21, 1862.

Sharpsburg M.D.
Sept. 21st 1862

Dear Brother,

I received your letter this morning. I wrote a letter to mother yesterday. & had a letter from Sarah and I will send and direct the letter to Binghampton. We are now lying about a mile from the battlefield. They say the rebels have recrossed the river.

The fight of Antietam was one of the hardest ever fought in America. We lost 9 killed and 9 wounded but the Rebels lost more than we. We ___ in good many horses. The Rebels where we ___ on our battery and came within a few yards of ___ when we were driven back. The bullets flew like hail and the shells burst all around us. The fight of Bull Run was nothing compared to this battle. The fight was in a corn field. Where we fought the battle field extended five miles. The corn field was fought over five times but we held the field at last. I went over the field after the fight and dead and wounded lay so thick you could hardly step. Some had legs, arms, and heads torn off. Some a groaning and breathing their last. It was awful. I never saw such a sight again in ___ and may never have it. ___ ___ as close as may be ___ again. I have ___ enough of war.

We have only 41 men fit for duty now and we cannot do much more fighting until we are recruiting up. When I came to the company, we had 132 men.

Battlefield at Antietam, Maryland. (Alexander Gardner, Library of Congress)

Page 2, Oney F. Sweet's letter to his brother, dated September 21, 1862.

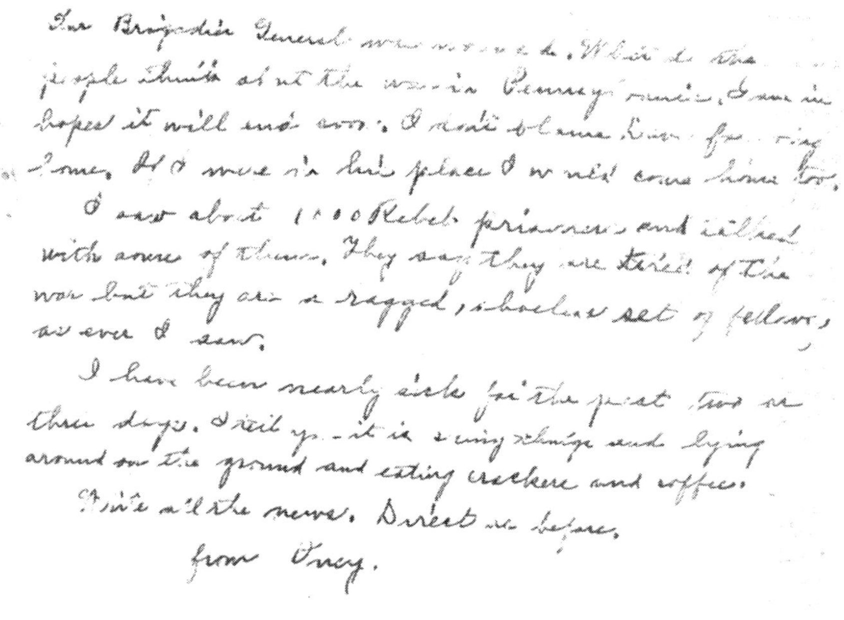

Our Brigadier General was wounded. What do the people think about the war in Pennsylvania, I am in hopes it will end soon. I don't blame him for coming home. If I was in his place I would come home too.

I saw about 1000 Rebel prisoners and talked with some of them. They say they are tired of the war but they are a ragged, shoeless set of fellows as ever I saw.

I have been nearly sick for the past two or three days. I tell you it is trying things and lying around on the ground and eating crackers and coffee.

This is all the news. Direct as before,

from Oney.

The battle along Antietam Creek near Sharpsburg, Maryland, on September 17, 1862, proved to be the bloodiest single day of the entire war. Casualties on both sides numbered more than 26,000.

Although not a clear Union victory, the fact that General Lee had been forced to lead his army back to Virginia constituted a reversal of fortune for the North. President Lincoln had been waiting for a strong showing by the Union troops before issuing his preliminary version of the Emancipation Proclamation, which he did five days later. (Library of Congress)

Brig. Gen. James B. Ricketts wrote in his report:*

> Battery F, First Pennsylvania, under Captain Matthews, and Captain Thompson's Independent Pennsylvania Battery, each consisting of four 3-inch rifled guns.** Taking advantage of the ground, both batteries opened with destructive effect, officers and men displaying great coolness while exposed to a severe fire of artillery and infantry.

Bates (1869) described it as:

> At daylight on the 17th, it opened the battle. The [Battery F] position at first was just in rear of the cornfield which has become historic, the Dunkard Church being just beyond. Soon the enemy's fire was concentrated upon it, and it was advanced across the inclosed field to the edge of the cornfield. The enemy several times charged this position, but he was as often repulsed by the storm of canister poured into his ranks.
>
> Towards the close of the engagement, Captain Matthews had his horse killed under him. Most of the battery horses were either killed or wounded. Four men were killed and fifteen wounded.
>
> The battery at this time, from severe service in the field, was in a sad state. It had been reduced from a six to a two-gun battery; the men were greatly reduced in numbers, and worn down with constant marching and fighting; the horses and equipments were in the most pitiable condition. Lieutenant Godbald was dead, Lieutenant Brockway a prisoner, Captain Matthews and Lieutenant Case absent, prostrated by disease, and the men largely scattered by wounds, sickness and desertion.

---

* James B. Ricketts, commander, Second Division, badly injured when a horse fell on him.
** James Thompson, Independent Pennsylvania Battery C, formed in September 1861.

Camp Near Sharpsburg, Md.
Friday Oct. 3d, 1862

Dear Sister:

I received a letter from you a few days ago. Since the battle of Antietam I have written two letters home and I do not know whether you got them or not. I see Jim Warner most every day. George Bennett has got back from the hospital. He is well now. I saw George Belcher the other day. Oscar Belcher is in the hospital. Charley Belcher was wounded over the eye in the last fight.

The last fight was a very hard one. I wrote all the particulars in those last letters and I hope you got them.

Charley Wells has not come to the camp yet.

Today is a very disagreeable day. Rainy. We will not get any pay until we get it for four months and that will be some time yet.

I wrote a letter to Uncle Jo day before yesterday. Has any of Spauldings boys enlisted? We only have two guns now, and not a great many men. There has a good many boys deserted since we came into Maryland.

Write soon and all the news.

From your Brother Oney F.S.

Camp Near Sharpsburg, Md.
October 7th, 1862

Dear Mother:

I received your letter a few minutes ago. If you should have time to make me 2 under shirts the same as I wore last winter before Case starts. He might not start on the 15th. If you don't have time all right. You put in box what you think best. Bread, cake, and some butter and preserves if you can pack them tight. A good big apple, 2 colored pocket hendkerchiefs.

Lakes' son came out all safe. I do not know why he don't write home oftener. The names of the boys that were killed and wounded you would not know any of them. One by the name of Benedict from Starucca was wounded in the hand. Lee Greenwood is in the hospital. Alf. Larrabee too. We have a great many sick. Lt. Gadbold is dead. He died last week in the hospital at Washington. You reccolect he had his leg shot off at the Rappahanock. Our capt. has gone home. Lt. Ricketts is here now. I will have to draw to a close. Write soon, I hope this will go through quick.

From Oney.

Oney F. Sweet's letter to his mother, dated October 7, 1862.

Camp Near Sharpsburg, M. D.
October 7th 1862

Dear Mother

I received your letter a few minutes ago. If you should have time to make me 2 under shirts the same as I wore last winter, before Case starts, (he might not start on the 15"). If you don't have time all right. You put in the box what you think best. Bread, cake and some butter and preserves if you can pack them tight, a good big apple, 2 colored handkerchiefs. Lakes son came out all safe, I do not know why he don't write home oftener. The names of the boys that were killed and wounded you would not know any of them. One boy the name of Benedict from Seneca was wounded in the hand. Lee Greenwood is in the hospital. Alf Larrabee too. We have a great many sick. Lt. Godbold is dead. He died last week in the hospital at Washington. You recollect he had his leg shot off at the Rappahanock. One Capt. has gone home. Lt. Ricketts is here now. I will have to draw to a close. Write soon. I hope this will go through quick.

from Oney.

Camp Near Sharpsburg, Md.
October 14th, 1862

Dear Brother:

I received your letter some time ago. I wrote to mother about a week ago. I was not well then I was sick for about 3 weeks and about a week I was very sick. I was taken sick after the last fight. I over-done myself. I am well now and feel like a new person. I bought some bread and butter and that done me more good than anything else. We have had two or three cold rainy days, but today is quite warm and pleasant again. I hope that box will come through safe. We only have two guns now. The captain is away recruting. Lt. Ricketts is in command of the Battery. Since the last fight we have had 8 or 10 men desert from the company. Some of them may come back after being home a while. We are in hopes we will lay on this side of the Potomac this winter and go into winter quarters. The boys does not want to go into Virginia again. We have some of our boys return from the hospital most every day. I suppose you are busy getting in the crops. Is there much game this fall? We have layed in the same camp ever since the fight. Nearly a month. We have expected to move every day for two weeks. There is some talk of our going to Washington to recruit but I do not believe we will. We will not get any pay before the middle of next month if we do then. Did you have a great many apples this fall? I suppose you are gathering them now.

I tent with Maynard Gates from Jackson and those cold days we put a fireplace in our tent and it made it quite comfortable. I will have to close for the present. Write soon and write all the news.

From your Brother Oney

Mathews Battery 1st Pa
October 25th, 1862

Dear Sister:

Do not send any box by the French boys but send the shirts, handkerchiefs and thread and a few cakes of maple surgar. I will write a letter this afternoon and write all the news. But I have got to send this off in one minute or I will not have another chance till Monday. I am well and hearty. On guard last night. A nice frosty night. In haste from

Oney F. Sweet.

Camp Near Warrinton, Va., November 7th, 1862

Dear Mother:

 I wrote a few lines to Sarah while we was at Sharpsburg and I wrote another the same day giving you all the news I could think of and I sent the letter off without putting a stamp on it and I do not know whether you got it or not. I am well. We are camped now at the place we was at last summer when Case's wife came to see him. We are nearly as far advanced as we was before. We are chasing the rebels pretty fast. Case has not come to the Battery yet and Charley Wells has not come. If you can find out where Charley Wells is let me know. I have eight letters for him. I hope you got my last letter for it was a long one.

 I will give you an account of our march. On Sunday 26th we got ready to march about noon and it was raining like old Harry. We marched until 10 o'clock at night and it was an awful night. I was wet and cold. I did not sleep a bit all night. I stood up by the fire all night. Monday, October 27th marched 7 miles. Tuesday, Oct. 28th marched to Berlein 9 miles. Wednesday Oct. 29th layed still, a cold day. Thursday Oct. 30th marched across the Potomac into Virginia, marched 6 miles. Friday, October 31st did not march. We was mustered for pay. Saturday November 1st marched 11 miles. Nov. 2nd did not march. Nov. 3rd marched at 3 o'clock in the morning. An awful cold night. Marched 15 miles. Tuesday marched 12 miles a cold day. Wednesday, Nov. 5th marched 18 miles. Nov. 6th marched here. Had snow storm. An awful day. We will not march today. There is snow on the ground now. We expect a fight soon. I will close and get some supper. Write soon.

Camp in a Wilderness, Va.
Nov. 22nd, 1862

Dear Mother:

I have written three letters home since I have received one, but we have not had a mail for about a week. Charley Wells came to the Battery the same day that I wrote the last letter home. We have had some hard marching since I last wrote. We are now 12 miles from Fredericksburg and we have layed here three days. We could not march any farther on account of bad roads. There is three thousand soldiers working on the road for two days and we will move out of here as soon as possible for we cannot get supplies here.

It has been rainy for two or three days. I am the healthiest now I ever was and I take everything easy for a person might as well make himself contented wherever he is. We expect to get paid every day.

I heard that the French boys started for the battery but could not get to where we are. Write all the particulars. Case has not come to the battery yet. I have got fat since I was sick. I saw George Belcher, George Bennett and Jim Warner the other day. They are well.

We have a plenty of fresh beef. They drive the cattle along with the army and when we stop they kill them. Today is quite a warm pleasant day. It is the first day the sun has shone for a week. I can not think of any more this time.

From Oney

Camp Near Brook Station, Va. Mathews Battery
Nov. 24th, 1862

Dear Mother:

I received your letter last night and I was very glad to hear from home. It was the 1st letter I have had from home since we came into Virginia. I was very sorry that I did not get the box. But there was no one to blame and I thank you as much as though I got it. There was many things in it that I would like to have, but I do not think I will have any more things sent unless I am very sure of getting it. I can get along very well if I should not get the shirts this winter. I have three good woolen shirts, two pair of drawers, three pair of stockings and a good overcoat and I can make myself as comfortable as the others.

I am sorry the French boys did not find us. For their sake I hope they will come soon. Dave has not come here yet. It is time that we got our pay and I hope we will get it soon for I want to get a good pair of boots for muddy weather. There is some talk that we will not get paid for some time yet.

We have marched one day since I last wrote to you. We are now 10 or 12 miles from Fredericksburg and as soon as the rail road is finished I think we will move on. Well Gillespie has been promoted to 2nd Lieut in Battery G of our regiment. He left this battery two days ago but he is camped near here. And I will see him soon and tell him about the things that was sent him.

Charley Wells brought me the sugar and it was the best thing I had tasted for some time and the towel came handy. If I had a thousand pounds of maple sugar I could sell it for 25¢ a pound here.

I sent a letter to you day before yesterday and I will write as often as I can. When we are on the march I do not have much chance to write. I have written two letters to Uncle Jos and I have had no answer. The stamp that I put on this letter is the last one I have and I wish you would send me a few in your next letter for we may not get paid for some time.

From your son Oney F. Sweet

Camp Near Brooks Station
Thursday night Dec. 4th [1862]

Dear Sister:

I received your letter a few minutes ago with the stamps and I am on guard tonight. So I will sit up and answer it. I will have to go on guard at eleven o'clock.

We expect to march from here tomorrow and I do not know where we are going. I hate to leave this place for we have got everything fixed up comfortable. We have a good tent with a fireplace in it and three of us are in it together.

We do not expect to ever see Case back to the battery again. We hear that he is Provost Marshal at Harrisburg.

Guss Roper was up here to see us last Tuesday. He stayed all night. He looks well and hearty. He is very sorry he did not enlist in artillery. His company is camped about 4 miles from here. We did not have any snow here but the ground is white in the mornings with frost.

I received Willie's letter a few days ago and I will answer it as soon as we get through with our march and I find out where we are going. Dave has not come here yet but he has not had hardly time to get here.

I will have to close for this time as it is nearly 11 o'clock. Write soon.

Direct Oney F. Sweet
Mathews Battery
Taylors Brigade
Gibbons Division
Washington, D.C.

Remember me to all enquiring friends.

Battle of Fredericksburg

December 11-15, 1862

Our men talked with some of the rebels and the rebels said they were tired of fighting and I know our men are tired of fighting and after a pay day there will be a great many desert.

—Oney F. Sweet

General Ambrose E. Burnside replaced Major General George B. McClellan as commander of the Army of the Potomac on November 7, 1862, and he immediately laid out plans to attack Fredericksburg. The ensuing conflict—fought on December 11-15, 1862, and engaging more than 170,000 combatants—ended with a Confederate victory and massive casualties on the Union side. (Library of Congress)

Bates (1869) wrote:

On the 1st of [December 1862]* while encamped at Brook's Station, on the Acquia Creek Railroad, Lieutenant Ricketts was ordered to Washington for an additional battery, and obtained two guns, fourteen men, and twenty-nine horses.

On the 10th, the battery moved to Falmouth, and reported to Captain De Russy, at Burnside's Headquarters, and was by him posted on the left bank of the [Rappahannock] river to cover the laying of the lower pontoons, and the crossing of the troops. On the 11th, the cannonading opened, and towards evening the battery was engaged with the enemy on the opposite side.

During the 13th, the batteries posted on the left bank performed very important services, driving away the enemy who had posted his guns so as to enfilade the Union column as it advanced to the attack. . . . On the two following days, while the troops remained on the right bank, the batteries were of great aid in enabling them to hold their position, and in covering their withdrawal.

See Oney F. Sweet letter dated January 3, 1863.

---

* The date "1st of September" in Bates (1869) is in error.

Letters & Diary, 1863

I never was fatter or healthier than I am now. I was weighed today and weighed 124 lbs, the most I ever weighed.

—Oney F. Sweet

Camp near White Oak Church
Jan 3rd, 1863

Dear Mother:

I have been looking for a letter from you every day for a week and I received a long one tonight. We are in the same camp as when I last wrote. I think you had not got my last letter when you wrote. I asked you to send me a silk pocket handkerchief and some thread by mail. I presume you have got it before now and the things are on the way.

I never was fatter or healthier than I am now. I was weighed today and weighed 124 lbs, the most I ever weighed. I was chopping wood this forenoon.

We have a good camp and comfortable quarters here, but I think Burnside will make another move soon and I hope he will be more successful than he was before. The soldiers do not like him much, they want Mc Clellan to command them. Burnside made a very foolish move but it was not as bad as it was first thought to be, but it was bad enough.

We don't hear anything only what we see in the papers. You know as much about our loss as we do. I think we lost about 13,000 killed, wounded and prisoners. 900 killed, 11,000 wounded and 1,000 prisoners. I believe our loss was a great deal heavier than theirs.

Our men talked with some of the rebels and the rebels said they were tired of fighting and I know our men are tired of fighting and after a pay day there will be a great many desert. But I never will desert until they put negroes in to fight and then I will. To-day's paper says they are going to put in the niggers in with white men. I say keep the niggers where they are.* I am sorry I ever enlisted in such a war as this. I never enlisted to fight for the damned nigger but I will stay now I am here. If the rebel soldiers and our soldiers understood each other they would all go home and leave Jeff Davis and Lincoln [to] fight it out.

Perhaps you may think by what I say that I am homesick but I am not. I am only tired to see the thing go on as it has been going. The French boys have not come here yet, or the Larrabee boys. Jim Warner is not in this company and I have not seen him since the fight.

---

* Sweet's daughter Marian, when going through her father's letters after his death, wrote: "This is the first time that I ever knew that my father felt antagonistic about negroes." She also commented on his statement about homesickness: "He must have been homesick for I never heard him express any such sentiments as this in his later life." She told her children and grandchildren that she grew up "hearing his war stories."

Christmas and New Years passed off without anything unusual taking place. I would not know it from any other day. We have had most beautiful weather for two weeks passed and I hope it may continue so.

I git the stamps all right. We was mustered for pay last Wednesday and we will get it in a few days or else we will have to wait two months longer. Some of the boys begin to think we are not agoing to get paid any more.

Charley Wells stands soldiering first rate. He is a cannoneer the same as me. There is but very few that have stood it better than I have and I don't let anything worry me. A good many get sick by thinking of home all the time and not taking care of themselves. Our doctors in the army are not worth a snap. But our doctor for the Battery is a pretty good one and he thinks a good deal of me. I never have taken but very little medicine.

I have been lousy once or twice when I had to wear my clothes 3 weeks without changing them. That was at Bull Run, but I got rid of them very quick by throwing all of my clothes away and putting on new ones. Nearly every one in the Battery was lousy, but if you have a chance to wash you can easily keep clean. This company is a very clean company to what some are. I have seen officers and men sit down and pick them off. I have seen good shirts by the hundred thrown away, and they were alive with them. I do the most of my own washing, some times I have a nigger wash for me. I had a shirt, pair of drawers, and a pair of stockings washed today. I have often thought I would write about this, but I thought maybe you did not know anything about such animals. I never heard of body lice until I came in the Army.

I do my own cooking. I used to have a nigger to cook for me, but I would rather do it myself. When I come home you will need no cook or washer.

Have you heard from Uncle Jo lately. I have written two letters and had no answer. Write soon. You don't know how I like to hear from home and any little thing is news to me. I think this is a long letter.

Oney

Monday, January 5, 1863

Cool and cloudy in the morning. Cleared off about 8 o'clock and was very warm and pleasant. The warmest and pleasantest day I ever saw this time of year. Report of a big fight in the west. Ordnance equipment received from Washington.

Tuesday

Warm and pleasant in the forenoon. Cool and rainy in the afternoon. Quite a hard rain in the evening. Watered Jim Quin's horses.* The Monitor foundered at sea off Cape Hatteras.**

Wednesday

Mild and very pleasant. Heard that our Battery was to be put in the Pennsylvania Reserve Corps. Received a letter from home stating that they had expressed a box to me and Charlie on Dec. 31st. A very cold night. Recd. orders to march in the morning at 8 o'clock a.m.

Thursday

Cool and pleasant day. Marched at 9 o'clock. Reached camp about noon. Joined the Reserves. Saw Battery A boys. All well. Strict orders from Major Brady, Chief of the artillery. Snowed in the evening. Putting up quarters.

Friday

Warm and pleasant day. Worked hard putting up winter quarters. Got done about noon. Major Brady came into our camp. George Bennett came over to see me. Henry Whitman and George Bennett came over to camp.

Saturday

Warm in the forenoon. Helped dig a sink. Cleared out the woods in front of Ricketts' quarters. Commenced raining about noon and rained all day. Rained very hard in the evening. Had no roll call. Washed some clothes today.

---

* James Quinn, private, mustered in July 8, 1861; mustered out with battery, June 10, 1865.

** The Union ironclad Monitor, with 16 crewmen, sank during a gale off Cape Hatteras, North Carolina, on the night of December 30-31, 1862. (Quarstein, 2006)

Camp Near Bell Plains, Va. Mathews Battery
Jan. 11th, 1863

Dear Mother:

I received your letter a few days ago stating that you had sent me some things in Charley's box. We have not got them yet but I think we will get them if we lay here a few days longer. Last Thursday we moved camp. We are now in the same division with Jim Warner and all the other boys. We have comfortable quarters built here. We hope we will lay here the rest of the winter but there is some talk of our leaving here in a few days.

Our camp is only a very short distance from Battery A. I was over to see Jim Warner and George Bennett. Also Henry Whitmarsh. They are all well. I heard by way of Jim Warner that Adeline Claflin was married. I was pleased to hear that she was married and had done so well. We heard here today that Mc Clellan had command of the army again, and I hope it is true.

There is a report here that this division is going to Washington soon. And if we go there we will not probably see any more fighting of any account. I do not believe the report, but I hope it is true. There is one thing sure there is something going to be done with this division.

Stephen Ridgeway, that is the fellow I tent with, his father came to see him today and brought him a lot of things. We live bully now and if my things come we will live better. There is a new law passed that you can send things by mail cheap.

We are looking for our pay every day now. I think we may get our box tomorrow. I will write as soon as we get it. I wrote you a letter last Sunday, I do not get any more letters from Sarah and Willie. Direct your letters as follows:

Battery F
1st Pa Artillery R.V.C.
Washington, D.C.

I am well and hearty and hope you are as ever. From your affectionate son
Oney F. Sweet

Sunday, January 11, 1863

Cleared off pleasant but it is a cool, windy day. Ridgeway's father came to see him. Had a letter from G. Riley Stiles. Wrote a letter to mother. Went over to Battery A in the afternoon and saw Goodson's boys. Heard that McClellan had command.

Monday

Very warm and pleasant day. Standing gun drill from 10 till 11 a.m. Battery drill from 1 till 2 p.m. Wrote to mother and G. R. Stiles. On guard, 3rd Relief Corporal Flory countersign Globins.

Tuesday

A warm and pleasant day. Wrote to Uncle Joseph, asking him to send me a paper weekly. Cool toward night. Steven Ridgeway was away with his father. Had bread, butter and chicken for supper. Received a letter from D. P. Maynard. Sent me two notes.

Wednesday

A warm and pleasant day. Had a drill in the forenoon. Cleaned off Pieces and Caissons in the afternoon. Windy toward night. The boys charged on a Suttler last night. A very windy night.

Thursday

A warm but windy day. Cloudy, winds southeast. Mr. Ridgeway started for home. Had to police our camp from eleven til one o'clock. Jim Warner came over to camp and eat supper with me. The wind stopped blowing at dark.

Friday

A cool, windy day. Wrote a letter to David P. Maynard. Had a drill in the forenoon. Made a bet with Jack Rake that we would leave this camp before the twenty-ninth of this month. One dollar bet. Went to bed at 1/2 past 8 o'clock.

Saturday

A clear, but pleasant day. Were inspected by Col. Wainwright, Chief of Artillery of 1st Army Corps. Passed inspection better than I expected we would. Received a letter from Willie. Received marching orders. A cold night.

The Camp Sutler

Made a brilliant charge on a Suttler near the landing.
                              —Oney F. Sweet

The phrase "charge on a sutler," variations of which appear in other diaries and letters of the period, seems to have a double meaning. On one hand, it could refer to charging on credit until payday items sold by sutlers, the camp merchants who provided non-military goods to the army. The phrase could also mean, as seems likely in Oney Sweet's case, the taking of goods, without payment, from a sutler perceived as being a war-time profiteer.

The sutlers had local monopolies under licenses from the government, and their prices reflected that—along with allegations of graft and corruption. In their defense, sutlers incurred extraordinary financial risk by being near the battle lines and, at times, in the line of fire; if soldiers died or deserted, the sutlers found it difficult, if not impossible, to collect on the debts.

In an account published after the war, a soldier with the 1st Regiment, Ohio Volunteer Cavalry, described how the setup worked:

> Sutlers usually were regular sharks, and their methods of doing business was by Sutler's checks from one pay-day to another. These checks were either tickets or metal [tokens] representing from ten cents to one dollar, and any soldier could go and get a limited amount of checks and the Sutler would charge him up on his books with the full amount of them, and then when the soldier made his purchases the Sutler would charge him up so as to get at least one hundred per cent profit—for instance, fifty cents a pound for cheese, one dollar for a plug of Navy tobacco, and three dollars for a canteen full of commissary whisky, warranted to kill at a hundred yards. When pay-day arrived, the Sutler was on hand at the table beside the Paymaster to collect, and he always got his full share of the greenbacks paid out. . . .

A sutler's bomb-proof "Fruit and Oyster House" during the siege of Petersburg, Virginia.
(Timothy H. O'Sullivan, Library of Congress)

Some of our trainmen gave the passing troops a hint one day that if they would give the thing a start, there would be no serious opposition from anyone in the regiment to confiscating the Sutler's stock, as it was getting pretty well run down anyway. No sooner said than done, for two or three fellows gave a few yanks at the guy-ropes and down came the tent and the goods were confiscated in a jiffy. (Curry, 1898)

continued on page 65

Horses & Mules

*I saw a horse sold here for three dollars which was sound
every way, but he was grey and the government rejected him.*

—Oney F. Sweet

Horses and mules played an indispensable role in the Civil War, not only
for the cavalry, but as draft animals for the artillery brigades, quartermaster
supply trains, and sutlers. A single field artillery battery like the one Oney F.
Sweet served in needed 100 or more horses to operate efficiently.

During the heat of battle, equines had a significantly higher casualty
rate than the men, not only due to their size, but because they became
primary targets for charging infantry as a means of immobilizing the
cannons and caissons.

Over the course of the war, there were at least three million horses
and mules used, and about 50 percent of them became casualties—either
killed in action, or broken down by hard service, and soon after they died
or were abandoned. (Armistead, 2013)

continued from page 64

Isaac L. Taylor, a soldier with the 1st Minnesota Volunteer Infantry
Regiment, penned a similar anecdote:

> This morning the boys "charge" on a sutler shop, carry
> off three or four thousand dollars worth of goods, tear down
> his building & carry off the boards. (Wolf, 1944)

A post-war Congressional investigation reported "flagrant abuses" and
that soldiers were "literally robbed" so the sutler's "purse might be swelled"
to "bribe army officials." The investigation also found that President Ulysses
S. Grant's Secretary of War, W.W. Belknap, "had received a liberal share of
the surplus profits of these army profiteers." (Compton, 1919)

Sunday, January 18, 1863

A cold but pleasant day. Wrote a letter to Willie. Had knapsack inspection at 11 o'clock. Went over in the hills and got some curiositys. Went over to Battery A in the afternoon. Expect to move tomorrow. A very cold night. Gloves were issued to the company.

Monday

A cold, but a very pleasant day. Had harness drill in the afternoon. Washed some clothes in the morning. Did not move as we expected. Went out and shot off revolvers at the mark. Made a brilliant charge on a Suttler near the landing.

Tuesday

A cold, cloudy day. Marched at twelve o'clock. Passed White Oak Church, Falmouth. Marched 12 miles and camped in the woods. A cold, rainy night. Put up our tent. The whole army is moving. An account in the paper that Burnsides had crosst the river.

Wednesday

A cold, stormy day. Rained nearly all day. Marched at daylight. A very bad road and we got stalled several times. Camped about noon in the woods. We could not get any farther. A very rainy night. Slept very good in our little tent.

Thursday

A stormy, muddy day. Harnessed up ready for march at eight o'clock. Very bad roads and don't think we will move today. Saw Bill McCall. He is Adjunctant of HPRVC. Received orders to on harness at one o'clock. Expect to fall back tomorrow morning.

Friday

Stopped raining. Orders to get ready for move back. Started on the march at eight o'clock. A very muddy day and bad going. Reached our old camp about three o'clock. Put up our tent and got dinner. Passed through Falmouth, saw some of the 141st regiment.

Saturday

A warm and pleasant day. On guard first relief Corporal Mead no countersign. Wrote a letter to mother. Cannoneers had to clear off camp for Battery G, B and A. Looks like a rainstorm. Went to bed early.

Camp near Bellplains Landing, Va.
Battery F 1st Pa Artillery
Jan. 24th 1863

Dear Mother:

Here we are back in our old camp. We marched from here last Tuesday expecting to cross the river and have another fight. We marched about 10 miles on Tuesday and on Wednesday we marched 5 miles and got stuck in the mud and could not go any farther. It rained Tuesday night, Wednesday and Wednesday night. It was the awfullest time you ever saw. Mud was hub deep and it was raining all the time. We had to fall back and we reached our old camp yesterday and we are now in our old quarters and I do not think Burnsides will undertake to move us again very soon. It was a great failure and a great many horses were used up, and it was the hardest times we ever saw. If I wasn't as tough as a knot I could not have stood it, but I feel as good as new today. I was on guard last night.

I think we would have whipped the rebs this time if it had not rained.

We drew buckskin gloves last Monday and they come good to us. We have not got the box yet and I have give up all hopes of getting it.

It has cleared off pleasant today and perhaps if the mud drys up or freezes up we will move and have a fight. I wish it would for I want to fight them and either whip or get whipped and see if it won't bring this war to a close.

One company of the Bucktails stacked their guns and swore they would not fight any more until they were paid.*

I will close. Write soon. I remain your Son.

Oney F. Sweet
Battery F
1st Pa Artillery Rgt. R. V. C.
Washington, D.C.

---

* Prior to leaving for Harrisburg, the men of the 42nd Pennsylvania Volunteer Infantry Regiment, 1st Pennsylvania Rifles, adopted the tail of a buck as their "regimental badge of honor." Recruits placed deer tails on their caps, and they became known as the Bucktails Regiment. (Bucktails)

Mud March

January 20-24, 1863

It was the awfullest time you ever saw. Mud was hub deep.
—Oney F. Sweet

General Burnside attempted to cross the Rappahannock River and mount a second attack on Fredericksburg, having failed to capture the fortified city on his first attempt in December. But a nor'easter blew in, bringing with it a deluge of cold rain, and turned the road into a quagmire.

A *New York Times* reporter described the scene:

> An indescribable chaos of pontoons, wagons and artillery encumbered the road down to the river. Horses and mules dropped down dead, exhausted with the effort to move their loads through the hideous medium. One hundred and fifty dead animals, many of them buried in the liquid muck, were counted in the course of a morning's ride. . . .
>
> The lads trudged along tired enough, but jolly withal, and disposed to be quite facetious over the "mud campaign," whose odd experiences will doubtless long for the theme of conversation around many a camp-fire.
>
> (*The Rebellion Record,* 1863)

President Abraham Lincoln, upon General Burnside's request, relieved Burnside of his command of the Army of the Potomac, saying that Burnside had lost the confidence of the army. Lincoln replaced him with Major General Joseph Hooker. Generals William B. Franklin and Edwin V. Sumner also lost their commands in the house cleaning.

(Library of Congress)

Sunday, January 25, 1863

A cloudy, rainy day. Cleared off about noon. Was quite unwell. Had no inspection. Received a letter from cousin Annie and a paper from Uncle Joseph, the New York Tribune.* The letter was dated August 15, 1862, mislaid. Brilliant charges. I was not engaged. A bad job.

Monday

Warm, but cloudy day. Standing gun drill from 10 till 11. Cleaned off the Guns and Caissons in the afternoon. Received the Mercury Herald, Harpers Weekly and Police Gazette from Uncle Joseph. A windy night. Rained during the night.

Tuesday

A rainy, stormy day. Heard that Burnsides was superseded. Hooker to take comand. Built stables for our horses. Orders from the President stating that Burnsides, Sumner and Franklin were relieved by their own request. George Bennett was over to see me in the evening. A rainy night.

Wednesday

A snow storm. Snowed about three inches. Wrote to Uncle Joseph and Annie. Received the New York World. Snowed nearly all day and night. Snowed about ten inches. Orders read to us that the Penn. Reserves are going to Washington in a few days.

Thursday

The sun shines and it has stopped snowing, but it is an awful disagreeable morning in camp. Went and got some wood. Heard that the batterys were not going to Washington with the infantry. Felt unwell all day, but did not go to the doctors.

Friday

A warm and beautiful day. Snow is disappearing very fast. Received a paper from Uncle Jo, the Herald. Jim Quinn kicked up quite a row in camp. Put him under guard. A soldier's delight: the mail, the paymaster and tobacco.**

---

* "cousin Annie" probably Annie L. Foster, cousin on his mother's side and the daughter of Uncle Joseph [Foster].

** See Song and Dance, page 83.

Saturday

A cool, but pleasant day. Went down to the landing with a horse after feed, but got none. The roads are in the awfullest condition I ever saw. Received a New York World from Uncle Joseph. Orders. The President's proclamation setting the Nigers free. Don't like it.*

Sunday, February 1, 1863

A warm and pleasant day. Some wind. Had Battery Inspection at ten o'clock. Major Johnson came to pay us. We were paid in the afternoon. Received a paper from Uncle Joe and a letter from Sarah. The paymaster was welcomed in this camp. On guard.

Monday

A cold, windy day. Received a paper from Sarah. Sent her fifty cents. Expressed home thirty dollars. Orders read to us stating that we were to receive furloughs. The boys are quite sure that we are going to Washington.

Tuesday

A cold, windy day. Received a paper from Uncle Joseph. An awful cold night. The boys drew for furloughs. Joe Misha and Tardy are going. I did not draw. Going to wait until we go to Washington.

Wednesday

A cold, but pleasant day. Wrote a letter to D. P. M. sending him two notes. Wrote to Uncle Joseph sending him A. V. Dan Gabley was over here. Received a paper from Uncle Joseph. A Very cold night.

Thursday

Cold and snowy day. Got no mail. Was in the Orderly's tent nearly all day. Bought a load of wood of the boy; 25¢ a load. The snow turned to rain in the night.

Friday

A warm, but very muddy day. Rained some. Went over to Battery A. They

---

* President Abraham Lincoln issued the Emancipation Proclamation on January 1, 1863. The proclamation declared "that all persons held as slaves" within the rebellious states "are, and henceforward shall be free." It did not free the slaves in states that remained in the Union. (National Archives)

have to go to the 9th Army Corps. Heard that we have to stay here. Received 3 papers and a letter from D. P. Maynard. Battery A started for Washington.

Saturday

A warm and pleasant day. Wrote a letter to D. P. Maynard. A plenty of licour in camp. Several fights. Steven felt good. Went to bed early. No mail for the Battery.

Sunday, February 8, 1863

A warm and pleasant day. Had Battery inspection at 10 o'clock. Lt. Brockway inspected us. Recd. a letter from Cousin Annie and one from mother. Heard that our box was in Washington. We are going to send for it. A charge made on Sutler.

Monday

Warm and pleasant day. Recd. a letter from mother and one from D. P. M. Had standing gun drill at two o'clock. On guard, 3rd relief. Corporal Christian on the horses.* Mother started another box for me by way of Lieutenant Brainard, 141st Reg. P.V.

Tuesday

A warm and pleasant day. Windy in the morning. Wrote a letter to Sarah, sending her an Express Receipt and one dollar. Cut some wood. Got no letters. A real summer's day.

Wednesday

A warm, cloudy day. Hail and rain. Done in the afternoon. Had inspection at ten o'clock by Major Brandy. A plenty of licour in camp. A high old time. 9 extra guards detailed. No mail.

Thursday

Cold, windy day. Had inspection by Colonel Wainwright at 12 o'clock. Passed ok. Quota of whiskey issued out to us. Got a mail but I got nothing. Went to bed at 12 o'clock. A cold night.

---

* John H. Christian, private, mustered in July 8, 1861; promoted to corporal; wounded at Gettysburg; mustered out August 8, 1864.

Friday

A warm and pleasant day. Had Battery drill at ten o'clock. Drove Shiphers team. Standing gun drill in the afternoon. A beautiful day. Received a paper from Uncle Joseph. Camp rumour that we are going to ship.

Saturday

A beautiful day. Warm and pleasant. Wrote to Annie Foster. Sent her a dollar. Got no mail. Had some washing done. Went to bed early.

Sunday, February 15, 1863

A cold, rainy day. Rained very hard in the morning. Rained some all day. Had no inspection. Got no mail. Cleared off about three o'clock.

Monday

Warm and beautiful day. Had Battery inspection at ten o'clock by Lt. Ricketts. Went over to have my likeness taken, but did not get it. Got no mail.

Tuesday

Cold, snowey day. Snowed all day. Snowed about twelve inches. Snowed in the evening. Got no mail. Went to bed early. Cleared off about 9 o'clock.

Wednesday

A warm, but very disagreeable day. Sloppy underfoot. Sent a letter to D. P. Maynard came here for him. Rained most all day. On guard, 3rd relief Corporal Nead on the horses.* An awful rainy night.

Thursday

A warm, but very disagreeable day. On guard, got no mail, got some washing done. Expected a big mail from Division Hd. Qtrs., but did not get it. New troops came in.

Friday

On a warm and pleasant day the 8th New York Cavalry left here. They have been camped near us for some time. Got a big mail. About thirty papers from Uncle Joseph and a letter from D. P. M. Policed the camp.

---

* Francis Need, private, mustered in July 8, 1861; discharged May 31, 1864, expiration of term.

Winter quarters of Union forces near Centreville, Virginia. (Library of Congress)

Saturday

A warm and pleasant day. Began to build a new house. Worked hard all day. Got it about half done. Recd. a paper from Uncle Joseph and a letter from Mother and one from Sarah.

Sunday, February 22, 1863

Snow about six inches deep. Snowed all day. Snowed 15 inches. An awful cold day. Got breakfast up at the house. Wrote to D. P. Maynard. The orderly put a few lines in it.

Monday

Stopped snowing. Sun shines. Wrote to Will G. Brewer, Robt. Ballantine and two home. Received a letter from Uncle Joseph. Saw Frank Chamberlain. A clear, pleasant day. Some new men detailed for the Battery.

Tuesday

A warm pleasant day. Worked at our house. Got it most done. Got 4 papers from Uncle Joseph. Snow is disappearing fast.

Wednesday

A warm and pleasant day. Rained all day. Could not work at house much. Got no mail. A muddy day. Wireman and Mowery's fathers came to see them.

Thursday

A cold, rainy day. On guard, Second Relief, Corp. Nead, Countersign: Cleveland. Moved into our new house and slept bully. I got no mail. Cleaned off the guns for inspection.

Friday

A warm and pleasant forenoon. Wrote to Uncle Joseph. Had my likeness taken and sent to mother. Cleaned off the guns for inspection. Got two papers from Uncle Joseph.

Saturday

A warm and pleasant day. Had inspection at 10 o'clock. I had to drive a team. Inspected and mustered by Major Braydy. Cloudy in the afternoon. Wrote to Dick T. Fitzgerald. Got a letter from Willie.

Bates (1869) noted that Colonel Wainwright, in command of the artillery of the First Army Corps, published to his command, on the 25th of February, 1863, a communication from General Hunt regarding the Battle of Fredericksburg, fought December 11-15, 1862, one of the largest and deadliest of the Civil War. Excerpts from this communication describe Battery F's role in the battle:

> Colonel :—The reports of the late inspections show that none of your batteries are in bad order; the only corps so reported. The batteries reported in the best order are, Reynolds' L, First New York; Ricketts' F, First Pennsylvania; and Lepperne's, Fifth Maine.
>
> HENRY J. HUNT,
> Brigadier General and Chief of Artillery,
> Army of the Potomac.

** Henry Wireman (also Wyerman), private, mustered in July 8, 1861; promoted to 1st Lt., December 6, 1864; mustered out with battery, June 10, 1865.

Sunday, March 1, 1863

A cold, rainy day. Myron French and Silby started for home. Sent a knife to father by Myron French. Wrote a letter to Willie, sent him one dollar. Got no mail.

Monday

A warm and pleasant day. Guss Roper came over to see me and staid all night. He has a box for me. Received two papers from Uncle Joe. A letter from cousin Annie and a letter from Will S. Brower.

Tuesday

A warm and pleasant day. Started to go after my box, but could not get along with the horse. Got a paper from Uncle Joseph.

Wednesday

A warm and pleasant day. Steph went over to the 141st to get the box for me but they had moved camp and he did not get it. Orders read to us stating that we would have a drill twice a day. A cold night.

Thursday

A warm and pleasant day. Had inspection of quarters at 10 o'clock by Lt. Ricketts. Had a drill at 11 o'clock and one at 2 o'clock. Got no letters or papers.

Friday

A cold, stormy day. Had a march inspection by Major Brady. I acted No. 3. Made no mistakes. Rained some and it was very cold. Got a paper.

Saturday

A cold, windy day. Got a load of wood. Bot two books from Dick C. Fitzgerald. Got a letter from D. P. Maynard. He has got his discharge Got a letter from cousin Annie. Her photograph. A paper from Uncle Joe. Heard that our box was at the 13th Mass.

Sunday, March 8, 1863

A warm and rainy day, but did not rain much. Had Knapsack and Quarters inspection by Major Brady at ten o'clock. Got our box from the 13th Mass. The things were nearly all spoilt. Got some things which were good. Wrote to D. P. Maynard.

Monday

Warm and beautiful day. Had standing gun drill at 10 o'clock. Harness drill in the afternoon. Steph was away all day. Got the NY World from Uncle Joseph. Corp. More returned to the Battery.

Tuesday

A rainy and disagreeable day. A detail made to go to Hd. Qtrs. No drill on account of storm. Got no mail. Stephan was sick and went to the Drs.

Wednesday

A cool, rainy day. Very disagreeable. Had standing gun drill at ten o'clock. Drivers drill in the afternoon. Cleared off pleasant. Got a letter from Robert B. and a paper from Uncle Jos. Seagt. French returned. He brought some little things for me from home.

Camp Near Bell Plains, Va.
Battery F 1st Pa Artillery
March 11th, 1863

Dear Mother:

I have at last got the box and heard from the other one. We got the one from Washington. We paid $1.50 to get it. The things was most all good. Some of the cakes was moldy, but the fruit and other things was splendid. I bought some sugar and stewed some apples and berrys. I have six shirts now. The night cap I think a good deal of and other little things. The needle case that Mrs. Burrows made me I lost at Bull Run. I also lost the Bible that Sarah gave me. And your likeness. I got Annie Foster's likeness the other day. We expect to get the other box in a few days. We have very bad weather here now. I suppose you have got my likeness before now. And also the knife which I sent by French. Write soon and all the news. I cannot think of much to write this time.

From your affectionate son

Oney F. Sweet

Thursday

A warm and beautiful day. Wrote a letter to mother. Drew for a furlough last night. Curry and S. Mowry drew (go). Curry sold his to Blackman for fifteen dollars. Wells and I went to the 141st PV and got our things. Got two papers from Uncle Joseph. Bought a map of the Battle of Antietam. Sent it home.

Friday

An awful cold morning. A very cold night. The orderly starts home on furlough. Also Lt. Ricketts.* Sent a map of the Battlefield of Antietam to mother. I got no mail. A very cold day. Had a short drill. Saw Frank Chamberlin.

Saturday

A cold, but pleasant day. Had no drill. Blakman and Mowry started for home on a furlow. Wrote to R. F. Ballantine and to Uncle Joseph. Got a paper from Uncle Jo. Got a load of wood. Licuor high in camp.

Sunday, March 15, 1863

A cold, but pleasant morning. Had a preparatory review at three o'clock p.m. Rained and hailed in the afternoon. Very cold. Thundered, stormy. Got the World from Uncle Jo. Rained a good deal in the night.

Monday

A cold, but pleasant day. Had Battalion drill in the forenoon by Major Brady. Had review in the afternoon by General Doubleday and staff. I acted No. 1. Passed off well. Got two papers from Uncle Jo.

Tuesday

A mild and pleasant day. Had gun drill at two p.m. Three papers from Uncle Joe, Herald, Leslies, and Mercury. Report in camp that the rebel Jackson was on our right with 100,000 men. The report is not credited. He will make things git if he is there.

Wednesday

A warm and pleasant day. Stephen went to see his cousin who is very sick. Had guns at ten a.m. Drilled at dismantling pieces. Wrote to GWB Phila. Got no letters or papers. Got some new horses. Heard heavy cannonading on our right.

---

* Upon the promotion of Captain Matthews to major on March 14, Lieutenant R. B. Ricketts was commissioned as a captain to succeed him. (Bates, 1869)

Thursday

A cold, but pleasant day. Went to the doctor 3 times. Morning, noon and night. On guard 3rd relief, Corporal Trump. Had Battery drill in the forenoon. Cleaned out the pieces in the afternoon. Got no mail. Snowed some in the night.

Friday

A cold, snowy day. Snowed and blowed. An awful day for being out. Got three papers from Uncle Jo and a letter from D. P. Maynard. Did not feel very well.

Saturday

A cold, snowy and rainy day. A very disagreeable day. Got no mail. Quite unwell. The snow has all disappeared.

Sunday, March 22, 1863

A warm and beautiful day. Went to the doctors. Got a dose of oil. Feel much better than I did yesterday. Got a letter from Sarah and one from mother. Three papers from Uncle Joseph.

Monday

A warm and beautiful day. Wrote to Sarah. Had Battery drill in the forenoon. Got a paper from Uncle Joseph. Went to bed with a severe headache.

Tuesday

A warm and beautiful day. Had Battery drill in the forenoon and Gun drill in the afternoon. Recd. marching orders. Snider returned.* Got a letter from R. F. Ballantine and papers. Papers from Uncle Joseph. Commenced raining at dark and very hard.

Wednesday

A warm, beautiful day. Wrote to R. F. Ballantine. Had Gun drill in the afternoon. Frank Chamberlin was over to see me. Jim Quin sentenced to 1 month hard labour. Got no mail. Saw George Dutcher.**

---

* Francis H. Snider, mustered in July 8, 1861; promoted to 2d Lt., January 31, 1864; wounded at Mine Run, Va.; discharged October 8, 1864.

** George E. Dutcher, private; transferred to Battery A; mustered out with battery, July 25, 1865.

Thursday

A warm, pleasant day. Had Gun drill in the afternoon. Played ball. We have to turn in our Sibly tents and have the shelter tents.* Sam Mowery returned.** Henry Tiffany returned to the Battery.

Friday

A warm and beautiful day. Had a drill in the forenoon. Had a picture taken of the Battery camp. Q.C. Blackman returned. Conrad started on a recruiting furlough.*** Got a letter from G. R. Stiles and a paper from Uncle Jo. Drew for furloughs. Steph got the Go.

Saturday

An awful rainy day. Rained very hard nearly all day. Wrote to David P. Maynard. My cold and cough is not so bad today. Got three papers from Uncle Joseph: Herald, Police Gazette and Budget of Fun. Cleared off near night.

Sunday, March 29, 1863

A warm, but windy day. Had knapsack inspection at 10 a.m. The boys played ball. Preaching at Battery B in the afternoon. Got no mail for myself. A very cold night. Report that we are going to Harpers Ferry under General Ricketts. It is merely a report.

Monday

A warm and pleasant day. Had Battery drill in the forenoon. Wrote to G. R. Stiles. Recd. a paper from Uncle Joseph. Got an answer from G. W. B. Phila. A cool night. A report that the Rebels were evacuating Richmond. Don't believe a word of it.

Tuesday

A warm, but disagreeable day. Snowed about five inches last night and turned to rain early this morning very fast. Went with the wagons after forage.

---

* Shelter tent: a rectangle of canvas laid over a horizontal brace to form an open-ended "A" or wedge shape.

** Sam Mowery, private; mustered in July 8, 1861; deserted June 29, 1863.

*** Enoch Blackman, private, [reenlisted] January 3, 1864; mustered out with battery, June 10, 1865.

Henry A. Conrad, sergeant, mustered in July 10, 1861; discharged on Surgeon's Certificate, January 15, 1864.

Went after the mail. Got only five letters, none for myself. Cleared off pleasant toward night. On guard, 1st Relief, Corporal Brockway.*

Wednesday, April 1, 1863

A cold, clear morning. Windy. All Fools Day. A great many fooled. On guard, 1st Relief, Commissary, Corporal Frank Brockway. Heard that this division was to remain here to guard the landing. Received a paper from Uncle Jo. Gus Roper came here and staid all night.

Thursday

A cold, windy day. Reviewed by General Hooker, Reynolds and Doubleday at 12 o'clock. Both infantry and artillery out. Rained real hard all day. Went to bed early. I got no mail.

Friday

A warm and beautiful day. Cleaned off the guns for inspection. O. G. Larrabee and Smith L. French returned to the Battery. They have been out in Ohio. Lt. R. B. Ricketts returned from home. Got a paper from Uncle Joseph. Quite a jubilee in camp. A cold night.

Saturday

Cold, windy day. Had inspection by Capt. Cowper in the forenoon. Wind blew hard all day. Capt. E. W. Mathews returned to the Battery. He is not entirely well yet. The boys were glad to see him. Got a letter from Sarah. Got eight stamps. Commenced snowing in the evening. A cold night. Got two papers from New York.

Sunday, April 5, 1863

A cold, disagreeable day. Snow about ten inches deep. No roll call in the morning. Wrote to Sarah. Snow nearly all disappeared. Rained some. Got no mail for the Battery. A cold night. No drill.

Monday

A cool, pleasant day. Inspection of quarters by Maj. Mathews and Lt. Brockway. Boys played ball. Cloudy and bad underfoot. No drill. Got two

---

* Franklin P. Brockway, mustered in as a private; promoted to 2nd lieutenant December 21, 1864; mustered out with battery, June 10, 1865.

papers from Uncle Jos. Contributions distributed by Maj. Mathews. I got a pair of socks. It's a very interesting occasion. 3 hearty cheers given for the Major.

Tuesday

A warm and beautiful morning. Cool and windy in the afternoon. Saw Billy Bartlett. Had Gun drill in the forenoon. Quite a hubbub last night in camp. Blagguarded Ricketts. Went over to the 161st Reg. Got two papers.

Wednesday

A mild and pleasant day. Had no drills. Went out in the woods with O G and got a load of wood. Got no mail. On Guard on the Guns, 2nd Relief, Corp. Brockway only stood four hours.

Thursday

A warm and beautiful day. The 1st Army Corps was reviewed by President Lincoln and General Hooker. Marched about four miles to the ground. It was a Grand Affair. Abe's wife and children were along. We left camp at 7 o'clock in the morning and returned at 5 p.m. Got a paper from mother and one from Uncle Joseph.

Friday

A warm and beautiful day. Stephen Ridgeway started on a furlough. Also Hagues and Shoop.* Wrote to mother. Sent my overcoat and gunner's haversack by Steph. He is going to express it home. Had a dance in the evening. Got a paper from Uncle Jos.

Saturday

A warm and beautiful day. Had no drill. Wrote to Uncle Joseph. Frank Chamberlain came over to our camp. Had several games of Euchre.* A very warm day, but some windy in the afternoon. Got a paper from Uncle Joseph. Lt. C. B. Brockway started on a furlough

Sunday, April 12, 1863

A warm and pleasant day. Had Battery inspection at ten o'clock by Maj. Mathews and Capt. Ricketts. Got a paper from Uncle Jos. A shower in the afternoon. Went to bed early.

---

* William Shoop, corporal, mustered in July 8, 1861; transferred to Battery G, March 26, 1864.

Monday

A cool, but pleasant day. O. G. Larrabee and Lake went to the 17th Penna. Cavalry. The Cavalry camped near us struck tents and marched down the river. Went down to the landing. Had fresh fish for dinner. Had Battery drill in the afternoon by Lt. Ricketts. Received marching orders. Got a paper from Uncle Jos.

Tuesday

A warm and beautiful day. Preparing for a march. Went over to the 151st. The caissons went down to Falmouth after ammunition. On guard, second relief on the Guns, Corporal Patterson.** A cool, windy night. Got a paper.

Wednesday

A cool, rainy day. Rained very hard nearly all day. Expect to march tomorrow. Payrolls came to be signed but were not right. A very disagreeable night. Got no letters or papers. Turned in our Sibly tents.

Thursday

A warm and pleasant day. Did not march as we expected. A cloudy afternoon. Went down to the landing after oysters. Got no letters or papers. Expected the paymaster, but he did not come.

Friday

A warm and pleasant morning. It looked like rain all the afternoon. Went with the wagons after hay. The boys played ball. Drew three days more rations. Saw Frank Chamberlain. Got no mail. Charlie Clark came back from Washington with the Major's mare.

Saturday

A warm and beautiful day. Had no drills. Signed the payrolls and got our pay. Major Burt paid us. Got a paper from Uncle Joseph. All well and all right.

---

* Euchre, a popular, trick-taking card game that originated in Europe. (*Encyclopædia Britannica*)

** William H. Patterson, corporal, mustered in July 8, 1861; wounded at Bristoe Station, Va., October 14, 1863; transferred to Battery G, March 26, 1864.

Song and Dance

Had a dance in the evening.

——Oney F. Sweet

Music, song, and dance played an influential role in the life of a soldier, from voicing their patriotism through lyrical expression to dancing for joy to alleviating boredom. Some men carried (or made) fiddles, guitars, and banjos to complement the military-issue bugles, fifes, drums, and assorted brass instruments. Many regiments had their own bands.

Soldier's Joy, also known as *Pay Day in the Army*, was a popular dance tune of the era. One verse sheds light on the soldier's life:

> *Twenty-five cents for the morphine, fifteen cents for the beer,*
> *Twenty-five cents for the morphine, gonna take me away from here.*

Legend has it that officers in Confederate and Union camps banned the love song *Lorena* because it made men long for home and desert. Perhaps "the best-loved song in the Confederate army," *Lorena* captured the hearts of homesick soldiers, and "it almost appeared to be a new national anthem." (Holsinger, 1999)

Other popular songs included *The Girl I Left Behind Me* and *Listen to the Mockingbird*. Soldiers of both camps also enjoyed a number of songs composed during the war years. *Weeping, Sad and Lonely*, or *When This Cruel War Is Over*, "was so destructive to morale that it was banned." (Heaps, 1960)

The Union and Confederate bands battled each other, and not without risk. In describing the action at Cold Harbor, Bates (1869) quoted Battery F's Captain Brockway:

> "At dusk a rebel band came to the extreme front of their line and played 'Dixie,' 'Bonnie Blue Flag,' 'Maryland' and other confederate airs, to which the men responded by lusty cheers. Our bands then went as close as possible to their lines and returned the compliment by playing 'Hail Columbia' and 'Yankee Doodle.' The rebels groaned for the one and poured in a volley while the other was played; but 'Home, Sweet Home' drew cheers from both sides."

Camp Near Bell Plains, Va.
April 20th, 1863

Dear Mother:
We were paid off day before yesterday and I expressed ($25.00) twenty five dollars home to you this morning. I have not had a letter from you since I wrote to you. We have been under marching orders for the last 8 days and we have 10 days rations on hand all the time. We will march from here very soon. As there is not much news in camp I will have to close. Write as soon as you get this and let me know if you got my overcoat, etc.

From your son
Oney F. Sweet

Since writing the above we have got orders to march tonight and it is raining like furry.

Sunday, April 19, 1863
A warm and pleasant day. Had an inspection by Col. Wainwright. Had everything in marching order. Rations and grain packed on the carriages. Got no letters or papers.

Monday
A cloudy morning, rainy in the afternoon. Expected to march. Expressed home $25.00. Wrote home. Got a paper from Uncle Joseph. A very rainy night. William Shoop returned.

Tuesday
A warm and cloudy day. Expected Ridgeway, but he did not come. Wrote to R.F.B. Sent him ten dollars. Got no letters or papers. Had the toothache.

Wednesday
A warm and pleasant day. Got a paper from Uncle Jo and a letter from Sarah. Some licour in camp. On guard, third relief, horses, Corporal Brockway. Rained some during the night.

Thursday

A cold, rainy day on guard. Steven Ridgeway and Sgt. Hage returned. Also Lt. Brockway. Got a paper from Uncle Joseph. Some fun with the boxing gloves.

Friday

Rained nearly all day. Cleared off near night. Got a paper from Uncle Joseph.

Saturday

A warm and pleasant day, but very windy. Raffled my watch off. J. Rake got it. Wrote to Uncle Jos. Sent him $2.00. Got two papers from Uncle Jos.

Sunday, April 26, 1863

A warm and beautiful day. Had Company inspection at 10 o'clock. Got a paper from Uncle Joseph. Some fun in camp.

Monday

A warm and most splendid day. Stephen went to the 98th P.V. Heard firing. Think it was a salute. Marching orders. Went to bed early.

Tuesday

A cloudy morning. Commenced raining about eleven o'clock. Orders to be ready to march at 12 or One o'clock. All ready and raining hard. Marched about ½ past one o'clock. Marched, passed by White Oak church. Halted about six hours and marched down to the river in the night. Got a mail. Two papers and a letter from R. F. Ballantine. Did not rain much.

Wednesday

A cloudy day. Opened fire early in the morning. Our troops crossed the river. Took about a hundred prisoners. One division 1st crosst. Not much fighting. Rained some in the night. Laid in positions all night. No mail.

Battle of Chancellorsville

April 30 - May 6, 1863

It is an awful feeling when you are going into a fight but after you once get in to it you don't mind it much.

—Oney F. Sweet

Parrott rifled guns of the Union army field artillery. (Library of Congress)

Thursday

A rainy morning. Cleared off about noon. The Rebs opened fire about four o'clock. We returned the fire. It was kept up until dark. A good many of our infantry were killed and wounded. Our men took up one of the pontoons in the evening and moved it up to the right. Laid in position all night when the Rebels fired with twenty pound parrots and the Whitworth gun.*

Friday, May 1, 1863

Got up very early. All quiet at nine o'clock. A very heavy fog hung over the river. All quiet all day. Our troops cheered over the river. Ricketts got his commission as captain of Battery F. On guard second relief, Corporal Brockway. Got a letter from home. All quiet during the night.

Saturday

A warm and pleasant day. The Rebels opened fire on us. We returned the fire and they ceased first. Our troops fell back across the river and took up the pontoons. We marched until about ten o'clock up the river to reinforce Hooker.

---

* Whitworth projectiles, because of their unusual shape, produced a unique, easily recognized sound.

We marched all afternoon. Reached the U.S. ford about dark. Did not onhitch our teams. Heavy fighting on the right all day.

Sunday, May 3, 1863

A warm and pleasant morning. The ball opened early and very hard fighting. We are about 4 miles from the fighting, a very hard fight. We started for the front but went back. I saw Guss Roper. He was wounded in the leg. Marched up to the front in the evening. Our Pickets driven in.* Expected a fight but it was all quiet except Picket fireing.

Monday

A warm and pleasant morning. All quiet the forenoon. Our men charged into the woods in front of us about four o'clock. Came back after finding that the Rebs were still there. Some artillery fighting. Went to bed. Aroused up about eleven o'clock by the pickets. Went to bed again. Gen. Whipple killed by a sharpshooter.**

Tuesday

A very foggy morning. A ration of whiskey given to us. Heavy firing about nine o'clock. Lasted about 20 minutes. A clear and pleasant day. All quiet the rest of the day. General Sedgewick driven off of Fredericksburg Heights. Heavy loss. A heavy shower. Comenced retreating about dark. Crosst the river about midnight. Got no sleep.

Wednesday

Rain all the forenoon. Took up our line of march early. Reached our old camp in the afternoon. I walked all the way. A very hard day's march. All covered with mud. Put up our tents and made ourselves comfortable. Got five papers from Uncle Joseph.

Thursday

I feel very near used up. A cloudy, rainy day. Fixed up our quarters. Got orders to march back to White Oak church. Started back about 3 o'clock and reached camp before dark. Heard that we were going to cross the river again,

---

* Pickets (or sentinels) were detached bodies of soldiers that guarded an army from surprise; "driven in" means they had retreated to the safety of the main force; thus, engagement with the enemy was considered imminent.

** Brigadier General Amiel W. Whipple, division commander, Third Corps.

May 6th [1863]

Dear Brother:

Marched all day through mud and rain and reached this camp at dark. I was so lame and sore I could hardly move. I had a good night's sleep and it was the first good night's sleep I had for 8 days and it was awful hard on our horses. The men are discouraged and I don't believe we ever will whip them. Some think that Hooker is going to make another move soon. I think old Jo is a good man but the rebels are too well prepared to receive us. The two year and 9 months men are going home soon. I will have to close for the present. Write soon, from your Brother Oney.

> *Battery F 1st Pa. Artillery*
> *3rd Division*
> *1st Army Corps, Washington, D.C.*

I never got that letter with the stamps.

but don't believe it. Also heard that Stoneman was near Richmond. Don't believe it.

Friday

A cool, cloudy morning, but did not rain. Got a mail. Got a paper from Uncle Joseph. Wrote to mother. Got a letter from Willie. Our folks have got the money and box. Got a paper from Uncle Joseph. Went to bed early. Drew for furloughs. Babe Shoop and Cap Frederick got the go.

Saturday

A warm and pleasant day. Detailed to dig sinks. Got some things at the commissary. Heard that our cavelry went within two miles of Richmond. Went to bed at 11 o'clock. Whiskey issued to the Company.

---

* Possibly William Frederick, private, mustered in July 8, 1861; mustered out with battery, June 10, 1865.

Camp Near White Oak Church, Va.
May 8th, 1863

Dear Mother:

I am safe and well except my legs are lame and sore. We have seen hard times and we have been whipped again. We were across the river. We did not have a man in our battery hurt but we was fighting and marching every day for 8 days. We was very lucky. I saw one battery that was all knocked to pieces and one battery lost 50 men. I received your letter on the battlefield and I hope that you have got the things and money before now. Write soon.

We expect to move from here every minute. I have not time to write any more, but I know you are anxious to hear from me. I will write all of the particulars of the fight as soon as I can. I saw Guss Roper on the battlefield. He was slightly wounded. He was doing well. There was many of our brave men killed. I think we never can whip them. They fight awful hard. They don't fear nothing. They march right up to a cannon's mouth. Write soon.

From your son Oney F. Sweet.
Direct Battery F 1st Pa Arty
3rd Division, 1st Army Corps.
Washington, D.C.

Camp Near White Oak Church, Va.
Battery F 1st Pa Artillery
May 10th, 1863

Dear Brother:

I received your letter last Friday and was glad to hear that you had got the money and box safe. Today is very warm. I will give you an account of our marches and fights. April 28th marched from our old camp about noon. Rained very hard, Marched down to the bank of river.

April 29 opened fire across the river. The rebels was on one side and we was on the other. Our men tried to build a bridge but the rebels would not let them. About noon our men crossed in boats and took over a hundred prisoners. Our men then laid the bridge and our infantry crossed. We had quite a good many killed and wounded. The artillery laid on this side.

April 30th a rainy morning cleared off about noon. The rebels opened fire with artillery about 4 o'clock. We returned the fire. Some of the shells burst in our battery but hurt nothing. Some of our infantry was killed by shells. We fired at a distance of two miles and a half.

May 1st all quiet. No firing. May 2nd the rebels opened fire on us. We returned it. Lasted about two hours. Our infantry came across the river and took up the bridges. We started to reinforce Hooker on the right. It was a very warm day. Marched all day up the river. Reached the crossing place about 8 o'clock at night. Did not unharness our horses. Slept about 2 hours. All this fighting was 6 miles below Fredericksburg.

Sunday May 3rd. Heavy fighting all day. We layed about 7 miles from the battlefield, until evening and then we were taken up to the front. We had just got into position when our pickets were driven in and I thought we would have some fun, but it amounted to nothing but picket firing.

At about 11 o'clock we were routed up again. I got but very little sleep as we had to be ready and at our post. I saw Guss Roper. He was slightly wounded in the leg. It is an awful feeling when you are going into a fight but after you once get in to it you don't mind it much.

May 4th all quiet except the rebels sharp shooters. They kept firing away at our men when we were only about 200 yards from the woods and the rebels were thick as flies in the woods. Genl Whipple was killed by a sharp shooter near our battery and a infantry man was killed in our battery. The bullets was whizzing by our ears all the time. It was a wonder we did not have some men hit. A brigade of our men charged into the woods to see if there was a plenty of rebels there and they found enough of them and came back.

May 5th 9 o'clock had a little fight lasted half an hour. Had a heavy shower in the afternoon and made the roads awful muddy. Commenced retreating about dark. Got across the river about midnight. Got no sleep.

I wished I could have stepped into our house and let you see me. I was mud from top to toe and I could have eat a hearty meal. We marched all night and it rained like old Harry.

Chancellorsville: In Retrospect

The ball opened early and very hard fighting.
—Oney F. Sweet

Excerpt from the report of Capt. R. Bruce Ricketts, Battery F, First Pennsylvania Light Artillery:

> At daylight on the morning of April 29, I was placed in position in the corn-field in front of the Fitzhugh house, by Colonel Wainwright, chief of artillery, First Army Corps.
>
> At 5 p.m. on the 30th, the enemy opened from a battery of 20-pounder Parrott guns, at a distance of about 3,600 yards, and continued firing until 7 p.m. During that time I fired 20 Hotchkiss shell, 25 Schenkl percussion, and 3 case-shot (Schenkl), at an elevation of from 10 to 14 degrees, and fuse from eleven to fifteen seconds. The distance being so great, and several batteries firing at the same time, it was impossible to determine with any degree of certainty what execution was done. I was able to ascertain, however, the proper elevation to be 14 degrees, and length of fuse fifteen seconds. (Moodey, 1890)

Bates (1869) wrote:

> On the evening of Sunday [3rd of May 1863], the day on which the heaviest fighting occurred, Battery F relieved Seeley's regular battery, which had lost in the day's work fifty men and as many horses. The enemy's line was only two hundred and fifty yards distant.
>
> Captain Ricketts was ordered to hold the position at all hazards. The horses were, accordingly, sent away to the rear, and the grape and canister was silently piled at the muzzles of the pieces, other ammunition being of little avail in so close quarters.

At ten o'clock p.m., our pickets were driven in and the guns were double-shotted. For a little time a perfect storm of bullets was showered upon the battery by the enemy's infantry; but the canister, which was poured forth in almost a continuous stream, was too terrible for them to withstand. Several times during the night the rebels advanced, but could not be induced to charge up to the muzzles of the guns.

On the same night our infantry threw up breast-works, and on the following day, Monday, a reconnoissance by Griffin's Division disclosed the fact that the enemy was heavily entrenched and awaiting an attack.

"Throughout the entire day," says Lieutenant [Charles] Brockway, "we were annoyed by their sharp-shooters. General Whipple was shot by one of them close to our battery. Some of Berdan's sharp-shooters routed them, except one persistent fellow stationed behind a large tree in the forks of which he rested his rifle. He put six bullets in the sapling which covered one of Berdan's men. He was finally shot by setting three men at work at him. On his person was found forty-eight dollars in gold, two hundred in greenbacks, fifty in confederate money, and three packs of cards. • • • At ten o'clock at night the enemy advanced in strong columns, and peal upon peal of musketry rang on the still night air. The 'zit,' 'zit,' of the Minnie balls, and their 'thud,' 'thud,' in the ground, was interspersed with yells and cheers from friend and foe. Again the enemy retired.

"The next morning they advanced in heavier columns and one continued roar was kept up, from muskets, rifles, Napoleon, Parrott, and Regulation guns. The rounds of double-shotted canister rattled among them and finally compelled them to retire." During the night the army withdrew to the north bank of the river.

---

* Minnie ball: a bullet originally designed by Captain Claude-Etienne Minié of France for muzzle-loading rifles and known as the "minié ball." Its elongated shape and conical point increased the accuracy and range of the bullet in contrast to the spherical "round ball" used up to that time. As the predecessor to the modern bullet, it changed warfare. (Smithsonian Institution)

Sunday, May 10, 1863

A warm and pleasant day. Missed roll call. Had inspection of knapsacks at ten o'clock. Wrote to Willie. Got a Herald from Uncle Joseph. On guard for missing roll call. 1st relief, Corporal Brockway.

Monday

A warm and beautiful morning. On guard, 1st relief, Corporal Brockway. Changed camp in the afternoon. Moved about a mile. We have a splendid camp. A very warm and pleasant day. Got a World from Uncle Joseph. Heard that General Peck was in Richmond. Doubt it.

Tuesday

A warm and pleasant day. Washed our gun. Very hot day. No news of any account. Got no letters or papers.

Wednesday

A very warm day and pleasant. Wrote to R. F. Ballantine. A shower in the afternoon. Read a report of Stoneman's raid. Brilliant affair.*

Thursday

A warm and pleasant day. A heavy shower came up in the afternoon and it was quite cold. Had a headache and got excused from guard. Battery B moved from camp near us.

Friday

A cool, but pleasant morning, except windy. Marched from our camp passed by Hookers Hd. Quarters and camped near where we camped one year ago. We are now in the Reserve Artillery of the Army of the Potomac. Direction for letters: Battery F, First PA Artillery, Major Tompkins district, Army of the Potomac, Washington, D.C.

---

* Major General George Stoneman led Union cavalry detachments in a raid behind Confederate lines in late April 1863. His troopers burned minor bridges and broke up the Virginia Central Railroad for several miles, but when Stoneman ran out of rations and retreated, he left the Fredericksburg and Richmond Railroad—Lee's main route of communication—almost intact. The Rebels repaired the slight damage wrought by Stoneman's troopers, and the raid had no practical effect. (Sears, 1996)

Saturday

A warm and pleasant day. Parker and I went over to the 11th P.Y. Policed camp. Went over to Hooker's Hd. Qrt. in the afternoon.

Sunday, May 17, 1863

A warm and pleasant day. Windy and a shower in the afternoon. Had a drill inspection in the afternoon by Major Mathews. A very poor drill. Got a letter from G. R. Stiles.

Monday

A warm and pleasant day. Wrote to Uncle Joseph. Sent him two dollars. Had a drill in the forenoon — standing gun drill. Got a letter from home and one from R. F. Ballantine.

Tuesday

A warm and pleasant day, but windy. Detailed to go after some cedars for the officers. Had Battery drill but I was not out. Got some things at the commissary.

Wednesday

A warm and pleasant day. Wrote off to G. R. Stiles. Had no drill. Went after brush. Had some boxing in camp. Saw three Rebel deserters. Got a paper.

Thursday

A warm and pleasant day. Got the World and Police Gazette from New York. Had no drills. Detailed to go after grain.

Friday

A warm and pleasant day. Had a drill in the forenoon. Got no letters or papers. Our Suttler came up with a load of goods.

Saturday

A warm and pleasant day. Had to police our camp. No drills. Bo Frederick, Dave Shoop and Major Mathews started on furloughs. No letters or papers. A very hot day.

Sunday, May 24, 1863

A warm and pleasant day. Had Battery inspection at ten o'clock. Inspection of quarters at 12 o'clock and clothing inspection at 3 o'clock p.m. No letters or papers. Cheering news from Vicksburg.*

Monday

A cool, cloudy day. Drivers drilled as cannoneers in the forenoon. Had Battery drill in the afternoon. Got two papers from Uncle Joseph.

Tuesday

A cool, but pleasant morning. Had gun drill in the forenoon. Moved camp in the afternoon. Moved near Bell Plain Landing. Have a very nice camp. No mail.

Wednesday

A warm and pleasant day. Policed camp. Signed the payroll. Got two papers and a letter from Uncle Joseph.

Thursday

A warm and pleasant day. Heard that the furloughs were stopped and that Hooker expects an attack. The Rebs are moving. Got no mail.

Friday

A warm and pleasant day. On guard 1st relief, Corp. Patterson, on the horses. Expressed thirty dollars home by Lt. Brockway. Got our pay. Wrote to mother and Uncle Jos., and got two papers from Uncle Jos. A plenty of licour in camp.

Saturday

A warm and pleasant day. Washed some clothes and we had to police camp in the afternoon. Got a paper from Uncle Joseph. Got a letter from D. P. Maynard.

---

* On May 21, 1863, General Grant had reported that Vicksburg was "fully invested" by Union troops; i.e., surrounded. (Hitchcock, 1868)

Camp Near Bell Plains, Va.
May 29th, 1863

Dear Mother:

   I have been looking for a letter from home anxiously and I presume you have been looking for a letter from me. Well we have moved camp three times since the fight. We have a very nice camp now in the woods. I had a letter from Uncle Joseph a few days ago. He had got the box of sugar. We were paid off this morning and if I have a chance I shall send you some money, but I do not like to send it by mail, but I may have a chance to express some in a few days. I sent Uncle Jo some last pay day and he never got it. I am well and hearty and all I ask is to keep so until my time is out. I am more afraid of disease than the bullet. It is more fatal in this army. Write soon.

From your affectionate son Oney F. Sweet
Address Battery F 1st Pa Arty
Maj Tompkins Division
Reserve Artillery
Army of the Potomac
Washington, D.C.

Sunday, May 31, 1863

A warm and pleasant day. Got two papers. Had knapsack inspection at 10 o'clock. Sgt. Hage put under arrest for not putting brush over the gun. Wrote to D. P. Maynard.

Monday, June 1, 1863

A warm and pleasant day. Put brush over the gun in the morning. Each sergeant has his own roll of his detachment. Got no papers. Wrote to J. H. Winslow.

Tuesday

A warm and pleasant day. Wrote to mother. Sent her express receipt. Wrote to R. F. Ballantine. Some licuor in camp. Got no papers or letters. Battery G came into our Battery.

Wednesday

A warm, but cloudy day. Looks like rain. Had to move tents. Got no papers or letters. Have our camp laid out very nice.

Thursday

A Warm and pleasant day. Called up at four o'clock to be ready to march within one hour. Got ready but did not go. Went into camp again. Heard that the Rebels were trying to cross the river. Got two papers from Uncle Joseph and a letter from Roper.

Friday

A warm and pleasant day. Heard heavy cannonading near Fredericksburg. The infantry on the move. Got a World. Expect to march tonight or in the morning.

Saturday

A warm and pleasant day. Cannonading near Fredericksburg. Rebels left the Heights. Got a paper and a letter from mother. Peter DeWitt's wife is dead.

Sunday, June 7 1863

A warm and pleasant day. Had Battery inspection by Capt. Ricketts. He took us out two miles from camp. Got a paper from N.Y. Unwell.

Monday

A warm and pleasant day. On guard, 2nd relief, Sgt. of the Guard French, Corporals Brockway and Thurston.* Got a paper from Uncle Jos., and a letter from J. H. Winslow.

Tuesday

A warm and pleasant day. Got two papers from Uncle Jos. Heard some cannonading near Fredericksburg. Nothing new from Vicksburg of any importance.

Wednesday

A warm and pleasant day. On police duty. The Suttler returned from Washington. Got no letters or papers. Expected to go down on river.

Thursday

A warm and pleasant day. Orders from General Hooker. Having us turn in our knapsacks and extra clothing. Got no letters or papers.

Friday

A warm and pleasant day. The First Army Corps marched by our camp. Heard some cannonading on the river. Got three papers from Uncle Jos.

Saturday

A warm and pleasant day. Detailed to go to Falmuth after grain. Wrote to mother. Marched from our old camp at 5 o'clock. Marched nearly all night. Passed Stafford Courthouse. Halted two hours in the morning.

---

* William M. Thurston, mustered in July 8, 1861; promoted to 1st Lt., April 22, 1865; mustered out with battery, June 10, 1865.

Camp Near Bell Plains, Virginia
June 10th, 1863

Dear Mother:

I received your last letter a few days ago. I wish I could get with Case, but I do not think I can. I suppose you have got the money and letter before now. I was sorry to hear that Peter's wife was dead. I think the young folks are all getting married that are at home. Remember me to Julian when you write. I think I will write to Aunt Sally one of these days

June 13th, 1863

Dear Mother:

I have been looking for a letter from you every mail. We are under marching orders and most of the troops camped near us have gone. Where we are going I cannot tell. We had to turn in our knapsacks and most all of our clothing. We are only allowed one blanket. I do not think we are going to advance. Write soon and all the news.

From your affectionate son Oney F. Sweet

Sunday, June 14, 1863

A cold but pleasant day. Marched very fast. Passed through Dunnfries about noon. Crossed Wolf Run. Marched all night. Halted about daylight for three hours. Got some sleep.

Monday

A very hot and dusty day. Marched to Fairfax courthouse. Got there about noon. Camped in an orchard. Passed the Pa. Reserves. Got two papers and one letter from Uncle Joseph.

Tuesday

A very hot day. On guard, 3rd relief, Sgt. of the guard Hage, Corporals Thurston and Harder. Heard that the Rebs were in Pennsylvania. Got no mail. Washed some clothes. Expect to march in the morning.

Wednesday

A warm and pleasant day. Harnessed up ready for a march but did not go. Went up to Fairfax courthouse. Heard the Rebs were near Harrisburg. Got six papers and a letter from mother and Willie.

Thursday

A warm and pleasant day. Had a shower in the afternoon. Got no mail. The 6th Corps and Hooker's Hd. Qtrs. passed us. Heard that there was a skirmish near Catletts Station.*

Friday

A warm and pleasant day. Wrote to mother. Hear that there was fighting near Snookers [Snickers] Gap. Went over to the 1st Va. Cavelry. Suttler came from Washington with a load. Had a heavy shower in the night. Got no mail.

Saturday

A cool and cloudy day. Looks like rain. Had some rain in the afternoon. Got three papers. No important news of the movements of the Rebels.

---

* Confederate Major John S. "Gray Ghost" Mosby led the notorious Mosby Rangers in guerrilla attacks on Union assets. "Moseby's guerrillas made their appearance to-day [May 30] at Catlett's Station, on the Orange and Alexandria Railroad. . . . Ten cars and a locomotive were destroyed." (*The New York Times*, June 1, 1863)

Camp at Fairfax Court House, Va.
June 19th, 1863

Dear Mother:

I received yours and Willies letters yesterday. We are only 14 miles from Washington. We marched from near Fredericksburg last Saturday and we got here Monday noon. We marched night and day and we was as dirty and sleepy looking lot of men as ever you saw when we got here. 15 men in the infantry dropped dead from sun stroke. When we came here we did not expect to stay here long but we have been here three days. Most all of the rest of the troops have marched on toward Maryland and we will soon follow. When we go we travel right along. The reserve artillery is all camped here.

I presume there is more excitement in Pennsylvania than there is in the whole army here. I am not afraid of the rebs getting far in Penn. You can put the money out at whatever you think best. Sheep or cattle I think is better than at interest. We have got a little colt in the battery. It is 5 weeks old. We had a shower here last night and it makes it cool and nice this morning.

The reserve artillery only goes into the big fights. They are kept in reserve until they are really needed. I think we will see a big fight soon. I hear cannons at a distance this morning. Write soon. Direct as before.

From your son Oney.
Send a few stamps.

Sunday, June 21, 1863

A cool and cloudy day. Had Battery inspection at 9 o'clock. Heard heavy cannonading toward Snickers Gap. Got two papers. Saw Neb Sloat.

Monday

A warm and pleasant day. Wrote to Uncle Joseph and Frank Spaulding. Got a World from Uncle Joseph. Saw about a 100 prisoners pass. The Suttler came up with a load.

Tuesday

A warm and pleasant day. Washed some clothes. Got no letters or papers. Our Cavelry whipped the Rebs at Snickers Gap on Sunday.

Wednesday

A warm and pleasant day. One Division of Reserve Artillery marched from their camp near us. Got a paper from New York.

Thursday

A warm and pleasant day. Started on the march about 8 o'clock. Marched all day. Rained in the afternoon. Halted near Edwards Ferry.* A rainy night.

Friday

A cool, rainy day. Crosst the Potomac about seven o'clock. Camped one mile from the ferry. A very rainy afternoon. Crosst the river on pontoons. The 12th Army Corps passed us.

Saturday

A cool, cloudy morning, looks like rain. Marched about nine o'clock. Marched through Poolsville, Barnsville and reached Frederick City at about dark. Camped about one mile from town.

Sunday, June 28, 1863

A cloudy day. Went to town. Was put in the guard house by the patrols. I am now in the guard house writing these lines. Soon got out. I went up town again in the evening.

Monday

A cloudy, wet morning. Aroused up at 3 o'clock. Did not march until 8 o'clock. Rained some, but cleared off about noon. Passed through Woodburry and several other small towns. Passed through a very fine country. Went out to a farm house and got supper.

Tuesday

A cloudy, rainy forenoon, but cleared off in the afternoon. Marched at 10 o'clock. Went to a farm house and got dinner. Very slow marching. Camped about 5 o'clock near Jonnytown. Rained some near dark. Mustered for pay.

---

* Edwards Ferry became a major crossing of the Potomac River throughout the Civil War. In June 1863, the Union army crossed there on twin pontoon bridges on the way to Gettysburg. (Maryland Historical Trust)

Battle of Gettysburg

July 1-3, 1863

Death on our own State soil, rather than give the enemy our guns.
—Battery F rallying cry

By thunder, if we can't whip them here we can't whip them anywhere. I shall never run from here.

—John Given, Ricketts' Battery F

Wednesday, July 1, 1863

A cloudy morning, but cleared off near noon. 12 o'clock and we are now in camp. Got two papers. We expected to march but did not.

Thursday

A warm and pleasant day. Marched to Gettysburg. Went into the fight about six o'clock and had a hard fight. Lost about twenty killed and wounded. Myron French, Riggin, Anderson, Miller killed.* The Rebels charged on our Battery about dark, but were repulsed.** Nead, Given and O. G. Larabee were taken prisoner.

Friday

A warm, pleasant day. Heavy fighting all day. Pryne and Christie wounded in the leg.*** The Rebs were repulsed at every point. General Longstreet wounded and taken prisoner.**** Very hard fighting all day.

---

* James H. Riggin; Elijah Y. Anderson; the military record states that Samuel Miller mustered out with the battery. Francis Need, discharged May 31, 1864, at expiration of term; John M. Given, died of his wounds; Oscar G. Larrabee, mustered out with the battery, June 10, 1865.

Sweet was wounded in one leg and lost his hearing in one ear. *The History of Franklin and Cero Gordo Counties* (Iowa, 1883) cites him as saying he saw twenty-three of his comrades fall around him in as many minutes.

In a letter published in *The National Tribune*, April 29, 1909, Sweet wrote: "I pulled the lanyard for every shot from that gun." In 1931, he told the Long Beach Press-Telegram, that his gun "fired 101 times" during the battle.

** The charge of the Louisiana Tigers. See Sweet's retrospective piece.

*** James Powryne, killed at Gettysburg, buried in the National Cemetery, section D, grave, 48; "Christie" probably John H. Christian.

**** On July 3, Confederate Major General George E. Pickett, serving under Lieutenant General James Longstreet, led his division in the renowned "Pickett's Charge" on Cemetery Ridge. Union artillery and rifle fire repulsed the attack, inflicting great losses on the Rebel army. (Hitchcock, 1868)

Contrary to what Sweet apparently heard, Longstreet was not wounded at Gettysburg, nor taken prisoner.

In 1931, Oney F. Sweet told the *Long Beach Press-Telegram*:

> *My first big fight was the second Battle of Bull Run, and there I showed the Johnnies I could beat them in a foot race. In fact, we seemed to make it a practice of running pretty nearly every time we came to grips with the rebels until Gettysburg. After, we didn't run any more.*

Report of Capt. R. Bruce Ricketts, Batteries F and G, First Pennsylvania Light Artillery.

Hdqrs. Batteries F And G, First Pa. Artillery,
August 30, 1863.

CAPTAIN : In compliance with your communication of the 29th instant, I have the honor to submit the following report of the part taken by my battery in the battle of July 2 and 3, at Gettysburg:

On July 2, my battery moved from Taneytown to Gettysburg with Captain Huntington's brigade, to which it was attached, arriving on the field about noon.

At 4 p. m. I was ordered by Captain Huntington to report to Col. C. S. Wainwright, First New York Artillery, who placed me in position on Cemetery Hill, to the right of the turnpike leading into Gettysburg. During the afternoon, I was engaged with the batteries on the enemy's left, and in shelling a column of the enemy that charged into the woods on my right, which was occupied by the Twelfth Army Corps.

At about 8 p. m. a heavy column of the enemy charged on my battery, and succeeded in capturing and spiking my left piece. The cannoneers fought them hand to hand with handspikes, rammers, and pistols, and succeeded in checking them for a moment, when a part of the Second Army Corps charged in and drove them back. During the charge I expended every round of canister in the battery, and then fired case shot without the fuses. The enemy suffered severely.

During the battle of July 3, I was engaged with the batteries on the enemy's left and center.

During the battle of the 2d and 3d, I expended 1,200 rounds of ammunition.

The casualties were as follows: Killed, 6; wounded, 14; missing, 3. Horses killed, 20.

First Lieut. C. B. Brockway, Battery F, First Pennsylvania Artillery, First Lieut. Beldin Spence, Battery G, First Pennsylvania Artillery, and First Sergt. Francis H. Snider, fought their sections with the greatest gallantry.

I am, captain, very respectfully, your obedient servant,

R. BRUCE RICKETTS,
Capt. First Pa. Artillery, Comdg. Batteries F and G.

Capt. C. H. WHITTELSEY,
Asst. Adjt. Gen., Artillery Reserve.

Excerpt from the report of Col. Charles S. Wainwright, First New York Light Artillery, commanding Artillery Brigade, First Army Corps, July 17, 1863, regarding the second day at the Battle of Gettysburg:

Captain Cooper's battery, which had suffered considerably, was relieved by Captain Ricketts' battery of six 3-inch guns. . . . As [General Rodes' Louisiana brigade] became fully unmasked, all the guns which could be brought to bear were opened on them, at first with shrapnel and afterward with canister, making a total of fifteen guns in their front and six on their left flank. Their center and left never mounted the hill at all, but their right worked its way up under cover of the houses, and pushed completely through Wiedrich's battery into Ricketts'. The cannoneers of both these batteries stood well to their guns, driving the enemy off with fence-rails and stones and capturing a few prisoners. I believe it may be claimed that this attack was almost entirely repelled by the artillery. My surgeon, who was in the town and dressed many of their wounded that night, tells me that they reported their loss in this attack as very great.

The music commenced. . . . If I remember thinking at all it was of mother at home.

— Oney F. Sweet

Bates (1869) described the role of Ricketts' Battery in the florid style of 19th century prose:

> Captain Ricketts had been advised that the enemy would doubtless make desperate efforts to take [Cemetery Hill], and was ordered to hold it to the last extremity. He had, accordingly, sent his horses well to the rear, but had his caissons harnessed and ready to move upon the instant of warning.
>
> As soon as he discovered that this compact and desperate rebel column was moving upon his position, he charged his pieces with canister and poured in the deadly volleys, four discharges per minute, throwing five hundred pounds of deadly missiles full in the faces of the foe. But these desperate men [Louisiana Tigers] had never failed in a charge, and nothing daunted, they closed up where their line was blown away, and rushed forward with deafening yells. The infantry supports, lying behind the stone wall in front, fled in despair, and the battery on the left [Wiedrich's] without its supports was overwhelmed.
>
> The batteries on the right were so posted that they could not fire after the enemy began to ascend the hill. The brunt of the attack therefore fell upon Ricketts. But he well knew that the heart of the whole army was throbbing for him in that desperate hour, and how much the enemy coveted the prize for which he was making so desperate a throw.
>
> With an iron hand he kept every man to his post and every gun in full play. The giving way of our line upon the left brought the Tigers upon his flank. Pouring in a volley from behind a stone wall that ran close to his left piece, they leaped the fence, bayonetted the men, spiked the gun, and killed or wounded the entire detachment, save three, who were taken prisoners. But the remaining guns still belched forth their

double rounds of canister, the officers and drivers taking the places of the fallen cannoniers.

The battery's guidon was planted in one of the earthworks, and a rebel Lieutenant was pressing forward to gain it; but just as he was in the act of grasping it, young Riggin, its bearer, rode up and shot him through the body, and seizing the colors, he levelled his revolver again, but ere he could fire, he fell, pierced with bullets, and soon after expired. The rebels were now in the very midst of the battery, and in the darkness it was difficult to distinguish friend from foe. A struggle ensued for the guidon. It had fallen into the hands of a rebel. Seeing this, Lieutenant Brockway seized a stone and felled him to the ground, and the next instant the rebel was shot with his own musket. A scene of the wildest confusion ensued.

The men at the batteries were outnumbered, and were being overpowered by a maddened and reckless foe. But still they clung to their guns, and with handspikes, rammers, and stones, defended them with desperate valor, cheering each other on, and shouting, "Death on our own State soil, rather than give the enemy our guns."

At this critical moment, [Colonel Samuel S.] Carroll's Brigade came gallantly to the rescue, and the enemy retreated in confusion. The men again flew to their guns and with loud cheers gave him some parting salutes, in the form of double-shotted canister. Thus ended the grand charge of [General Jubal Anderson] Early's Division, headed by the famous Louisiana Tigers, who boasted that they had never before been repulsed in a charge. They came forward, 1700 strong, maddened with liquor, and confident of crushing in our line, and holding this commanding position. They went back barely 600, and the Tigers were never afterwards known as an organization.

Oney F. Sweet wrote the following piece for *The National Tribune*. Date of publication, if published, is unknown.

THE BATTLE OF GETTYSBURG (July 1-3, 1863)

In Retrospect

By Oney Foster Sweet

The battle of Gettysburg has been studied and written about more than any other battle of the civil war. There were fifty or more battle fields where the fighting and losses were as great as any one day at Gettysburg. The battle of Shiloh was the most stubbornly fought battle. No army was ever so completely whipped as at the second battle of Bull Run, when the Union army took to its heels. At Fredericksburg there was a terrible slaughter of northern troops and small loss to the southern forces. At Antietam, the bloodiest battle of the war, the armies were nearly equal and the losses were nearly so and both armies lost more on September 17, 1862, than was lost on any one day at Gettysburg. Greeley's history says that ten thousand Union soldiers fell in twenty minutes at Cold Harbor. At the Wilderness General Grant had the largest army in any one battle during the war. In the battle of Franklin, Tennessee, General Thomas fought the most systematic battle of the war. Then why so much about Gettysburg? Why does every boy and girl know of Gettysburg? Because it was fought on northern soil. It was fought by nearly equal numbers. It was at a critical period of the war. A Confederate victory meant everything to the Confederacy at this time and would give them great chances for their cause. Robert E. Lee and his fine army of veterans had never seen defeats such as the Army of the Potomac had received at their hands in the seven days on the Peninsula, at Second Bull Run and at Chancellorsville, and because it was at the high water mark of the rebellion. The next day Vicksburg fell and the Confederacy went gradually down to Appomattox. This is why you hear so much about Gettysburg.

The unwritten part of our war is greater than all that has been written. Two soldiers side by side in a hot place in our battles did not see the same things. The generals did not see what the privates saw. The general in command and the corps commanders, if they were where they should have been at Gettysburg, saw a good deal. But they saw little of the

Bodies of dead on right of Federal line, Gettysburg, Pennsylvania. (Library of Congress)

real stuff. Colonels, majors, captains, lieutenants, and privates saw what the battle really meant in the positions which they filled. It was in the first day's fighting on the first of July that General Reynolds, the commander, was killed. There is not much written of this day's fighting because it was a defeat for our army. However, the Union army never fought harder or against heavier odds than for five hours on this day. The first corps contested every inch of the ground (one and one half miles) and made it possible to turn defeat into victory on the second and third of July. That old Wisconsin Brigade and all the corps did the fighting of their lives against heavy odds.

I was not there myself. I was thirteen miles away at Taneytown. Sedgwick's old sixth corps was forty miles away. All corps were ordered to concentrate at Gettysburg on the second. At daylight we made tracks for Gettysburg. We reached there before noon. Our battery of six 3½" rifled guns were placed in position about noon. These were between the tombstones of Gettysburg cemetery. The view was fine—grand. Off to the left were Little and Big Round Top. To our front were ripe fields of wheat, some partly cut, orchards, farm houses, and barns. The village of

Gettysburg was at our right—Gettysburg lying on the slope. The town was full of wounded from the first day's battle. The rebels had possession of nearly all of the town. Our skirmishers were advanced as far as they could get into the town. We could look to our front and west over the valley and see the Lutheran cemetery, General Lee's headquarters, and overlook part of the ground fought over the day before. There was no fighting at any part of the line at this time. There was an unhealthy stillness about. Except for the occasional crack of a sharp shooter's rifle all was quiet. We did not fire a shot from this point.

At about two o'clock we were ordered and moved nearly north out of the cemetery, across the Baltimore Pike and assumed our positions with our guns pointing nearly north. This brought the town to our left and front and Culp's Hill to our rear and right—this position in history and maps is what is called East Cemetery Hill. Our line of battle was in the shape of a fish-hook. Our position was on the extreme point of the right center.

We were not long at peace. We heard artillery firing on our left, this side of Round Top and to the left of where Pickett's charge came next day. About this time the music commenced in our front from a 20# battery and others, and we gave them the best we had. We soon discovered it was to draw our attention and fire from [Confederate Gen. Richard S.] Ewel's corps which was massing on our front and right to assault Culp's Hill. We could plainly see their columns as they passed through a ravine. We directed part of our shots at them while part of our guns entertained their artillery.

The fighting on our left had become terrific and it was a roar of musketry and artillery. The fighting became warmer and close on our right. The assault to take Culp's Hill was now full blast. It was now about sunset and the fighting on our front became hotter and our pickets in a wheat field began to fall back. Our main line began to give way. A brigade of rebels known as the Louisiana Tigers had formed in a street of Gettysburg, marched to the edge of town and given that never to be forgotten yell "Yep, Yep, Yep." The chief of artillery had ordered all the captains of batteries at this point to fight and man the guns as long as they could and make no effort to save the guns as our support, the infantry, in the Baltimore Pike would do the rest. When this racket commenced and our infantry was forced back through us we ceased shelling and prepared to give them grape and cannister.

This we did about this fast: load, ready, fire. We did the best we could. We cut them up, we broke them up, yet they kept coming—not in compact

A Confederate sharp-shooter, killed by a shell at Gettysburg.
(James F. Gibson, Library of Congress)

line, but scattering like a mob. It was now dark, and our guns had done their deadly work. And they had done theirs. A few of them had reached two of our guns. General Carrol's brigade then made its rush through our guns, forced the rebels back to their original line—Carrol's brigade losing few men—and East Cemetery Hill was saved! Confederates give their loss at this point as over seventeen hundred. We lost killed and wounded twenty-seven men and forty horses. In our battery horses were a bigger mark than men.

All was quiet along the Army of the Potomac. We were ordered to lie down by our guns and to sleep. We did not know what might come next. I could not sleep. At about eleven o'clock the moon came up over Culp's Hill. It was very bright. Maynard Gates, a comrade, and I walked down the slope in front of our guns. The dead lay quite thick but we had seen them much thicker at Antietam.

At daybreak of the third the musketry at our right commenced very early and heavy. It was General Stacome's troops retaking some breastwork lost the night before on Culp's Hill.* The fighting was severe and continued

* Major General Henry W. Slocum, commander, Union army's 12th Corps.

until about eight o'clock. The day was bright, clear, and hot. From nine o'clock until one were the most solemn hours I have ever experienced. A death stillness. But the battle was not ended. Everyone seemed to be moving carefully as if holding his breath and not knowing what to expect next—whether from our right or left—would come what we knew not. It seemed like two dogs facing each other, showing their teeth, neither one making a move for four long hours. We all seemed to feel that something was going to happen, but what and where and how?

At ten o'clock the dead silence was broken. It came as a relief from that terrible stillness and anxiety which had become monotonous. It was the signal shot fired from near the Lutheran cemetery. The shell burst quite high over the cemetery, about where we went into position first. In five minutes Cemetery Ridge was alive from Rebel shots from one hundred and fifty guns or more and about the same number of our guns were answering back. This was the beginning of that famous charge of Pickett. We were about three fourths of a mile to the right of where the charges came so we did not see or do much, but being on high ground we could see the swaying of the troops and the immense smoke. The artillery and musketry were terrible and fairly jarred the earth where we were. At three o'clock the battle was over and Pickett's veteran Virginians for the first time were badly defeated.

We moved from our position July 5th and I saw but little of the battle field except where we were. In 1888, I spent four days going over the battle field. I again visited after the monument had been placed where our gun stood that day, and on it with my own were the names of the boys who fought beside me that memorable day.

In a battle—in the greatest danger—there are funny things happening—funny sayings—funny actions, but we don't think them very funny at the time. After the battle is over we can talk and laugh over them.

Every company has its odd and peculiar characters. Most of them have a nickname. On our gun we had such a character. He was six feet tall with broad shoulders—a perfect soldier. He talked very slowly. His jokes were dry. I never saw him when he seemed the least bit excited. On account of his coolness and slowness we nicknamed him "Reverend."

At Antietam when the minnie balls were coming pretty thick out of a corn field I was putting a shell into the gun. He was ready to ram it. He said, "Sweet, do you hear them calling you cousin?" I don't believe I even smiled then as the bullets were pretty thick. If I remember thinking at all it was of mother at home.

Now this boy (John Given) when we went into position on Cemetery Hill in his dry way expressed the feelings of every man in the army from General Meade, General Hancock, General Sickles down to the lowest private (there were no jealousies at Gettysburg).*

This big slow boy looked the position over right, left and front. He pulled off his shoes and set them down by the wheel of the gun carriage. He was foot sore from marching after Bobby Lee. He was mad and determined. Larrabee, one of the gunners, said, "Reverend, you better keep your shoes on, we may have to get out of here lively." As you know, Lee had generally made us "git." Given said, in his droll way, "By thunder, if we can't whip them here we can't whip them anywhere. I shall never run from here." He never did. When he got his death wound he would not try to get back. This spirit is what whipped Bobby Lee at Gettysburg.

---

* Major General George G. Meade initially commanded the Second Brigade of the Pennsylvania Reserves and later took command of the Army of the Potomac to lead the Union forces to victory at Gettysburg.

General Winfield Scott Hancock commanded the Second Corps, and later directed the Veterans' Volunteer Corps.

Major General Daniel E. Sickles; some people have claimed he disobeyed General Meade's order during the Battle of Gettysburg, resulting in the Third Corps being overrun. Sickles lost his right leg in the battle. (Hitchcock, 1868)

Retrospective piece written by Oney F. Sweet and published in *The National Tribune,* April 29, 1909.

RICKETTS' BATTERY
It Was One of Those at Gettysburg Which Came to Stay

Editor National Tribune: In reading A.H. Huber's article concerning the 33d Mass in *The National Tribune* of March 11, there comes vividly to my mind the part that Ricketts' Battery played in that part of the history of Gettysburg on the evening of July 2, 1863.

So far as I know I am the only one living who was on the immediate gun which was the first of Ricketts' guns reached after Wiedrick's Battery ceased firing.* I pulled the lanyard for every shot from that gun and at the same time tried to see everything that was going on, but I assure that I saw but little. My position was No. 4 on the left gun close to the stone wall running up and down the hill with Wiedrick's guns to the left. Wiedrick's guns had ceased firing for a few moments.

When I saw from the flash of their guns the rebels creeping up, I have always thought that the first men to reach our guns came from over the stone wall. Our gunner did not seem to see them but was giving them canister straight to the front down the hill. As soon as our gun was over powered, of course they would be coming in an oblique direction and would soon reach the second and third gun. This was as far as they got when Carroll's Brigade drove them back. As it was quite dark, there was an exciting time for a few moments.

Huber's mention of Stevens' Battery prompts me to write from my viewpoint how they helped save East Cemetery Hill that night. While Ricketts' men were holding on for time and Carroll came in the nick of time, Stevens was pouring shot and shell across our front where no support could form or live. This made it easy for Carroll's men to drive the enemy clear back to where they started from.

It needed us all that night to save East Cemetery Hill that Pickett could have a chance to try his hand at routing us. A little incident occurred on our gun which shows why we won at Gettysburg and whipped Bobby Lee and the feeling and sentiment that prevailed from Gen. Meade down to

---

* Captain Michael Wiedrick, 1st New York Light Artillery, Battery I.

the last private. Our first position was in the old cemetery where we had a splendid view of the ripe wheat fields, the Round Tops, the valleys, the well painted farmhouses and barns, the little town at our feet, a scene grand enough to inspire one and doubly so with the battle impending. We were soon moved across Baltimore pike and took position where we remained until July 5.

Our No. 1, the man who rams the shot, stood over six feet and in the prime of life. When we got our gun unlimbered and in position, he took off his shoes from his sore feet and coolly set them beside the wheel. O.G. Larrabee, the man who thumbed the vent,* said, "John you had better keep your shoes on. We may have to get out lively. "By G," answered John, looking over the surroundings, "If we can't whip them here we can't whip them no where. I'll never run from here."

And he never did run. He was wounded in the mix up and taken prisoner. He lived only to get home and die of his wounds. The sentiment of the officers and men at Gettysburg was the sentiment of John Givens.

Oney F. Sweet, member of Ricketts' Battery from '61 to '65, Hampton, Iowa.

---

* "thumbed the vent" refers to a maneuver by the No. 3 gunner to cover the vent hole with a piece of leather over his thumb while the gun was swabbed out and reloaded, "in order that all sparks might be extinguished by the air pressure" and prevent a premature discharge; "the responsibility for any accident was placed upon him." (Sherburne, 1908)

Saturday, July 4, 1863

A shower in the morning and very warm. The Rebs have fallen back. We have possession of the town. I was in town and we took a great many prisoners. No fighting all day. Think the Rebs have retreated.

Sunday, July 5, 1863

A cloudy day – had showers. The Rebels have retreated towards the Potomac. We marched from the battlefield and marched to Littlestown and camped. Had a heavy rain in the night.

Monday

A rainy day. Did not move camp. Went to town. Made arrangements for going home.

Tuesday

A cloudy rainy day. Our Battery marched. Houser, Gates, Harder and myself started for home on a French.* Walked through Hanover and stopped for the night near York.

Wednesday

A very rainy day. Walked to the river and slept in a barn. Went thru Dover. Had a very good time.

Thursday

A warm and pleasant day. Crosst the river and stopped at Middletown nearly all day. Got clothes there. Walked to Highspire and took the cars for Harrisburg. Did not sleep much all night.

---

* John Houser, private, reenlisted March 14, 1864; mustered out with battery, June 10, 1865.

A French Leave: absent without leave (AWOL) but voluntarily returning to duty within the all-important 30-day grace period, was a common practice during the Civil War, but it was always dangerous. This was the closest he had been to home since enlisting, and he took the opportunity to visit his family and friends. The arrangements probably included some sort of unofficial sanction by his C.O. since this same R. B. Ricketts stood by him throughout his army service. (George O. Sweet)

Friday

Took the car for Innbury. Got Innbury at 7 o'clock. Got to Scranton at 10 at night. Stayed all night at a hotel.

Saturday

A warm and pleasant day. Left Scranton at 10 o'clock. Saw Case. Got home at six o'clock. Mother was pleased to see me.

Sunday, July 12, 1863

A cloudy day. Went around to see the neighbors. Went to Ames woods to swing with the girls.

Monday

A warm but cloudy day. Went to Arvines. Mr. Sisnor's uncle Raymonds stopped at home that night. Dave Maynard, Henry Ingalls and two others went to war for three months.

Tuesday

A cloudy day, but warm. Mother and me went up to Mr. Wellses. Had a pleasant time.

Wednesday

A warm and pleasant day. Went up to Mr. Gates. Maynard was not ready to go. Went up to Mr. Perry's and French's.

Thursday

A warm and pleasant day. Gates and myself started for the Battery. Stayed over night at Scranton. Saw Case and wife. He gave me a pass.

Friday

Left Scranton at six o'clock for Danville. Rained all day. Stayed overnight at Danville. Had a pleasant time.

Saturday

Started for Harrisburg at 9 o'clock. Got to Harrisburg at noon. Went up to Eckerts. Stayed there, then went to the Gateses. Saw Will G. Brower.

Sunday, July 19, 1863

A hot and pleasant day. Went up to Camp Curtin and stayed all day. Had a good time in the evening.

Monday

A hot day. Started for Chambersburg at two o'clock. Got to Chambersburg at six o'clock and went to a farm house and stayed all night.

Tuesday

Walked to Hagerstown. Passed through Green Castle. Saw Dave Gill and the other boys. 35th Regt. Penn. CM, Co. D. A very hot day.

Wednesday

A warm and pleasant day. Walked through Sharpsburg, and Harpers Ferry and stopped over night at a hotel at Oxford.

Thursday

A warm but cloudy morning. Got across the Potomac at Berlin. Walked three miles and got dinner at a farm house. Got in with the 13th New York Cavelry and rode to Snickersville. Camped for the night.

Friday

Started early. Rode all day. Camped near Peidmont Station. Slept in a wagon. The main army lays near here.

Saturday

A warm and pleasant day. Found our Battery about noon in the 2nd Army Corps. Glad to see the boys. Reported available for duty. Rickets told us to go to duty.

Sunday, July 26, 1863

A warm and pleasant day. Marched from White Plains to near Bealton Station. Passed through Warrenton.

Monday

A cloudy morning, but warm. Had a heavy shower in the afternoon. Heard that we was to be court martialed but have not had any orders to that effect. Wrote a short letter home stating that I had returned to the Battery.

Tuesday

A hot day. On guard. Corp. Brockway and McFarland on the lines, third relief. Thunder showers near night.

Wednesday

A cloudy rainy day. Our court martials were made out. Got no mail.

Thursday

A cool day with showers. Wrote to mother and Will G. Brower but did not send them off. Marched about four o'clock. Marched nine miles to Elk Run.

Friday

A cloudy morning. Marched at eight o'clock. Marched 7 miles to Morrisville. Camped for the night. There is gold mines near here. Got two papers.

Saturday, August 1, 1863

*A very hot day, the warmest day this season. Sent a letter to Will G. Brower and one to mother. Had inspection of clothing by Captain Hazard.**

---

* John G. Hazard, 1st Rhode Island Light Artillery. (See October 23, 1863.)

Camp Near Warrenton, Va.
July 30th, 1863

Dear Mother:

I now seat myself to give you an account of our travels in returning to the battery. On Wednesday I started from home and when I got up to Gates he was not ready to go until the next day and I thought I would spend the day in Jackson. I enjoyed myself first rate. I was to Mr. Frenches and took supper with Mr. Perrys folks. I would like to have gone to Susquehanna.

On Thursday we started and stayed over night at Scranton. Saw Mr. and Mrs. Case. Case gave us a pass which helped us along. On Friday morning we left Scranton and met the other boys at Danville and they said we must stay over one day there and there is a good many boys in our company from that place and they all had heard of me and wanted to see me. And I had a very pleasant time. On Saturday morning we started on and reach Harrisburg about noon. We had to lay over there until Monday on account of the cars and we spent a very pleasant time. As I am pretty well acquainted there.

On Monday we went to Chambersburg. That was as far as the cars run. We stopped at a farm house one night and the rebels had taken 19 horses from the farm. On Tuesday we walked all day. We run on to Dave Gill and the other boys and we stopped about 3 hours to see them. That night we slept in a barn. The boys don't have it near as hard as we do. On Wednesday we walked to the Potomac River. We walked about 30 miles and if ever I was tired it was that 40 miles into Virginia.

On Thursday we crosst into Virginia and we got along with some cavelry and rode all day. Friday we rode all day and overtook the army but we could not find our battery. Our battery had been put into the 2nd Army Corps.

On Saturday we travelled and looked and about noon we found one of the baggage wagons that belongs to our battery and the driver told us to wait and our battery would come along the road and soon we saw it and such a shaking of hands you never saw. They thought we would never come back. Our Captain told us to go to our old posts on the run.

The next day we marched and camped here. This makes four times we have been at this place. This is the place Mrs. Case was to see us last summer. We are now about 60 miles into Virginia.

I wrote you a few lines day before yesterday to ease your mind, but you wanted me to give you a full account of our return and I have done it. There will not be anything done with us only lose our pay while we was gone. We run *a great risk in going home. If we had been caught we would have been treated as deserters and it was a wonder we got across the river but we had passes from several men. We was very lucky all the way in going and coming. Charley Wells is well.*

I forgot to get any stamps while I was home. Send me some in your next. We have not got any mail since I got back. Write soon and all the news. How does father and Willie get along with their haying?

> *Direct Battery F 1st Pa Arty*
> *2nd Army Corps*
> *Washington, D.C.*

Sunday, August 2, 1863

A very hot day. Got a mail. Got my photographs from Danville. Got nine papers and a letter from Uncle Joseph and Sarah. Wrote to Uncle Joseph and Sarah. Sent each of them my photograph. Sent two to mother.

Monday

A very hot day. Got a paper from Uncle Joseph. Drew new clothing, but I did not get any.

Tuesday

A very hot day. Got an old letter from mother. It had been to North Carolina. It had a dollar's worth of stamps in it. Moved camp about fifty yards this forenoon and moved about one mile in the afternoon.

Wednesday

A very hot day. Moved camp about noon. Moved near water. We now have a very pleasant camp. Got a mail but nothing for me.

Thursday

A very hot day. Washed some clothes. Got a "World" from Uncle Joseph. Charlie Wells got a letter from home. An answer to his, written since I returned.

Virginia August 3rd, 1863. Sunday

Dear Mother:

I received your letter in due time and was glad to hear from you and Willie. Enclosed you will find two dollars and I wished I could send more. I have some money left yet but we cannot tell When we will get paid again. Perhaps in two months and perhaps not in four. I shall send you all I can spare and you are welcome to it.

We expected to march from here before this. We shall leave here very soon I think. Today is a very hot day, one of the hottest this season.

What do the people think about drafting in Gibson?

You must be getting pretty well along with the haying. We can get a plenty of milk and potatoes here by paying a good price for them. I had bread and milk for breakfast and bean soup for dinner.

We are camped in one of the healthiest countrys in Virginia. It is hilly and if there is any wind stirring anywhere we have it here. And we have excellent water. We have only 3 sick in the company. I am glad we are not any farther south and I do not think we will get much farther until cold weather, but I think we will see some hard fighting and very soon too. We look for Bryant back here every day.

I had a letter from Annie Foster some time ago and I answered it the other day.

This is a great country for flies and bugs. In the night the bugs crawl all over a person. The other night one crawled into my ear and I had a hard time to get him out. The river runs by our camp and I gernerally go in once or twice a day.

You say that I never speak about Julia.* I don't know what I could say about her. I often think about her, and sometimes I will forget that I have but one sister. I seen her so little. I suppose she must begin to talk by this time. Willie and Sarah write often you have nothing much to do.

Direct as before. From your son Oney.

---

* Julia Sweet, Oney Sweet's youngest sister, who was a toddler when he enlisted.

Some of the people that have blowed and talked so patriotic but would not volunteer will have to come now. I am glad I volunteered when I did.

—Oney F. Sweet

Oney Sweet's daughter Marian, in a letter to her grandson William J. Ketchum, commented on his mention of the draft:

Our family considered it a disgrace to be drafted and to hire a substitute was even worse. Times have somewhat changed since then, but to this day none of our family have been drafted, altho there should be no stigma attached as I see it now.

I was born in 1872 just seven years after the war closed and I was brought up on War history and politics. . . . My father told good stories and always had a group of listeners in his store evenings. I only wish I had been a better listener but the stories meant so little to me then. My mother wrote out many of his war stories and they were published in the [Iowa] Hampton Recorder but so far as I know there were none preserved by the family. . . . Folks all over the county clammered for these stories at the time.

Our father drilled my sister Edna, my brothers Will and Robt and myself to give entertainments in marches and songs. We wore little uniforms and he took us to entertainments and that perhaps accounts for my liking for military music and exhibitions to-day.

Camp Near Culpepper, Va.
August 7th, 1863

Dear Sister and Brother:

I wrote to Mother last Monday and on Tuesday morning we marched early in the morning and marched 9 miles and on Wednesday we marched ten miles and reached here about noon the same day. We had to get up early in the morning so as to march in the cool of the day. We would start about four o'clock. It was most awful hot. The sweat run off the horses like water. We have a splendid camp here. We have our horses and tents in the woods.

The town is about two miles from here. It is very pretty little town. We are now not a great many miles from the rebels and we may be attacked at any moment. Yesterday we were ordered to hitch up double quick and we expected to have a little brush, but before we got far the orders were countermanded and we layed quiet in camp all day. The rebels are in full force at Gordonsville and that is about 25 miles from here and we are the nearest army to them. The cars [trains] run from Washington to this place and while we lay here we will get a mail regular.

I suppose there has been a good deal of excitement and some loud talk in Gibson for the past few days about drafting. Some of the people that have blowed and talked so patriotic but would not volunteer will have to come now. I am glad I volunteered when I did. Write all the news.

We have to drill one hour every morning before breakfast and it gives us a good appetite. I think I write as full as often as you do. I shall write as often as I have anything to write about. We can not tell how long we will lay here, but I don't think long. Write soon and remember me to all inquiring friends. From your Brother

Oney F. Sweet

The Draft in the Civil War

Compulsory military service during the Civil War began in the second year, after Congress enacted the draft law on July 17, 1862. The law instituted a "pseudo draft" to add 300,000 soldiers to the ranks. Six months later, Congress made some changes to the controversial law and formalized the draft under the National Conscription Act, enacted on March 3, 1863.

As with volunteers, draftees could collect the enlistment bounty of $100 from the federal government—provided they agreed to serve for three years—and, in some cases, they could receive state and local bounties as well. In many cases, those who volunteered could choose the regiment in which they would serve. (Keenan, 2012)

The conscription policy allowed draftees to purchase substitutes for varying amounts, which created the nightmare of "substitute brokers." The law also permitted draftees to purchase an exemption for $300; critics of the policy dubbed the war a "poor man's fight." (Lord, 1960)

When officials began enforcing the draft law, violence erupted throughout the northern states. Most draft violence took the form of assaults on enrollment officers while they visited households to count white males between the ages of 18 and 45 years. They were beaten, chased off property, pelted with eggs, scalded with boiling water and shot at. (Towne, 2013)

Pennsylvania did not escape the resistance or the violence to the draft. Stories surfaced of alleged conspiracies to aid the Confederacy, several officials were murdered while carrying out their duties, and desertions were common. (Shankman, 1977)

Friday

A very hot day. Had my shoes soled. Wrote to D. P. Maynard and G. R. Stiles. Wrote to Delapo, 51 80 PB New York. Got a "World" from Uncle Joseph. Had a heavy shower in the night.

Saturday

A very hot day. Got no mail. Capt. Rickets and Orderly Sgt. Snider put under arrest by Genl. Hays.

Sunday, August 9, 1863

A most awful hot day. Got a paper from Uncle Joseph and also a line from him stating that he had received my letter of August 1st. Pay Master came. We got our pay.

Monday

A warm and pleasant day. Jim Smith, suttler, came up. Wrote to Sarah. Sent home some photographs. Wrote to Uncle Joseph. Sent him two dollars. Got three papers.

Tuesday

A very hot day. Got no mail. The hottest weather I ever saw.

Wednesday

A quiet, cool, pleasant day. Washed some clothes. Got two papers. "World Herald" and "Police Gazette."

Thursday

A cool, but pleasant day. Got a letter from Delapo. The suttler went to Washington after goods. Got a "World" from New York.

Friday

A warm and pleasant day. Wrote to Delapo and to T. L. Case. Got no letters or papers.

Saturday

A warm, pleasant day. Got a "World" Battery G got paid. A report that we are going to Alexandria.

"You damned son of a bitch . . ."

On July 24, 1863, Sergeant Francis H. Snider had sent a "statement of fact" to Capt. Ricketts, claiming that General Alexander Hays had "openly abused" him while he was discharging his duties. Excerpt from the letter:

> *General Hays commanding the 2nd Army Corps and staff came from the rear of the column . . . and in a loud tone of voice coupled with an oath said, "There are some more of those damned wagons and carts interfering with this train." . . . He swearing and talking in a loud manner, to the effect that we had stolen property with us, alluding to the Battery Cart containing the Fresh Beef for the Company. . . . He ordered both carts to be taken. . . . I spoke to him and said "General (saluting him at the same time) that is government property drawn with the Battery at Washington." . . . He instantly turned in his saddle . . . and drawing back his right arm struck me a violent blow on the left side of my face, and . . . said, "You <u>damned son of a bitch</u> how dare you interfere with me when I give an order." I said, "General have you a right to strike me?" He answered, "Yes Sir I have when you dispute my orders." I said to him, I have not done so Sir you asked me a question and I answered it in a respectful manner, and I shall test the matter. . . . One of the officers who was with the general . . . attracted my attention by touching me with his whip, . . . saying "For Gods sake man say no more. . . . I then rode forward and reported to you. . . .*

Capt. Ricketts apparently forwarded the letter to headquarters, and both he and Snider were arrested. Charges appear to have been dropped because Sweet says no more about it, and both Capt. Ricketts and Sgt. Snider had returned to camp by the following week. Snider was later promoted to lieutenant.

Editor's note: Unable to find any mention of this incident in historical records; the letter has sold at auction in recent years.

Sunday, August 16, 1863

A warm, pleasant day. Wrote to Sarah. Sent her a pocket book and two dollars. Wrote to J. H. Winslow. Two certificates and $2.30 for a pen and a chain. Got the "World." Uncle Joseph had received my letter with two dollars.

Monday

A warm and pleasant day. Got no letters or papers. Commenced to put up a shade over Rickett's tent.

Tuesday

A warm, pleasant day. Expressed home fifteen dollars. Sent it to Bealton Station. Charlie Wells and Joseph Micho went to the hospital.* Got three papers from New York.

Wednesday

A warm, pleasant day. Got a World from New York. Got a letter from V. D.

Thursday

A warm and pleasant day. Got about 20 papers, all old ones directed to the reserve artillery. Got some clothes washed. Orders to march at a moment's notice. Report that the Rebs are on this side of the Rappahanock.

Friday

A warm and pleasant day. Reviewed by General Warren in the forenoon. A soldier shot for desertion. Reported that the Rebels are in our rear. Got only one letter for this Battery.

Saturday

A warm, pleasant day. A good deal of liquor in camp. Jim Smith, the suttler, came up with a load of goods. Got a paper and a letter from mother.

Sunday, August 23, 1863

A warm and pleasant day. Had Company inspection at ten o'clock by Capt. Ricketts. Wrote to mother. Got no mail. Sent mother an express receipt for $25.

---

* Joseph Micho, private, mustered in July 8, 1861; transferred to Battery G, March 26, 1864.

Hd. Quarters Battery F 1st Pa Arty.
August 24th, 1863

Dear Mother:

I received your letter of August 17th last night and I was pleased to hear from you and I was better pleased to hear that you had received my letters for I know you was anxious to hear from me. I have been well ever since I returned but there has been a good many sick in the battery. Charley Wells went to the hospital last Tuesday. He had a very bad diareah. I have not heard from him since he left. I do not know what hospital he is in.

We had some of the hottest weather I ever saw. Ask Guss Roper if he got my letter when he was in the hospital in Washington.

I expressed $15.00 home last Tuesday in care of C. P. Hawley. I will enclose you the receipt in this letter.

We have been under marching orders for the past 10 days. There was a soldier shot within a half a mile of our camp last Friday. He was shot for desertion. He deserted twice and then came out again as a substitute. We was very lucky in getting back safe.

I want Sarah to write and answer all my letters.

From your son Oney F. Sweet.

Remember me to all.

P. S. Has the draft taken place yet in Susque. So? Give me a list of those drafted.

Monday

    A warm, pleasant day. Got no mail. Only one letter for the Battery. Right section went out on picket.

Tuesday

    A warm, pleasant day. Gates, Harder, Houser and myself were court martialed by Genl. Warren at his headquarters.* Capt. Ricketts was on the board. He was our witness. We do not know our sentences yet. Got a "World," a "Herald" and "Police Gazette." Had a letter from H. Winslow, containing a gold pen and chain. Wrote to Uncle Joseph, sent him five dollars.

Wednesday

    A warm, pleasant day. Some of our men were court martialed. The suttler went to Washington after a load of goods. Wrote to Robert F. Ballantine. Got a "World" from New York. Ridgeway got a letter from Charlie Wells. He is at Campbell Hospital, Ward 1, Washington, D.C.

Thursday

    Cool night, but a pleasant day. Got a large mail. Got a letter from mother and Sarah and G. R. Stiles.

Friday

    A cool night, but a warm, pleasant day. Two soldiers shot for desertion in the 2nd Corps. Got no letters or papers. Harder and the orderly went to the Penna. Reserve Corps. The Penna. Reserve presented General Mead with a splendid sword and equipment at his headquarters.

Saturday

    A cold rainy morning, but cleared off pleasant and was quite warm in the middle of the day. Got a "World" from N.Y. Wrote to Salsbury Bros. & Co., Providence R.I. Sent $20.

Sunday, August 30, 1863

    A cool, pleasant day. Inspection at ten o'clock. Wrote to 74 Bleecker Street,

---

    * General Gouverneur K. Warren, commander, Second Corps. It's not clear what these men did to be court martialed, but 22-year-old Sweet's mention of "a good deal of liquor in camp" three days earlier may have had something to do with it, or it may have been related to his French leave. (See the diary entry for October 4, 1863.)

New York and to Dawne and Moore for a badge, 208 Broadway, New York. Got a "World" from N.Y.

Monday

A cool morning, but warm during the day. Received orders to march at six o'clock. Marched to Bankford on the Rappahannock. Marched a distance of twenty miles. Camped near Banks Ford for the night. One section on pickett.

Tuesday, September 1, 1863

A warm, pleasant day. Went on pickett at six o'clock a.m. and was relieved at 12 by the eight section. Mustered for pay at 1 o'clock. No news of any importance.

Wednesday

A warm, pleasant day. Everything quiet. No news. Over three days' rations have run out and don't know where we will get any more. Expected to start back to our old camp today.

Thursday

A warm, pleasant day. Started back for our old camp at six o'clock. Reached our old camp at 10 o'clock a.m.

Friday

A cool, windy morning. Got a letter from Willie, D. P. Maynard and Charles Wells. Got three papers from New York. Uncle Joseph has got the money I sent him last week.

Saturday

A warm and pleasant day. Wrote to D. P. Maynard. Got a "World" from New York. Heard from C. Monro & Brown.

Sunday, September 6, 1863

A warm, pleasant day. Had Company inspection at 10 o'clock by Capt. Ricketts. Wrote to Charles Wells. Received a letter and package from Salsbury. Received a "World" and Police Gazette.

Monday
  A warm and pleasant day. Got no letters or papers. Had a drill in the forenoon and one in the afternoon. Took care of a team, the first duty I've done for six weeks.

Tuesday
  A warm, plesant day. Had drill twice a day. Got two papers from New York, no news of importance.

Wednesday
  A warm, pleasant day, windy in the afternoon. Had drill twice after and forenoon. Got a "World" and a letter from Case. Got some goods from New York, H & S. Belts issued to us. Suttler came with a load.

Thursday
  A warm, pleasant day. Drill twice a day. Wrote to mother and Willie. Orders read to us that Forts Gregg and Wagonir had surrendered.* Got a World, drew haversack.

Friday
  Had a Battery drill in the afternoon. Cool, but pleasant. Got a "World" and a letter from R. F. Ballantine.

Saturday
  Got marching orders to be ready at 10 o'clock. Marched at that time. A very hot day. Marched to Rappahanoak Station. Camped near the 1st Army Corps. A heavy shower in the afternoon. Saw several cases of sunstroke. Got no mail.

Sunday, September 13, 1863
  A rainy morning, but cleared off hot and pleasant. Marched at 7 o'clock. Crossed the Rappahannock. Our Cavelry had a skirmish with the Rebels. Skirmished all the way to Culpepper. Captured 3 pieces of artillery and a good many prisoners. Camped near Culpepper. A shower.

---

  * On September 7, 1863, rebel forces evacuated Morris Island (Charleston, South Carolina). Union General Quincy A. Gillmore seized Fort Wagner and Battery Gregg, and took 75 prisoners and 19 pieces of artillery. (Hitchcock, 1868)

Battery F, 1st Pa Arty
Sept. 9th, 1863

Dear Brother:

I received your letter a few days ago and was glad to hear from you. We are in our old camp. Last week we went on an expedition down the river. We was gone 4 days. We was 20 miles from here. We had a very pleasant time as it did not rain any, but if it had rained we would have suffered as we had no tents with us. I received a letter from Case today. I had a letter from Charley Wells last week. He said he was getting better slowly. We have cool pleasant weather here now. I suppose you have been busy and had to work hard this summer, but now you will have a little rest until it is time to gather corn, apples, and potatoes. I will have to close for the want of something to write. Answer soon.
From your brother.

Dear Mother:

When you have leisure time I wish you would make me the following articles: and perhaps you will have a chance to send them to me or express them: one undershirt, two woolen shirts for winter, two pair woolen stockings, one towel a good one, one pocket handkerchief and if Sarah is a good enough sewer tell her to make a housewife for thread, needles, etc., and oblige your affectionate son Oney F. Sweet.*

---

* "housewife": a pocket-size container for small articles, such as thread. (*Merriam-Webster*)

Monday

A rainy morning, but cleared off pleasant and hot. Laid in camp all day. A report that our Cavelry was within two miles of Gordonsville. Wagon train came up. Got a World and a Police Gazette. A letter from Charley Wells and one from Sarah.

Tuesday

A cloudy morning, cleared off pleasant. Marched at two o'clock. Camped two miles south of Culpepper. Went into position at 1st Division Hd.

Wednesday

A warm and pleasant day. Did not march. Saw General Meade, Sykes and Pleasanton.* Cavelry had some fighting on the Rappahannock.

Thursday

A cloudy morning, but cleared off pleasant. Marched at daylight. Passed Cedar Mountain. Went within one mile from the river, marched back two miles and went into camp. Rained very hard.

Friday

Very rainy morning. Cleared off about ten o'clock. All quiet along the lines at 3 p.m. Cavelry moved to the right. Got a World.

Saturday

Warm, pleasant day. Wrote to Charlie Wells and Robert F. Ballantine. Moved camp in the afternoon. We are now in full view of the Rebs. A cold night.

Sunday, September 20, 1863

A cool, but pleasant day. Had inspection at ten o'clock. Wrote to D. P. Maynard and Will G. Brower. Went up on the hill to look at the Johnies. Suttler came up and sold out on tick.

---

* General George Sykes, commander, 5th Army Corps.
General Alfred Pleasanton, commander, Cavalry Corps, Army of the Potomac.

Monday

A cool, pleasant day. Wrote to Sarah. Got a World. Had tomatoes and fresh pork for supper. Got news of a battle between Casey and Bragg. Fight a hard one. Not ended.*

Tuesday

A cool, but pleasant day. Drew 8 days rations and received orders to be ready to march at a moment's notice. Heard from O. G. Larribee who is at home, but sick. No new news from the West. Got a World and Police Gazette.

Wednesday

A cool, but pleasant day. Wrote to O. G. Larribee and J. G. Shan & Co., 48 & 50 New York. No news from the South West. Some fighting on our right, but not heard any particulars. Got a World. A cold night.

Thursday

A warm and pleasant day. Policed camp. Twelve o'clock, signed the payrolls. Three p.m. received our pay: twenty-six dollars. Expressed home twenty-five. Marching orders expected to march, but did not. Inspection by Capt. Hayward at four o'clock.** Got a World.

Friday

A warm and pleasant day. Drew rations. Wrote to mother. Sent her express receipt. Got a World. General Rosenkranz driven back on Chattanooga.

Saturday

A pleasant day, but cool and windy. Received a World, a letter from Charlie Wells and one from G. R. Stiles. A cold night.

---

* Battle of Chickamauga, Georgia, September 18-20, 1863; Colonel Thomas S. Casey, commander of the 110th Illinois Infantry, and Braxton Bragg, commander of the Confederate Army of Tennessee. (Hitchcock, 1868)

Gen. William S. Rosecrans, commander of Union forces at the Battle of Chickamauga, the most significant Union defeat in the Western Theater, and noted for having the second highest number of casualties in the war, following the Battle of Gettysburg. (Hitchcock, 1868)

** Editor's note: Could not positively identify Capt. Hayward (also "Hayard"), later referred to as major and colonel; possibly William H. Hayward, 1st Ohio Volunteer Artillery.

Sunday, September 27, 1863

A most beautiful day. Had a Battery inspection at 10 o'clock by R. B. Ricketts. Inspection of quarters at twelve noon. Wrote to Charlie Wells. Took care of Reed's horses. Got a World and a letter from R. F. Ballantine.

Monday

A warm, pleasant day. Got a World and a letter from Will F. Brewer. A cool night. Tomatoes and fresh beef for supper.

Tuesday

A warm and pleasant day. No news of any importance. Got no mail.

Wednesday

A pleasant day. Orders read to us that we could reenlist for three years and get forty dollars bounty.* A beautiful moonlight night. Did not go to bed until twelve o'clock.

Thursday, October 1, 1863

A cloudy day, but warm. New potatoes, tomatoes and corn for supper. Got a letter from Sarah and three papers from R.F.B. Three papers from New York.

Friday

A rainy day. Rained very hard all the forenoon. A deserter was shot in front of our Battery. Our Company was ordered out to witness the same. Got no mail.

Saturday

Cleared off warm and pleasant. Made a bed in our tent. Wrote to Robert F. Ballantine. Got no mail for the Battery.

Sunday, October 4, 1863

A warm and beautiful day. Wrote to Sarah. Had a Battery inspection at 10 o'clock. Did not feel very well. Went to bed early. Received three papers from New York.

---

* The War Department had issued a general order on June 25, 1863, offering a bounty of $400 and a 30-day furlough to "veteran volunteers" who reenlisted for three years or until the end of the war. (Lord, 1960)

Monday

A warm and pleasant day. Had gun drill at 10 o'clock. General Warren relieved from command of 2nd Corps.* A report that we are going back to Culpepper and be relieved by the 6th Corps. Our sentence read to us.**

Tuesday

Warm and pleasant day. Marched at six o'clock. Passed 5th LE Army Corps. Marched through Culpepper, camped about two miles north of Culpepper. Have a nice camp. On guard: Segt Leggett, Willman, Corp. Baum and Chandler.***

Wednesday

A cool, but pleasant day. On guard. Got two papers from New York. Looked like rain. Rained very hard in the night. Boys worked at putting up their tents. Got a Tribune.

Thursday

A drizzling rain all day. Had knapsack drill in the afternoon.**** Was not on police duty. Got a World and Police Gazette. Pat Curry under guard at Hd. Quarters.

---

* General Warren took General Hancock's place following the Battle of Gettysburg. General Hancock's wounds necessitated an absence of several months. (Fox, 1889)

** According to military records, the court sentenced him "to forfeit 2 months pay and carry a loaded knapsack weighing fifty pounds two hours each day for twenty days so as not to interfere with his other duties in the Battery." (National Archives) (See the diary entry for August 25, 1863.)

*** "Segt Leggett" unable to identify.

"Segt Willman" possibly Henry A. Willman, 1st Regiment, Rhode Island Light Artillery.

"Corp. Baum" possibly Morgan Bahn, sergeant, reenlisted[?] July 29, 1864; mustered out with battery, June 10, 1865.

William E. Chandler, corporal, Battery G, mustered in June 6, 1861; promoted to sergeant, Nov. 1, 1862, to 1st sergeant, Aug. 14, 1863; mustered out with company, June 13, 1864.

**** Knapsack drill: soldiers practiced packing their knapsacks or haversacks, then wearing them in formation and while marching. A knapsack might have contained an overcoat, change of underclothing, socks, woolen blankets, rubber blanket, food, and other items, and weighed 35 pounds or more. (Vermont in the Civil War)

Friday

A warm and pleasant day. Worked all day putting up our tent. Got it nearly done. Got a World and a letter from O. G. Larrabee. 8 days' rations issued to us. An order to be ready to march at a moment's notice.

Saturday

A cold, but pleasant day. Orders to march. Left camp at eleven o'clock and went to support 3rd Corps. Expected to have a fight. Unharnessed and went to bed. Received a letter from Charlie Wells. He is at home on a furlough. Got my watch from Winslow.

Sunday, October 11, 1863

Half past twelve a.m. Orders to march immediately. Locked up and was ready at one o'clock. Marched through Culpepper. Held up three hours on account of baggage wagons being blocked up. Marched to within three miles of the Rappahannock and halted. Crosst the Rappahannock and marched to Bealeton Station and camped for the night.

Monday

Monday a cold morning. Twelve o'clock had orders to march. Marched to Rappahannock and crosst. Marched to within a short distance of Brandy Station. Marched in line of battle. Camped at dark. Aroused up at twelve o'clock and recrosst the river and marched to Bealeton Station and halted two hours.

Tuesday

Election day for Governor of Pennsylvania. Marched toward Sulphur Springs. Halted three hours in the middle of the day. Marched 'til dark. Camped for the night. 3rd Corps had skirmish near us. A cold night.

Wednesday

Marched at four o'clock. Reached Cedar Run at daylight. Crosst and had a little skirmish. Fired 108 shots. Rebels were all around us. Things looked rather dubious for a few minutes but we soon drove the Rebels and opened the road. We took the advance of the Corps and went into position near Catletts Station. The rear guard had some fighting. Had a fight at Bristow Station. Whipped the Rebels, took five guns. Had six wounded. W. H. Patterson was wounded.

Report of Capt. R. Bruce Ricketts, First Pennsylvania Light Artillery, commanding Batteries F and G.

HEADQUARTERS BATTERIES F AND G,
October 22, 1863.

SIR: I have the honor to make the following report of the part taken by my command in the engagements at Auburn and Bristoe Station, October 14, 1863:

At daybreak on the morning of the 14th of October, while my battery was marching in rear of the First Division, Second Army Corps, the enemy opened fire on us from a battery stationed on a hill near the road leading from Auburn to Bristoe Station. I immediately engaged their battery and soon silenced it. I was then ordered to report to General Hays, commanding Third Division, Second Army Corps, and marched with that division to Bristoe Station, where the Second Army Corps was again attacked by the enemy's artillery and infantry. I placed my battery in position, by order of Capt. J. G. Hazard, commanding Artillery Brigade, on a hill near the rail road bridge crossing Broad Run, and opened on a column of infantry near the railroad with canister and shrapnel until they broke, when I engaged a battery in my immediate front, which was silenced and five of its guns were captured and brought off by our infantry skirmishers. I expended during both the engagements 633 rounds of ammunition.

The casualties were as follows.*

There were 3 horses killed and 5 wounded.

Lients. B. Spence, C. B. Brockway, and C. H. Mitchell fought their sections with great coolness and bravery.

I am, sir, very respectfully, your obedient servant,

R. BRUCE RICKETTS,
Captain, First Pennsylvania Artillery.

Lient. G. L. DWIGHT,
Acting Assistant Adjutant-General.

---

* Nominal list (omitted) shows 1 officer and 6 men wounded.

(*The War of the Rebellion,* 1890)

Excerpt from the report of Capt. John G. Hazard, 1st Rhode Island Light Artillery, commanding Artillery Brigade.

> HDQRS. ARTILLERY BRIGADE,
> SECOND ARMY CORPS,
> Near Warrenton, Va., October 23, 1863.

COLONEL: I have the honor to transmit the following report of the part sustained by the Artillery Brigade on the 14th instant, in the actions of the corps at Auburn and Bristoe Station, Va.: . . .

Battery F, First Pennsylvania Artillery (6 3-inch rifled guns), Capt. R. Bruce Ricketts commanding. . . .

The advance of the corps, the First Division, moving on the road passing through Auburn toward Bristoe Station, was fired into on crossing Cedar Run, a little after daybreak, by a battery of the enemy, in position on an eminence to the east of the road. Ricketts' battery, immediately in rear of the division, was placed in position and soon silenced the battery engaged. . . .

The arrival of Ricketts' and Arnold's batteries was most timely. Ricketts was immediately placed in position in rear of that first occupied by Brown, while Arnold's took an advantageous position in rear of the First Division. The fire of these batteries upon the charging lines of the infantry was most effective and deadly, and assisted greatly in securing their demoralization.

(Moodey, 1890)

Thursday

Marched acrosst Bull Run about two o'clock. Halted near Centreville. Got some sleep. Marched early in the morning. Halted and onharnessed near Centreville. A pleasant day. Marched two miles and camped. Some fighting. Heard that we whipped the enemy. On guard, 2nd relief. A cool, rainy night.

Friday

Rained very hard. Marched at eleven o'clock. Marched down near Bull Run and relieved some Batterys. Bull Run very high. A Brigade of Cavelry crosst near night, but they had no fight and recrosst at dark. A rainy night.

Saturday

All quiet in the front. Some cannonading on our right. A brigade of Cavelry and Pontoons went down to the run. Orders from General Meade giving great praise to the 2nd Corps in covering the retreat. No mail. Drew eight days' rations.

Sunday, October 18, 1863

A beautiful morning. Boots and Saddles blown at four o'clock.* Ready to march at daylight. Did not march. Got a large mail. Got a letter from R. F. Ballantine, one from mother, also a good many papers.

Monday

Boots and Saddles blown at four o'clock. Marched at daylight. A rainy morning. Crosst Bull Run, passed Manassas Junction. Camped near Bristow Station. Went over the battlefield. The railroad is all ripped up.

Tuesday

Boots and saddles blown at four o'clock. Marched at daylight. Crosst Broad Run three times. Passed near Gainsville. Very bad roads. Marched five miles through woods and fields where there is no road. Camped at dark on the field where we had the skirmish on the morning of the 14th.

Wednesday

Aroused up at daylight. 3rd Corps passed us. We laid in camp until they passed. Saw Charley Roper and Lt. Brainard. Got a World. Wrote home. Did not march.

---

* Boots and saddles, a bugle call used as the first signal for mounted drill or other mounted formation. (*Collins English Dictionary*)

Thursday

A warm, pleasant day. Wrote to R. F. Ballantine and I. N. Purcell, 205 Pearl St., New York. Did not march. Drew clothing.

Friday

A cool, but pleasant day. Marched at seven o'clock. Marched nine miles. Camped near Warrenton. Got a World. A rainy night. General Rosencranz relieved. General Grant in camp in charge of the Army of the Cumberland, Ohio and Kentucky.*

Saturday

A very disagreeable day, rainy and cold. Put a flew in the tent. Cleared off in the evening. Recd. marching orders. A report that our pickets were driven in. Got a World.

Sunday, October 25, 1863

A cold morning, but pleasant. Company inspection at 10 o'clock by Lt. Spence. Knapsack drill from one till three by order of Lt. Mitchell. On guard tonight; Corporals Moore and Rudssill. Got a World.

Monday

A cold but pleasant. On guard, second Relief. Wrote to Charlie Wells. Got marching orders. Got all ready and the order was countermanded. A cold night. Got World and Police Gazette from New York. Sick.

Tuesday

A cold, but pleasant day. Fixed up our tent. Knapsack drill in the afternoon. A very cold night, but we have good, warm quarters. Got no papers. No news of any importance. Inspection by Capt. Hazard. He is to be relieved and take command of his old Battery.

---

* Major General William Rosecrans never again held a major field command following his defeat at the Battle of Chickamauga. Major General Ulysses S. Grant assumed command of the Army of the Cumberland, Army of the Tennessee, and reinforcements from the Army of the Potomac at Chattanooga. On March 3, 1864, President Lincoln promoted Grant to lieutenant general and elevated him to general-in-chief of the Armies of the United States. Grant made his headquarters with the Army of the Potomac. (Hitchcock, 1868)

Wednesday

A cold, but very pleasant day. Went over to the 20th Mass., to get my wach fixed. King wach maker. Knapsack drill in the afternoon. Got a World and Mercury from N.Y.

Thursday

A beautiful day, not Very cold. Took the morning reports over to Artillery Hd Quarters. Drew fresh beef. Had no knapsack drill; don't know the reason. Got a World. Got a list of the drafted men in Susque County. A gay time in camp. Gil Stiles, Alvin Sweet and many others are drafted.

Friday

A Warm day, but looks like rain. Had standing gun drill twice After and forenoons. No knapsack drill. Wrote to G. R. Stiles and Uncle Joseph. Rained in the night. Got a World. A high old time. Ricketts serenaded by a band.

Saturday

A warm and pleasant day. Muddy under foot. Mustered by Capt. Hazard at 9 o'clock. Battery inspection at 3 o'clock by Chief of Artillery. A very thorough inspection. Got no mail. Wrote to Frederick A. Brady, 24 Arm Street, New York.

Sunday, November 1, 1863

A warm and pleasant day. Had inspection by Lt. Spence. The cars run up to Warrenton today for the first time. Got a Susque County paper and two Worlds.

Monday

A warm and pleasant day. Knapsack drill in afternoon. Gun drill in the forenoon. I took care of a team. Got a World.

Tuesday

A warm, pleasant day. Knapsack drill. Went after new horses; did not get them. Got a Herald and Police Gazette. The boys brought lots of tobacco into camp. Drew new clothing. I got a pair of boots and a blanket.

Wednesday

A warm, pleasant day. Standing gun drill in the forenoon. Lt. Spence drilled us. Wrote to Sarah and Will G. Brower; also to Schultz, Troy, New York. Got a World. Expected marching orders.

Thursday

A cool, windy day. On guard 2nd relief; Sgts. Stradford, Corporals Chandler and Pitcuke. Looks like rain in the afternoon. Drew Ordnance stores. Got World, a letter from R. F. Ballantine and one from Frederick Brady.

Friday

A warm, windy day. Had a Battalion drill by Col. Munroe.* Got a World. Got marching orders.

Saturday

Aroused up at five o'clock. Marched at six o'clock. Passed Warrenton Junction and Bealton Station. Reached Kelley's Ford near dark.** Camped for the night. Some fighting. A good many prisoners taken. Got a World. A very windy day.

Sunday, November 8, 1863

Aroused up before daylight. Marched at daylight. Crosst the river and formed a line of Battle. Marched to near Rappahannock Station. Halted for dinner. Marched on to Brandy Station. Camped for the night. Some fighting in the front. Got no mail.

Monday

Did not march. Laid in the line of battle all day. A very cold day. Got a World.

Tuesday

A cold, but pleasant day. Marched at daylight. Marched 4 miles and camped. A plenty of rails fixed up our tents comfortable. Sick with a cold. Got a World.

---

* "Col. Munroe" probably Lieutenant Colonel J. Albert Monroe, 1st Rhode Island Light Artillery.

** Kelly's Ford: Fauquier County's "hallowed grounds," the site of twelve battles and countless troop movements, raids, skirmishes, and encampments. With its proximity to Washington, DC, the county played a key role in Union and Confederate strategy. (Fauquier County Historical Marker)

Camp Near Warrenton, Va.
Nov. 3rd, 1863

Dear Sister:

It has been a long time since I have heard from you and I have not written home for some time. I have not had any paper or envelopes to write with. I lost all of my paper on the retreat.

I received a Montrose Republican with a list of the drafted in it and I saw many that I knew, but I do not think many of them will go soldiering but will pay the $300 and stay at home.* When you write let me know who go and who stay at home. We are having most beautiful weather and we are looking for another march and probably another fight, but I would like to stay in this camp all winter. Did mother send those shirts by express and how did she direct them?

I heard one of our lieutenants say the other day that we would get home next May. I hope we will and I hope the war might be over by that time but I am afraid it will last a long time yet. The cars now run to Warrenton. We are camped near the railroad. This is the 5th time we have been at this place and we know the country pretty well through here. I send you a photograph of our orderly sergt. Frank Snider. Sarah I will have to close for I have no more paper. We expect suttlers up from Washington every day and then we can buy a plenty of paper.

From your ever true brother Oney.

When you write give me all the news. On our last marches we had hard times. We never got a good nights rest for ten days. We would lay down along the road side and just get asleep when we would have to get up and jog along. We had one pretty hard fight and several skirmishes. We marched along side of the rebels for 30 miles not over two miles apart and our infantry was skirmishing all the time. The rebels were trying to get in ahead of us and they did at one place but we whipped them and opened the road again.

The government offers $400 to old soldiers that will reenlist for three years more but I want to get out of this before I bind myself again. I suppose the draft has made a great deal of grumbling in Gibson.*

---

* Draftees could purchase an exemption for $300. See The Draft in the Civil War, p. 127.

Wednesday

A Very cold day. Marched at three o'clock. Joined the Artillery Brigade. Camped near Corps Hd. Qtrs. Got a letter from O. E. Larrabee. He is at Camp Tyler near Baltimore. I do not feel well. A very bad cold.

Thursday

A cold morning, but clear and pleasant. Signed the payrolls. The Battery got paid. Two months' pay. I got none. Fixed up our tent. Got a World from Uncle Joseph.

Friday

A warm and pleasant day. A plenty of liquor in camp. Knapsack drill in the afternoon. Got a World and a letter from home. Got some stamps. Got a Mantour Amer. from Will G. Brower.

Saturday

A warm, pleasant day. On guard, first relief, Sgt. Wireman and Corp. Ridgeway and Hanes. Got a World and a letter from Charley Wells. A very rainy night.

Sunday, November 15, 1863

A rainy, muddy day. Marching orders. Brigade suttler came up with a load of goods. Cleared off pleasant. Got a World from New York.

Monday

A warm, but disagreeable day under foot. Wrote to mother. Got a World. Had inspection by Capt. Ricketts.

Tuesday

A warm, pleasant day. Had inspection at 10 o'clock by Col. Munroe. He drilled us. Got a World. All quiet in camp. Got a Police Gazette.

Wednesday

A warm, pleasant day. Expressed home twenty-five dollars by the Suttler. More's father and brother came to see him. Got a World.

Camp Near Kelley's Field, Va.
Nov. 16th, 1863

Dear Mother:
I received your letter last night and I was glad to hear that you was all well. We have had some hard times since I last wrote, but we was not in the last fight. It was very cold weather and I caught a very bad cold but I have got nearly over it now.

We expect to march from here every day. I was glad to get the stamps for I was out. I forgot to enclose the photograph in the last letter but I will put it in this.

I will also enclose a new kind of government money. Send me the express receipt for those shirts so I can send it to Washington and get them. I do not expect to get paid for the clothing I lost. We lost clothes at Bull Run and we never got paid for them but they tell us we will when we are discharged.

Most all of the battery has reenlisted but I have not and I do not think I will, but I think the war is nearly over. We had a very rainy day yesterday. I have not much news to write. I have two shirts now — old ones. I hope I will get those you sent me.

Will Arvine pay the $300 or will he come a soldiering?* Will Gill come? Write soon and send the express receipt.

From your affectionate son Oney F. Sweet

---

* Sweet's daughter Marian said in a letter to her grandson William J. Ketchum: "Arvine Sweet was father's cousin. Father [Almon Sweet] hated a man who would pay to get a substitute to take his place if drafted. They could do it in those days."

Thursday

A cloudy but warm day. Expect to march soon. Took a team out to pasture. Knapsack drill in the afternoon. Dedication of Gettysburg cemetery.* General Meade was absent from the Army to attend. Got a letter and paper from Uncle Joseph.

Friday

A cool, windy day. Sent $50.00 to Washington to buy a five by twenty and have it sent to Robert F. Ballantine. Wrote to Uncle Jo and to R. F. Ballantine. Wrote to F. A. Brady for diaries. Standing gun drill in the forenoon. Knapsack drill in the afternoon.

Saturday

A very rainy day. On guard, 1st Relief, on the prisoners. Rained all day. Capt. Ricketts started home on a furlough. Got a World and Herald.

Sunday, November 22, 1863

A warm, pleasant day, but very muddy. Inspection at ten o'clock. Wrote to A. G. Larribee and Charley Wells. Got World. Got marching orders.

Monday

A warm, pleasant day. Wrote to mother. Got marching orders. Got a World and two papers from Newark.

Tuesday

A very rainy day. Aroused up at four o'clock. Was harnessed up until eleven o'clock and then we went into camp. Rained some all day. Got no papers or letters.

Wednesday

A cloudy day. Rained. Took care of a team. Cleared off pleasant. Went to bed early.

Thursday

Aroused up at four o'clock. Marched at seven o'clock. A most beautiful day. Marched to Germaine ford on the Rappidamn. Crossed about noon. Found

---

* President Abraham Lincoln delivered his oft-quoted Gettysburg Address on Thursday, November 19, 1863, at the dedication of the Soldiers' National Cemetery at Gettysburg, Pennsylvania.

Paper Money

I will also enclose a new kind of government money.

—Oney F. Sweet

Expenses mounted as the war continued, and the U.S. government had reached a financial crisis. Congressman Elbridge G. Spaulding, a banker from Buffalo, New York, introduced a bill that would allow the U.S. Treasury to issue $150 million in notes as legal tender.

On February 25, 1862, President Lincoln signed the Legal Tender Act, into law, which also legitimized the first federal currency issued in 1861. The notes were declared to be "lawful money and a legal tender in payment of all debts, public and private" (except for customs duties). Because of their distinct coloring, the notes became known as "greenbacks." (Mitchell, 1903)

This act created a national currency and changed the monetary structure of the Unites States. Although opponents of the paper money predicted that runaway inflation would follow, the "gold premium" did not rise significantly except during Union military reversals. (McPherson, 1988)

The paper money now used every day in the United States grew out of the Civil War. In 1863, the National Banking Act allowed the widespread chartering of national banks, and, for the first time, the country had a uniform paper currency. (Gordon, 2013)

The reverse of a one-dollar "greenback" issued as legal tender in 1862.

no Rebels, but pickets. A very bad place to cross. Marched three miles on the plank road and camped for the night.

Friday

Aroused up at 3 o'clock. Marched at daylight. Turned off the plank road, then struck the pike to Orange C.H. Came onto the Rebels about noon. Some fighting. We threw up breast works. Orderly Leagh Snider wounded by a sharpshooter. All quiet at dark.

Saturday

Moved forward at daylight. Marched about two miles and ran onto the Rebels. They have a very strong position. Can see them plain. Threw up earthworks in the evening. Fell back to Robinson's Tavern. Rained all day. Roads all very bad.

Sunday, November 29, 1863

Marched at daylight. Roads very bad. Marhed past Gregg's Hdqtts. Came upon the Rebels. Skirmished with them all day. A very thick woods and bad place to fight. Nothing but skirmishing all day.

Monday

The Rebels have a very strong position. There was to be an assault by 4 divisions on the Rebs' works. We were to follow the charge. We have no positions for artillery. We stayed within five hundred yards of the Rebs in a thick woods but they could not see us. The charge was not made. We moved back and went into camp.

Tuesday, December 1, 1863

Aroused up at daylight and was moved up to the front. Was not in position. No fighting all day. Can see the Johnnies very plain. At eight o'clock we began to retreat. Marched on the plank road. A very cold night. Reached the Rappidan at daylight. Crosst and halted and got breakfast. The Johnnies followed us to the river. Marched twenty-five miles.

Wednesday

Got into out old camp at Berry Hill. Laid still all day. Got rested up some. Got a mail. Got a letter from Sarah and Charley Wells. 4 Worlds. Warren's Hdqtrs burned down.

Thursday

Moved camp at three o'clock. Marched about a 1/2 mile. Worked at winter quarters. Got a letter from D. P. Maynard and one from mother. Two Worlds. A report that we are to march tomorrow.

Friday

Aroused up at 4 o'clock. Marched at 8 o'clock. A pleasant morning. Marched 5 miles to Stevensburg and camped in line of battle. A very cold night. Near our camp is an apple tree where a Rebel deserter was hung. He deserted to our army and was afterwards caught.

Saturday

A pleasant day, but very cold. All quiet. Got a World. A full account of the victory in the Southwest.* A very cold night.

Sunday, December 6, 1863

A pleasant day but very cold. Expected to March and put up winter quarters but did not.

Monday

A pleasant but cold day. Washed some clothes. Wrote to Sarah and mother. Got a letter from will G. Brower and a dollar's worth of stamps. A cold night.

Tuesday

A very cold day but pleasant. Got ready to march at noon. Marched near Corps Hdqtrs. Camped in a very good place. Got no mail. Smith, the suttler, came up with a load of goods.

Wednesday

A cold, but pleasant day. Worked at winter quarters. Got orders to march. Monroe ought to be rode on a rail. On guard, third relief, on the horses. Corp. Chandler and Brockway. Got no mail.

---

* On November 23, 1863, the Union forces fought their way out of besieged Chattanooga, Tennessee, overrunning the Rebels at Orchard Knob. The next day, General Grant captured Lookout Mountain after six hours of fighting. On November 25, General George H. Thomas broke the center of the Confederate line. The three victories in three days opened the Deep South to a Union invasion. (Hitchcock, 1868)

Camp Near Stevensburg, Va.
Dec. 7, 1863

Dear Sister:

    I received your letter a few days ago. We have seen some very hard times since I last wrote.

    Nov. 26, Thanksgiving Day we were aroused up at 3 o'clock, cooked breakfast, and marched at daylight. We crossed the Rappidan about noon. Camped at dark. An awful cold night. That was the way I spent my Thanksgiving.

    Nov. 27 marched before daylight. Oh it was a cold morning to get up and stand around a fire. I would like to have been sitting by mother's stove that morning. We marched on a plank road 3 miles and then we had a turn pike. At about noon we came upon the Johnnies and there was sharp skirmishing. We did not fire any. Our orderly seagt., the one I sent you a photograph of, was wounded in the thigh by a sharp shooter. After dark we went to work and threw up breast works to protect us if we had a fight.

    Early next morning the rebels were gone and we advanced in line of battle. I saw several dead rebs and several graves. At about 8 o'clock we came in sight of the rebs again. They were drawn up in line of battle and we could see them very plain. They had a strong position. We opened on them and they opened on us. Several shells struck near the battery but hurt nothing. It rained quite hard all the forenoon. At near dark we fired several shells at them but they did not fire back.

    We expected a big battle would come off next day but at 12 o'clock we was aroused up and marched back. Other troops took our place. We had to leave all of our blankets behind and we marched around on to the extreme left of the line. At noon we found a plenty of rebs but our skirmishers drove them back. We was in a large woods and we could not get any position for artillery. I did not sleep much that night. I had no blankets and it was awful cold.

    Early next morning the rebels were found in a very strong position and at 8 o'clock there was to be a charge made by 20,000 men, but after Genl Warren examined the rebels works he sent for Genl Meade and the charge was not made. There would have been a great slaughter of men.

    Our battery was to follow the charge and if even one of us had come out safe it would have been a wonder. The men were ready but nearly every one that saw the rebels works dreaded the job. We layed in line of battle until Dec. 1st and at dark we retreated.

I never saw so much woods in my life as we marched through. If it had been an open country we could have whipped them. We had no position for artillery. I think that march was the hardest yet. The prospect is now that we will go into winter quarters. I hope so.

From your ever true brother Oney.

Thursday

A cold, but pleasant day. Moved camp at twelve o'clock. Moved a half mile. A very good place to camp. Water near. Got a World.

Friday

A cold, but pleasant day. Worked hard all day. A report that Pleasanton takes command of this Army. Got a World.

Saturday

A cold, but pleasant day. Nearly finished our house. Worked hard all day. Got a World. A busy day in camp. Got two shirts from home.

Sunday, December 13, 1863

My birthday. Finished our house and have everything comfortable. Got a new York Times. Some of the boys worked at the officers' Quarters. I have a very sore hand.

Monday

Have a very sore hand. Off duty. A cold, but pleasant day. Got a World.

Tuesday

My hand is very bad. Cannot sleep nights. Got a World and a letter from home.

Wednesday

A cold but pleasant day. Off duty. A very bad hand. Got a World.

Thursday

A cold day. McGoldrick, Fields and Quin started home on a furlough.* Got a World from N.Y. 0. G. Larrabee returned to the battery.

Friday

Cannot sleep nights. My hand is very bad. Got a World. A cold day.

Saturday

Off duty. My hand is very bad. Had it cut open.** Got a World.

Sunday, December 20, 1863

A cold day. Got a World, a letter from R. F. Ballantine. He has got the 5-20, and he sent me Annie's photograph.

Monday

In camp all day. Went up to Lt. Brockway's quarters with several others and reenlisted in the Veterans' Volunteer Corps on condition that the Battery went back to the States in a body to reorganize, and was sworn in for three years or during the war. In the evening: the day cold.

Tuesday

A very cold day. Nearly all of F and of A, great many of G, have re-enlisted in the Veterans'.

Wednesday

Lt. Spence went home on a 3 day furlough. A cold day. My hand is getting better.

Thursday

A very cold day. Expect to soon start on a furlough home. A very sore hand.

---

* Michael McGoldrick, private, reenlisted January 3, 1864; not on Battery F muster-out roll; possibly transferred to infantry.

George Fields, private, mustered in March 27, 1862; discharged on Surgeon's Certificate, March 15, 1863.

** Apparently Sweet injured his hand while building the "house" for winter quarters.

Veterans' Volunteer Corps

Went up to Lt. Brockway's quarters with several others and reenlisted in the Veterans' Volunteer Corps.

—Oney F. Sweet

In 1863, commanding officers in the Union army requested that a new corps be formed to keep the battle-savvy veterans from going home when their enlistments expired. The commanders wanted the veterans to bolster the ranks of the inexperienced recruits and draftees flooding into the army.

As an enticement to reenlist, the federal government offered a bounty (bonus) of $400 and a 30-day furlough to those who agreed to serve three more years or to the end of the war. (Lord, 1960; Guerin, 1865)

That amount of money was the equivalent of two and a half year's pay for Oney Sweet, based on his pay rate of $13 a month. When he and some of his Battery F comrades reenlisted in December 1863, they were to be reassigned to the elite Veterans' Volunteer Corps. However, the War Department did not formally authorize the veterans' corps until November 28, 1864, when it was placed under the command of General Hancock. (Guerin, 1865)

Meanwhile, Oney F. Sweet remained with Battery F, awaiting reassignment.

Friday

Christmas. A very pleasant day, but cold. Had a very good dinner. Some of the boys feel very gay.

Saturday

A cold, but pleasant day. Got a World. John C. Heinan whipped by King in twenty-five rounds.* A very fair, stand-up fight.

Sunday, December 27, 1863

A very disagreeable day. Rained all day. Got a World and a letter from Will Stiles.

Monday

Very rainy, muddy day. In camp all day.

Tuesday

A clear, pleasant day. Wrote to mother. Harder on guard at Hd.

Wednesday

A pleasant day, but cold. Off Duty. McGoldrick and Fields returned to the Battery from furlough. Got a World from New York.

Thursday

A very disagreeable day. Rained all day. Got no mail. Jim Quinn returned from a 10 day furlough. The old year is nearly gone and many events have occurred since the last 31st of December. Address: Victor Delapo, P. O. 5180, New York.

---

* U.S. prize fighter John Carmel Heenan, known as "The Benicia Boy," had challenged British heavyweight champion Tom King to claim the world title. Heenan lost the controversial fight on December 8, 1863. (James, 1879)

Camp Near Brandy Station, Va.
Dec. 29th, 1863

Dear Mother:

I received your letter in due time. I worked very hard at putting up winter quarters and the day I finished my house I got a very sore hand. I had a gathering in it.* I did not sleep for several nights. It is not well yet. But much better. I can write but I have not done any duty for two weeks.

I got the shirts the day before my birthday.

I well remember one year ago, the battle of Fredericksburg.

I spent my Christmas the same as every other day in camp. It was a fine pleasant day.

Nearly all of our battery have reenlisted for three years more but I have not yet. There is only about 15 that have not reenlisted. I think this war cannot last much longer. I had a letter from Robt. Ballantine a few days ago. He seems to think that this war cannot last longer than a year more but I think I shall take a mothers advise this time.

My hand hurts me so to write I will have to close. I will write again soon.

Henry Tiffany has reenlisted. We have good winter quarters and live very good. I was glad to get the shirts etc.

From your most affectionate son Oney F. Sweet

---

* gathering: an abscess, a localized collection of pus surrounded by inflamed tissue. (*Merriam-Webster Dictionary*)

Memorandum

Clothing Account

pair of gloves	*90¢*
canteen	*34¢*
pants	*$5.00*
shirt	*$1.00*
knit blouson,	*$2.50*
socks	*45c*

For Oney

The confessions of men
I feign would believe
But mama has told me
They all will deceive.

Anna

Poem possibly written by Anna Barriger, a frequent correspondent.

Letters & Diary, 1864

As we rode over the battlefield to view the terrible results wrought by his own shot and shell, [General Hancock's] face wore an expression of pity and anguish. The sight after Gettysburg and Antietam had not been more grewsome.

—Oney F. Sweet

[flyleaf notation]

*Oney F. Sweet, 1st PA Veteran Battery, founded
7 January 1864 in Camp Brandy Station, Virginia.*

2nd Army Corps.

*Joined the Veterans' Corps. Mustered into the Veterans'
Corps, January.**

---

* Editor's note: Unable to find specific details of this in his military record.

Friday, January 1, 1864
In camp all day

[Editor's. note: There are no diary entries for the early part of January and February; as part of Sweet's reenlistment agreement, the War Department granted him a 30-day furlough.]

Friday, February 19, 1864
Left New Milford at 3 o'clock. Willie was there. On 30 day furlough.

Saturday, February 20, 1864
In Scranton all day.

Sunday, February 21, 1864
In Scranton all day. Saw Jim H.

Monday
Left Scranton in the morning. Saw Mother. Arrived in Philadelphia. Went to the theater.

Tuesday
In Philadelphia.

Wednesday
In Philadelphia

Thursday
Returned to Camp Chester Hospital, near Chester, PA.

Friday
In camp all day. Wrote home.

Sunday, February 28, 1864
Arrived at Washington at 2 o'clock. Went uptown. Slept in the soldiers' retreat.

Monday

Left Washington at 10 o'clock a.m. Got to camp near dark. Everything was all right in camp.

Tuesday, March 1, 1864

A very disagreeable day. Rained all day. Wrote home.

Wednesday

Cleared off pleasant. Wrote to Uncle Joseph. Lt. Brockway returned.

Thursday

A warm, pleasant day. A report that Kilpatrick was on a raid to Richmond.

Friday

Warm and pleasant. On guard at Hd Quarters.

Saturday

In camp all day. On police duty.

Sunday, March 6, 1864

Had battery inspection at 10 o'clock. Wrote to D. P. Maynard. Kilpatrick within General Butler's lines. He captured eight guns and destroyed a great amount of stores.*

Monday

A warm and delightful day. In camp all day.

Tuesday

Rained very hard in the morning. Cleared off about 12. In camp all day. Wrote to Uncle Joseph and R.F.B.

---

* Brigadier General H. Judson Kilpatrick led a detachment of Union cavalrymen in an assault on the Confederate capital at Richmond, Virginia, in late February, early March. Kilpatrick's men were stopped northwest of the city and the Rebels routed a supporting column, under the command of 21-year-old Colonel Ulric Dahlgren, to the east. Dahlgren was killed. Brigadier General Matthew Calbraith Butler led a Confederate cavalry division in Virginia. (Luebke, 2011)

Saturday

   Started for the front. Arrived at Baltimore 3 o'clock a.m. Broke into the soldier's retreat and got breakfast.

Wednesday

   A warm, pleasant day. In camp all day. Played ball in the afternoon. Looked for a letter from home, but got none.

Thursday

   A warm, pleasant day. Received a paper from Uncle Joseph. In camp all day.

Friday

   A very rainy day in camp all day. Received the New York Times. Wrote to Mother.

Saturday

   A clear, pleasant day, but very windy. Recd. the Times and a letter from Uncle Jos. On police duty for missing roll call. The boys stole the linch pins out of the wagon and caused some fun.

Sunday, March 13, 1864

   A warm, pleasant day. Inspection of Company Guards and Horses by Captain Spence. Captain Ricketts sick with fever. No mail for me in days.

Monday

   A warm, pleasant day. Recd. a letter from Sarah with stamps. Three papers and a letter from D. P. Maynard.

Tuesday

   A cold, windy day. Wrote to Sarah. Recd. a World and Police Gazette from New York. In camp all day.

Wednesday

   A cool, pleasant day. Wrote to D. P. Maynard. Recd. a Times and a Montrose Republic. On guard 3rd relief on the guns. Seagt. Trump, Corp. McFarlin.

Thursday

A warm pleasant day. Got no letters or papers. On guard. Captain Ricketts out again. He is not strong yet.

Friday

A very windy day. On police duty. At about two o'clock Chief of Artillery came to the batterys and ordered them hitch up and pull out as quick as possible. We thought we was going to have a fight, but we only went out a mile and returned. Many reports were in circulation in regard to the move. Recd. a World from N.Y.

Saturday

A warm pleasant day. Went out target shooting. Very poor shooting done by the whole battalian. Got a Times.

Sunday, March 20, 1864

A warm pleasant day. Windy in the afternoon. Inspection and drill. Wrote to S. L. Case.

Monday

A warm pleasant day. Signed the pay rolls. Recd. a paper. Genl. Grant in command of the Potomac Army.

Tuesday

A cold day. Snowed 10 inches. Very cold. Got a load of wood. Sending the sick to the hospitals. Received pay $13.00. Recd. a letter from R.L.B. & a paper from P.O.

Wednesday

A cold windy day. Wrote to G. R. Stiles. Snow disappeared nearly. Recd. a paper.

Thursday

A clear pleasant day. Sent my carpet bag to Alex Kearns. Wrote to mother. Recd. a letter from D. P. Maynard.

Friday

A clear pleasant day. In camp all day. Recd. a Times from Uncle Jos.

Saturday

A clear pleasant day. In camp all day.

Sunday, March 27, 1864

A warm pleasant day. Inspection of Company and Quarters.

Monday

A warm pleasant day. Mounted inspection by Capt. Thomson, Ricketts and Spence. The two batterys seperated. G to go to Washington, F to move camp. This camp unhealthy. Recd. a letter from Case. He says my Local bounty is all right for me.

Tuesday

A very disagreeable day. Moved camp. On guard 3rd relief. Seagt Chandler, Corp. Chamberlin.* Wrote to Case.

Wednesday

A pleasant day. Fixed up guard quarters. Got no mail. Tent with Larrabee, French and Kyler.**

Thursday

Warm pleasant day. Made a stove in our tent. Wrote to D. P. Maynard and R. F. Ballantine. No mail.

Friday, April 1, 1864

All fools day. A miserable day. Corpl. of the Guard to night Sergt. Mathews. A very stormy night. Wrote to C. P. Hawley. Sent him an _____

Saturday

An awful day. Rained enough to flood. Can't believe it. 22 recruits arrived. George O. Dutcher came to the battery.

---

* Jesse Chamberlain, mustered in July 16, 1861; mustered out with battery, June 10, 1865.

** "Kyler" possibly Patrick Doyle, private, mustered in January 16, 1864, mustered out with battery, June 10, 1865.

Sunday, April 3, 1864

A fine day overhead. Muddy under foot. On police duty. Built new guard house. Received a paper. Received a letter from mother.

Monday

A very disagreeable day. Rained all day. Mud knee deep. Got no mail.

Tuesday

A very rainy day an awful day in camp. No mail.

Wednesday

Cleared off, but very muddy. Wrote to Mother, Law Root and Gabriel Claflin.

Thursday

A very rainy day. Got no mail.

Friday

Rained all day. The ridge near our camp washed away. On guard second relief. Corps. Ridgeway and Pritchert.

Saturday

A very disagreeable day. On guard. No mail.

Sunday, April 10, 1864

On police duty, but no policing done on Sunday. No mail. Washed away the bridge near our camp.

Monday

A very windy day. No mail. Battery inspection by Capt. Ricketts in the afternoon.

Tuesday

Cleared off pleasant. Received a large mail. Received a letter from Case and one from G. R. Stiles. Drill for afternoon inspection by Chief of Artillery. Wrote to Sarah.

Wednesday

A very pleasant day. Drew clothing. Recd. a mail and one paper. Gun drill twice a day. Wrote to G. R. Stiles.

Thursday

A warm, pleasant day. Battery drill in the afternoon. Carried the guide on suttlers. They have to leave the Army tomorrow. In camp all day.

Friday

A warm, pleasant day. Gun drill. Wrote to Mother, to George G. Dewitt. On guard.

Saturday

A pleasant forenoon, but rainy in the afternoon. In camp all day.

Sunday, April 17

Cleaned up the carriages for inspection but did not have any. On police duty.

Monday

A warm, pleasant day. Drill twice a day. In camp all day.

Tuesday

A beautiful day. Went out on target practice. Saw some very good shooting.

Wednesday

A warm, but windy day. Artillery review by General J. Hancock I Battery out. Returned to camp about noon.

Thursday

A warm, pleasant day. Battery drill. Washed carriages. Got a paper and letter from D. P. Maynard. Wrote to D. P. Maynard and Georgie Baker, W. H. Athington. Received a letter from Law A. Root.

Friday

A warm, pleasant day on guard. General Grant reviewd 2nd Army Corps. Was not out. Wrote to Law. Received a letter from Sarah.

Camp Hancock, Virginia
April 15th, 1864

Dear Mother:

I received your letter which was lost last night. I cannot account for its not reaching me before, if it was directed as others have been. I wrote to Sarah last Tuesday. I write as often as once a week, but when we get on the march you will not get them as often. We have had fine weather the past few days and the mud is nearly dryed up.

In Sarah's last she says you have moved and that it does not seem like home but it will in a short time. Everything goes as it should. Which part of the house are you living in?

If you have got the town bounty and have use for it you can have it without interest to use as long as you want it.* I think I will put some of it in cows and sheep, that is, if you don't want it.

Is there any one living in the house in the burg?

I am going over to see Guss Roper in a few days. He is now with his regiment but he is not entirely well. George Dutcher saw him yesterday.

I will not answer Sarah's last letter as it was so short. She must write again. In my other letters I wrote you all the news and will have to close this for the want of news.

We are expecting to be reviewed by Genl Grant in a few days if the weather holds fine.

Send me some stamps.

I had a letter from Case a few days ago. He said my papers to get my bounty was all right.

From your ever true and faithful son Oney F. Sweet

---

* Towns paid a "bounty" to men who joined the local militia, whether as volunteers or draftees, then the towns filed for reimbursement from the federal government. Sweet may have received as much as $300 as his federal bounty and $100 as a local bounty when he enlisted. See The Draft in the Civil War, p. 127; see the diary entry for November 3, 1863.

Saturday
A warm, but windy day. On police duty. Wrote to Sarah and to Charlie Wells. Lt. Snider returned to the battery.

Sunday, April 24, 1864
A warm, pleasant day. Brigade inspection by Col. Tidball.*

Monday
Warm, pleasant day. On guard. A soldier hung for committing rape on an old woman.

Tuesday
Detailed to go to Artillery Brigade Hd. Quarters for mounted orderly.*

Wednesday
A warm, pleasant day. Windy night. Tent blew down. Some of the artillery moved camp.**

Thursday
A cold, windy day. Moved Hd. Quarters over near Stevensburg. A letter from G. R. Stiles. A paper from Uncle Joseph.

Friday
A warm pleasant day. Burnside came up from Washington with 45,000 troops.

Saturday
A warm, pleasant day. Mustered for pay. No mail.

---

* Colonel John C. Tidball, 4th New York Heavy Artillery, commanded the artillery of the Second Corps of the Army of the Potomac during the Overland Campaign, including the Battle of the Wilderness. (Moodey, 1890)

** Oney F. Sweet was reassigned as an orderly and courier for General Hancock at Second Corps headquarters as Grant mobilized the Army of the Potomac. The next day, as noted in Sweet's diary entry, the Union army began to leave winter quarters, which marked the beginning of the Overland Campaign in May and June 1864.

Overland Campaign

Soon after midnight, May 3d-4th [1864], the Army of the Potomac moved out from its position north of the Rapidan, to start upon that memorable campaign.

—Lieutenant General Ulysses S. Grant

At this point, Oney had been reassigned to headquarters as a mounted orderly. He accompanied officers on their rounds and carried dispatches to artillery batteries at the front. At times that meant going beyond the battle line to assess the position and strength of the Confederate forces.

He maintained close contact with his comrades in Battery F and carried dispatches to Capt Ricketts, as referenced in Bates' description of the Battle of the Wilderness. The report from Capt. Ricketts further illuminates the daily life of the Battery F gun crews, to which Oney continued to feel closely attached.

Sunday, May 1, 1864
A warm, pleasant day. Went over to 4th Division, 2nd Corps. Bierly's old Division, 3rd Corps.

Monday
A very warm day. A hurrycane in the afternoon. Blew down tents and made quite an exciting time in camp.

Tuesday
Warm, pleasant day. Considerable riding to do. Marched at dark toward the Rapidan River. A hard night's march.

Wednesday
A very warm day. Crosst the river at 7 o'clock. Found no force of rebells. Camped on the old Chancorville [Chancellorsville] battleground. Headquarters at the Chancorville house.

Battle of the Wilderness

May 5-6, 1864

> *A good deal of hard fighting. . . . Nothing gained by either party.*
>
> —Oney F. Sweet

Thursday

Marched at daylight. Marched six miles toward Orange Court House. Run onto the rebells about noon. A lively time forming line of battle. Heavy fighting near dark.

Friday

A warm day. Very heavy fighting all day. Heavy loss on both sides. Genl Hayes killed. The rebells attacked our lines very strong but were repulsed with heavy loss. Our battery lost one killed and two wounded and burst one gun.

Saturday

A good deal of hard fighting. All along the line we held our own with the rebells. Nothing gained by either party.

General Gouverneur Warren's Fifth Corps crossed the Rapidan River ford on May 4, 1864, and entered a dense woodland known as the Wilderness. After three days of fierce combat and suffering some 20,000 casualties—including the death of General Alexander Hayes on May 5—General Grant ordered General Meade's army to pull out after dark and head for the Spotsylvania Court House. (Hitchcock, 1868)

Bates (1869) wrote:

At noon of the 5th [of May 1864], the enemy was met. The ground which he had selected was in a dense chaparral which covers the county for miles, and is known as the Wilderness. . . . Ricketts' Battery was sent to General Getty, commanding a division of the Sixth Corps. It was found, on advancing, that only a single section could be used at a time, and that must advance en echelon. At half past four the order to march was given, and a movement of a few yards showed the enemy's infantry to be in great force in front, with a battery of Napoleon guns masked in the road beyond. Brockway's section replied, using percussion shells, and soon blew up one of his limbers, killing a number of men and five of his horses.

The enemy hurled canister, but the percussion shells proved superior and his guns were soon withdrawn. For a moment there Was a lull, then his infantry charged, slowly pressing our men back, yelling, as they advanced, like demons. Shells were used against them until the head of their column entered the road, when canister was dealt and the guns were nimbly handled. The plank road was well suited to it, as the splinters did as much execution as the shot. A peck of bullets per minute was too much for rebel digestion, and his column was forced to give way. . . .

After two hours of constant firing Brockway's section was withdrawn and Snyder's substituted. Upon witnessing the withdrawal the enemy made a rush for the guns. Unfortunately one of Snyder's guns burst on the first discharge, and Lieutenant Campbell's were ordered up; but General Hancock, who had now arrived, ordered the battery to be withdrawn. Later in the day Carroll's Brigade re-captured the abandoned gun and caisson.*

During the two following days heavy fighting occurred, and, to add to the horrors of battle, the breast-works, which were composed of logs and rails, and the woods took fire, the wild torrent of flame and smoke enveloping friend and foe. The wounded, helpless and beyond the reach of human aid, perished miserably amid the flames.

---

* Extract from General Hancock's Official Report.—— General Birney immediately moved forward on General Getty's right and left, one section of Ricketts' Battery (Lieutenant Brockway) company F, First Pennsylvania Artillery, moving down the plank road just in rear of the infantry. The fight became very fierce at once—the lines of battle were exceedingly close, and the musketry continuous and deadly along the entire line. • • • The section of Ricketts' Battery which moved down the plank road when Birney and Getty attacked, suffered severely in men and horses. It was captured, at one time, during the fight, but was re-taken by detachments from the Fourteenth Indiana and Eighth Ohio volunteers, of Carroll's Brigade. It was then withdrawn.

Report of Capt. R. Bruce Ricketts, Battery F, First Pennsylvania Light Artillery.

HDQRS. BATTERY F, FIRST PENN. LIGHT ARTY.,
July 1, 1864.

SIR: I have the honor to forward the following report of the part taken by my battery in the campaign of May and June, 1864:

May 4. Crossed the Rapidan at Elys Ford with Second Army Corps and marched to Chancellorsville.

May 5. Marched to Wilderness battle-field. The sections of Lieutenants Brockway and Snider engaged on the plank road. One gun was temporarily lost; recaptured by a part of Carroll's brigade, under Captain Butterfield. One gun burst and was afterward buried at Todd's Tavern. Casualties: One man killed and 2 severely wounded; 6 horses killed and 6 wounded. Ammunition expended, 135 rounds.

May 6 and 7. Not engaged.

May 8. Marched to Todd's Tavern.

May 9. In position near Todd's Tavern. Not engaged.

May 10. Marched with Mott's division and took position on left of Sixth Corps, near the. Ny River. Ammunition expended, 28 rounds. Casualties: One horse killed.

May 11. Marched with Mott's division to near army headquarters. Not in position.

May 12. Marched with Second Army Corps to left of Sixth Army Corps. In position on left of Landrums house. Not engaged.

May 13 and 14. In position but not engaged.

May 15. Marched with Second Army Corps and bivouacked in rear of Fifth Corps.

May 16 and 17. Not engaged.

May 18. Marched to the right with Second Army Corps. In position on the right of the line with Motts brigade. Not engaged. Withdrew during the night and bivouacked in rear of Fifth Corps.

May 19. Not engaged.

May 20 and 21. Marched with Second Army Corps to near Milford Station via Bowling Green.

May 22. In position on left of the line with Birneys division. Not engaged.

May 23. Marched with Second Army Corps to North Anna River. In position on left of railroad crossing. Ammunition expended, 218 rounds.

May 24. Crossed the North Anna River. In position on left of Gibbons division.

May 25 and 26. Not in position.

May 27 and 28. Marched to the left. Crossed Pamunkey River.

May 29. Marched 6 miles.

May 30. In position on right of brick house on General Birney's line. Not engaged.

May 31. Fired 19 rounds. Casualties: One man wounded.

June 1. In same position. Fired 140 rounds. No casualties.

June 2. Marched with Birney's division to Cold Harbor.

June 3. In position with Eighteenth Army Corps. Fired 230 rounds. Casualties: Two horses killed, 3 wounded.

June 4. In same position.

June 5. Fired 36 rounds.

June 6. Same position. Not engaged. Casualties: One man severely wounded.

June 7. In same position. Not engaged.

June 8. Relieved from duty with Eighteenth Corps. Took position on General Barlow's line.* Not engaged.

June 9. Not engaged. One man killed.

June 10 and 11. In same position. Not engaged.

I am, sir, very respectfully, your obedient servant,
R. BRUCE RICKETTS,
Captain First Penn. Light Arty., Corndg. Batty. F.

Lient. U. D. EDDY,
Acting Assistant Adjutant-General.

---

* General Francis C. Barlow, commander, 1st Division of Major General Hancock's Second Corps.

Battle of Spotsylvania Court House

May 8-21, 1864

> *Went with Col. Tidball and Col. Morgan outside our pickets*
> *toward Spotsylvania C.H. I do not like such business, scouting.*
> —Oney F. Sweet

Sunday, May 8, 1864

A very warm day. We followed up the rebells, they having retreated towards Spotsylvania Court House. Some fighting near dark.

Monday

General Meade issued orders for the army to rest, but the rebells would not let us rest. They attacked our right but were repulsed. Genl. Sedgwick was killed.*

Tuesday

A warm, pleasant day. Heavy fighting all along the line. Saw Generals Grant, Meade, Warren, Wright and Hancock all together. General Barlow was driven back across the Nye River.

Wednesday

No fighting of any account. At 12 o'clock the 2nd Corps moved to the left.

Thursday

At daybreak the 2nd Corps made a charge and took 5,000 prisoners and twenty-five guns. Genl. Johnson and Stuart was taken.** I saw them. Very hard fighting all day. The Rebells tried hard to retake the position but could not. Heavy loss on both sides.

---

* Major General John Sedgwick, killed by a Confederate sharpshooter, possibly Ben Powell of McGowan's South Carolina Brigade. (Sedgwick Genealogy)

** Confederate generals Edward "Allegheny" Johnson and George H. Steuart.

*The awfullest sight I ever saw. Men were piled up 4 and 5
deep on both sides.*

—Oney F. Sweet

The Battle of Spotsylvania Court House began on May 8, 1864, when
General Hancock's troops surprised the Confederate forces, which had
built a U-shaped "Mule Shoe" breastworks. Hancock had attacked its apex,
or salient, which the troops afterward called the "Bloody Angle."* Major
General John Sedgwick, the highest ranking casualty of the Civil War, died
from a bullet wound on May 9 while directing artillery placements.
(Hitchcock, 1868)

**Confederate dead laid out for burial near Mrs. Alsop's house, Spotsylvania, Virginia,
May 20, 1864.** (Timothy H. O'Sullivan, Library of Congress)

---

* salient: a section of fortification that juts out to form an angle.

Retrospective piece written by Oney F. Sweet and published in *The National Tribune*, October 3, 1909:

WITH HANCOCK DURING AND AFTER A BATTLE
Superb, Masterful When the Fight Was On, Pitying When It Was Over

Editor National Tribune: As history's pass record in their dull way at best the events of the civil war, there often comes regret on my part that to-day's generation of students cannot feel as we who experienced those stirring scenes of the human side of that great struggle.

When in these late days the memories of those years come drifting back and to me the incidents become as tho they occurred but yesterday, I realize that to average youth, patriotic tho it may be, the historian has brought but dull statistics and hackneyed description. Of the hot-blooded young fellows who fell at my side in private uniforms, they know as a number killed, while I see again their tanned faces grow blanch and hear their dying cry of farewell to friends about. Of the more famous few, whom school books have pictured and orators have lauded, they may know as heroes, but not as men.

When I was an Orderly with [Maj. Gen. Winfield S.] Hancock's Second Corps during the assault at Bloody Angle on May 12, 1864, I presume that I was then as close to a great General as at any time during the war, and I recall with what enthusiasm as a hero-worshiping boy barely in my 20's, I caught eagerly for every word, every movement, every pose of the man.

Seeing a class fail in school one day because it could not remember his name, it was hard for me to appreciate their excuse for stupidity for it was he, flushed and thrilled with the passion of conflict, whom I once heard cry out, "Men, if you will charge with a yell, you can take yon breastworks without firing a shot."

But, after all, those words seem dull in print, I had heard him utter them. I had seen the enemy a few rods ahead beneath the southern skies. I had seen the rush, the yell and the victory. Aye, there was the difference. And it wasn't yesterday; it was 40 years ago.

Aye, 40 years ago. During the night of the 11th of May, the Second Corps was moved to a position for the assault on a salient which had been discovered on the right center.* Grant had determined that the attack should be made there, the hour being set for 4 o'clock the next morning.

> *[T]he historian has brought but dull statistics and hackneyed description. Of the hot-blooded young fellows who fell at my side in private uniforms, they know as a number killed, while I see again their tanned faces grow blanch and hear their dying cry of farewell to friends about. Of the more famous few, whom school books have pictured and orators have lauded, they may know as heroes, but not as men.*
>
> —Oney F. Sweet

The night was dark. It rained heavily, the road was difficult, so it was midnight before we reached the point where we were to halt. Morning dawned with a heavy fog, delaying the start more than an hour. Hancock put Barlow on his right, in double column, and Birney to his right. The instruction was to capture the pickets without firing a shot. The ground over which we had to pass to reach the enemy was ascending and wooded to within 300 yards of the enemy's intrenchments. In front of Birney there was also a marsh, but the troops, notwithstanding these difficulties, pushed on in quick time, without firing a gun, captured the pickets, and when within 400 or 500 yards of the enemy's lines, broke out in loud cheers and with a rush went over the breastworks. History says that we captured 40 guns and 2,000 men. It was a hand-to-hand conflict, the men on both sides being too close to fire.

During all this time Hancock sat with his staff knowing that his men to be successful must move with death-like stillness. After the yell came, he became alert and eager to hear from the front. There was no finer appearing man on horseback in the army. At the time he wore a common blouse without showing any rank except on his collar and the regulation army hat. A man in the prime of life, there was in the flash of his fine eyes the expression on his features and the poise of his erect figure, the something which master men reveal when in their real element.

The first news from the fight was brought by one of our men, who could not be discerned until he had almost reached us. He had neither hat nor gun, and the blood was streaming from his face. The General, catching sight of him, leaned eagerly forward in his saddle.

"My man," he asked with authority, "what is the news from the front?"

Looking up and seeing Gen Hancock, the fellow replied," We have captured half the rebel army and all of their artillery."

Having received this most satisfactory message, Hancock spoke in a kindlier tone. "My man," he said sympathetically, "follow this road back and you will find a hospital."

With that he moved a short distance to the front up the road, and in a few minutes prisoners began to stream along. Among them were Gens. Steuart and Johnson, former schoolmates of Hancock's at West Point. It was one of those circumstances so common in that conflict, where even families were pitted against each other. Johnson shook the hand which Hancock offered, but the haughty Steuart refused to do so.

From that time on, as history will show, the battle raged, the rebels trying all day to retake what we had captured. Hancock, busily giving orders, was in his element. His fine face glowed, and he evidently found delight in the fray. The ever-present danger, the uncertainty of the outcome, the readiness with which each order from his responsible position was carried out, put him on his mettle.

It was on the following morning, when the enemy had, in discouragement, given up the breastworks, that his mood changed utterly. As we rode over the battlefield to view the terrible results wrought by his own shot and shell, his face wore an expression of pity and anguish. The sight after Gettysburg and Antietam had not been more grewsome. With the dead bodies lying all about, distorted and ghastly, his whole attitude changed from what it had been with the men shouting and the flags flying and the struggle for supremacy filling his veins. With an almost guilty air he turned away from the carnage sooner than the rest of the staff was willing. Evidently he was seconding the expression as made by a fellow officer that "war is hell."

—Oney F. Sweet, Courier for Chief Artillery, Second Corps, from the Wilderness to Appomattox, Hampton, Iowa.

Friday

No fighting of any account. Wrote to mother. Heavy loss on both sides in yesterday's fight.

Saturday

The army is moving to the left. No fighting of any account. Saw Genl. Burnside was on the battlefield. The awfullest sight I ever saw. Men were piled up 4 and 5 deep on both sides.

Sunday, May 15, 1864

Marched at 12 o'clock to the left. Went into camp fifteen miles from Fredericksburg. No fighting.

Monday

No fighting or movement. Went to Fredericksburg. Was on the heights where Hooker charged in '63.

Tuesday

A very warm day. Went with Col. Tidball and Col. Morgan outside our pickets toward Spotsylvania C.H.* I do not like such business, scouting.

Wednesday

The Rebells made an attack on our right. The 2nd Corps marched back to where they charged on the morning of the 12th. They had some severe fighting, drove the Rebells back to their breastwork. Hd. Quarters at the Anderson House.

Thursday

Marched to the extreme left. The Rebells tried to capture some of our supply trains coming up from Fredericksburg, but the Heavy Artillery gave them a good thrashing.

Friday

No fighting of any account. Got a mail, a letter from Charlie Wells and one from home.

---

* Lieutenant Colonel C. H. Morgan, Tidball's chief of staff.

** General Grant had converted a number of heavy artillery units to infantry to bolster the ranks of foot soldiers on the battlefield. (Cannan, 2007)

Saturday

The 2nd Corps started on a flank movement, marched to the left, passed through a splendid country. Marched twenty-five miles. Passed through Bowling Green, Milford Station, crosst the Matapony River and formed line of battle fortified the positions. Some skirmishing with Rebell Cavelry. Took some prisoners.

Sunday, May 22, 1864

No fighting of 2nd Corps. Fifth Corps had a fight. Did not move out of our position.

Monday

Marched at daylight. Marched eight miles. Found the Rebells strongly fortified on the banks of the North Anna.* Attacked them and took the bridge before they had time to destroy it.

Tuesday

Some hard fighting. The 2nd Corps crosst the North Anna and had a hard fight. Gibbons division fought like tigers.** I was with Major Hayard and was in it all day.

Wednesday

A warm day. Was all along the line. No fighting, but sharpshooting. Put some mortars in position and shelled the Rebells in the woods.

Thursday

A rainy morning. Opened on the Rebells with artillery and mortar. The Rebells did not reply. Our army preparing to fall back across the North Anna River. Did not get any sleep.

Friday

Our army all safely on the north side of the river at daylight. The Rebells made their appearance on the other side. Started to the left on another flank movement. Camped 5 miles from the Pamunkey River.

---

* Battle of North Anna, May 23-26, 1864, ended when Grant, to avoid the "slaughter of our men," withdrew and moved Totopotomoy Creek. (Hitchcock, 1868)

** Union General John Gibbon commanded the Second Division of Hancock's Second Corps.

Saturday

Marched at daylight. A very hot, dusty day. Crosst the Pamunkey River and formed line of battle. Both flanks rests on the river. Cavelery had a hard fight. Drove the Rebells. Our loss was heavy. 17 miles from Richmond.

Sunday, May 29, 1864

Moved in line of battle 5 miles nearer Richmond. Only 12 miles from Richmond. Found the Rebells strongly fortified. Some skirmishing.

Monday

A very hot day. Preparing for a big fight. No fighting on any account. Got a mail. A letter from Sarah and several papers. Wrote home.

Battle of Cold Harbor

May 31-June 12, 1864

I have always regretted that the last assault at Cold Harbor was ever made. . . . No advantage whatever was gained to compensate for the heavy loss we sustained.

—General Ulysses S. Grant

The small crossroads of Cold Harbor, ten miles north of Richmond, became the focal point of the action in late May. The two-week engagement left more than 18,000 soldiers killed, wounded, or captured. (Hitchcock, 1868)

Bates (1869) wrote:

At Cold Harbor, Ricketts' Battery was attached to the Eighteenth Corps, and was sharply engaged. . . . "During Sunday, June 5th," says Captain Brockway, "we still maintained our position, though heavy firing continued during the day. . . . On the 8th, the battery was relieved from duty with the Eighteenth and returned to the Second Corps, having been in line of battle without relief for six days.

Tuesday

A very warm day. Hard fighting. Heavy artillery fighting. Genl. Barlow carried the 1st line of works but could not drive them any farther. Army headquarters in the rear of 2nd Corps.

Wednesday, June 1, 1864

A very warm day. The 2nd Corps did not have much fighting, but the 5th Corps had a hard fight. I was down at the 5th Corps when they were fighting. Marched at dark towards Cold Harbor, following 6th Corps passed the other Corps.

Thursday

Arrived at Cold Harbor at noon formed our lines on the left of 6th Corps. Some fighting. The cavelery had a hard fight on this ground and drove them two miles. 10 miles from Richmond, near Gains Hill. Smiths Corps, the 18th, is here. Came from Butler's Army.*

Friday

A very hot day. The 2nd Corps attacked the Rebells at daylight, but could not drive them. Hard fighting all day. Took many prisners. Was at the front all day. At about dark very heavy musketry. Wrote home.

Saturday

A very warm day. No very heavy fighting, but picket and skirmishing all day. Some artillery.

---

* Major General Benjamin Butler, commander of the Union's Department of Virginia and North Carolina, Army of the James, Tenth and Eighteenth Corps.

General William Farrar Smith, commander, Eighteenth Corps. (Hitchcock, 1868)

Battle of Petersburg

June 15 - 18, 1864

Siege of Petersburg

June 19, 1864 – April 3, 1865

> *Our battery is in the breast works. . . . I am up there nearly every day.*
>
> —Oney F. Sweet

[Editor's note: Sweet did not make any diary entries from June 5 through July 30. We know from later entries that he served at Petersburg during that period.]

Sunday, July 31, 1864

No fighting of any account. Not very much work to do. Washed and cleaned up. Feel very good. A shower in the afternoon. Yesterday and today, I think, are the hottest of the season. A report that the 2nd Corps is going to Washington.

Monday, August 1, 1864

Most awful hot day. Wrote to Sarah, mother and C. P. Holly. Expressed $25 to C.P., by mail, and sent 5 dollars to Sarah and Willie. No fighting of any account. Wrote for some photographs.

Tuesday

Hot day. No fighting, but heavy shelling. Received a Waverly magazine from Law. Orders for the Battery to harness and hitch up. Did not move. Unharnessed at daylight.

Wednesday

A very hot day. Everything quiet. No fighting of any account. Recd. a paper from Uncle Jos.

Thursday

A very hot day. No fighting of any account. Business very light. Lt. C. B. Brockway going home on furlough.

Friday

A very hot day. Wrote to Law Root and Anna Beriger. Heavy fighting on the right. Don't know the result.** Lt. Brockway did not go home on furlough. No mail. The flies are very troublesome. Never saw them so thick.

Saturday

A very hot day. No fighting of any account. Saw Gus Roper he is looking very well.

---

* A terrific fight in front of Petersburg, lasting from 5:30 to 7:30 P.M. It commenced by a charge of the enemy, which was repulsed with slaughter. (Hitchcock, 1868)

Sunday, August 7, 1864

A very hot day. Sent a pocket book home and wrote to Uncle Joseph. The rebells blew up one of our forts and charged. Was repulsed with heavy loss.

Saturday

A warm, pleasant day. In camp between the Appomattox and James Rivers near Butler's HdQTRS 2nd Army Corps (Infty) shipped on board transports at City Point.

Sunday, August 14, 1864

Marched at three o'clock a.m. Crosst James River at daylight. Infantry onloaded from transports and formed lines of battle. Expected a big fight, but only a little skirmishing. 10th Army Corps took 4 64 pound Howitzers and some prisoners.

Monday

A very hot day, considerable skirmishing but no very hard fighting. Advanced our lines some. Genl. Grant was with Hancock nearly all day. A shower near right.

Tuesday

A very warm day. Some very hard fighting. A charge was made. Took 500 prisoners _____ colors two Genls. dead, Chamberlin and Geardy.* 2nd Corps was not engaged only the 10th Corps. Received a letter from Anna Barriger.

Wednesday

A cloudy day. Looks like rain. A flag of truce went into the Rebels' lines 4 times to bury the dead. Received a letter from R. F. Ballantine. Hard fighting in front of Petersburg. Afterward it rained quite hard.

Thursday

Cleared off pleasant. Rebels attacked us. We repulsed them with heavy loss. 2nd Hd Quarters moved back near the river. A rainy night.

---

* Probably Confederate generals John Chambliss, Jr., killed in action at the James River, and Victor Girardey, killed in action during the Second Battle of Deep Bottom. (Bergeron, 1991; West, 1986)

Massaponax Church, Virginia, "Council of War": General Ulysses S. Grant examining a map held by General George G. Meade. (Timothy H. O'Sullivan, Library of Congress)

Friday

A cloudy, rainy day. Everything quiet. 3rd Div AR and our Battery marched to Petersburg. No fighting here, but heavy fighting on the right. The 5th Corps is on the Weldon R.R. Rebels attacked them, they were repulsed.

Saturday

A rainy day. No fighting here. Received a Times. Marched at dark. Recrossed the James and Appomatox rivers. Marched very fast. Reached our old camp at twelve o'clock. Infantry did not reach their camp until daylight. Wm. Wapples died of Colerea.*

---

* William W. Wapples, private.

Sunday, August 21, 1864

A cloudy day. Received marching orders at 10 o'clock. Marched at 11 o'clock to the Jones house and from there to the support of the 6th Corps. Maj. Hayard returned from furlough. 5th Corps had some hard fighting. Gave the Rebells a good whipping.

Monday

A very rainy day. Off duty with game leg. Wrote to Sarah. No fighting of any account. A rainy night. The roads are in awful condition.

Tuesday

A warm, pleasant day. Wrote to R.F.B. and sent some photographs to Sarah. No fighting of any account.

Wednesday

A warm, pleasant day. Wrote to Anna Barriger and sent her a photo. No fighting of any account. Second Corps at Reams Station destroying the road for many miles. Saw the boys in Battery A First Artillery.

Thursday

A very warm day. Everything quiet. Wrote to H. H. Hope. Second Corps had a hard fight near Reams Station. We lost nine guns and many artillery officers. The Corps fell back to the Jones house.

Friday

A warm, pleasant day. Headquartered at the Jones house. No fighting. Received a letter from Uncle Jos. A plenty of business. Major Hayard takes command again.

Saturday

A warm, pleasant day. No fighting of any account. Considerable mortar firing and shelling in 18th Corps.

Sunday, August 28, 1864

A warm, pleasant day. No fighting of any account. A busy day in camp. Used my horse up. Road him too hard. Recd. a letter from Charley Wells.

Monday

A very warm day. Wrote to Charley Wells. No fighting of any account. My horse sick. Done duty with another horse.

Tuesday

A warm, pleasant day. Done no duty. Recd. a letter and photo from Law. No fighting of any account. Some shelling of Petersburg.

Wednesday

Wrote to Uncle Jos. and Law Root. Off duty. Sick horse. No fighting. Mustered for pay two months. A warm day. Cool nights. Received a letter from G.R.S. He is at Rockton, Illinois. Saw Guss Roper. Let him have $10.00.

Thursday, September 1, 1864

A warm pleasant day. No fighting of any account. Fort Morgan captured by Farragut.* An attack is expected by our left. Wrote to G. R. Stiles. Received a letter from Anna Barriger.

Friday

A very hot day. The old members of Battery B, 1st N.Y. started home. Wrote to Anna B. A man shot for desertion. He belongs to K 4th, U.S. Arty. Everything is quiet along the lines. Wrote to George C. Jenks for envelopes and paper. Received a letter from Hope V. Co a paper.

Saturday

A cloudy day. Looks like rain. Very warm. Wrote to Robt. F. Ballantine. Reported capture of Atlanta.** Have no particulars. Recd. a letter from Sarah and a paper from Uncle Joseph. Everything is quiet along the line.

Sunday, September 4, 1864

Three years ago today I enlisted. A cloudy, cool day. Wrote to Sarah. Sent her 3 photographs. Warren Hanes & Ridgeway. No fighting of any account. Maj. Hayard started home on twenty days leave.

---

* The Battle of Mobile Bay: Admiral David Farragut captured Fort Morgan at Mobile Point, Alabama, on Aug. 23, 1864. (*The New York Times*, Aug. 29, 1864)

** Union General William Tecumseh Sherman captured Atlanta on Sept. 2, 1864, and began his "March to the Sea." In a telegram to Washington, Sherman said, "Atlanta is ours, and fairly won." (*The New York Times*, Sept. 5, 1864)

Battery F received 13 recruits. Recruits are arriving every day for this army at a rate of 3,000 a day.

—Oney F. Sweet

Monday

A warm, pleasant day. The Rebells opened with artillery on the Jersusalam plank road. Our batteries replied. First and Second Division 2nd Corps marched down the plank road at near dark. The Rebells cheered along the line.

Tuesday

A heavy shower last night. A cold, cloudy day. Rained considerable. Rained very hard in the evening. The capture of Atlanta is Confirmed. Many prisoners were taken. Wrote Carrie Edwards. Sent her a photograph.

Wednesday

Cleared off pleasant. A warm, pleasant day. The railroad from City Point along the line for the transportation of supplies for the troops is nearly completed. An attack by the enemy on our left is looked for every day. Received a N.Y. Times with an account of the Capture of Atlanta, GA.

Thursday

Last night was very cool. A pleasant, sunshiny day. Everything is quiet. The railroad is in running order up to the Jones house. I am quite unwell. A rainy night. No letters or papers for me in tonight's mail.

Friday

A cool, cloudy day. Off duty. Sick. Everything quiet along the line during the day. In the night we undertook to advance our picket line. We gained nothing. It caused considerable fighting and heavy artillery firing. Got a paper. No letters.

Saturday

A beautiful morning. Off duty. Feel very unwell. A good deal of artillery firing and picket firing along the 3rd Div. line. Our picket line now is in the Rebell's old line. Battery F received 13 recruits. Recruits are arriving every day for this army at a rate of 3,000 a day. I got no mail.

The Rebells blew up one of our forts and charged. Was repulsed with heavy loss.

—Oney F. Sweet

Dead Confederate soldier, Petersburg, Virginia. (Library of Congress)

Sunday, September 11, 1864

A pleasant day. Cool night. Had a bugler at the Hd.Qtrs. Picket firing all day along the 3rd Division line. Off duty. Recd. a letter from Anna Bariger and two papers from New York. My esteemed friend Augustus Roper was killed while on pick. duty at two o'clock p.m.*

Monday

A very changeable day. Pleasant, rain and cloudy. Wrote to Anna Bariger. Everything quiet along the line. Returned to duty. Business not very heavy. Received paper and envelopes from G. C. Jenks. The railroad completed.

---

* Augustus J. Roper, sergeant, killed by a Confederate sharpshooter near Petersburg, Va., on September 11, 1864.

I never saw before this summer so many flies. They are worse to bite than mosketoes.

         —Oney F. Sweet

Hd Quarters Artillery Brigade 2nd Corps
Camp near Petersburg, Virginia
September 10th 1864

My Dear Mother:

I have not written you a long letter in some time. I will now commence one. I wrote to Sarah last week and I have been looking anxiously for hers and Willies photographs. Perhaps tonight's mail may bring a letter from her. I suppose there are many leaving home for the war now. They come into the army at the rate of three thousand a day. They are drilled and may at any time be called upon to help the old soldiers fight. We need them now. There are hundreds leaving for home every day, their time being out.

It has been very sickly here this summer but the sickly season is nearly over, we begin to have the cool weather now. I never saw before this summer so many flies. They are worse to bite than mosketoes.

We have a rail road running from City Point along the line to supply the troops with rations. It was all built in 10 days a distance of 10 miles. That is building a railroad in double quick.

We are very close to Petersburg. We can shell it and have shelled it for the last two months but the rebels do not seem willing to let us have it yet. Genl. Grant will keep at it until he gets it and the opinion is here that he will take it this fall. We feel confident of closing this war within a year. The people of the north talk of peace. We want no peace until we can have it in the right way and we will have peace if the people of the north will keep their mouths closed and support the Administration. The rebels are on their last legs and all that makes them hold out is the Copper Heads *of the north.**

---

* The "Copperheads" were a vocal faction of northern Democrats who opposed the war, preferring to negotiate a settlement rather than fight. Republicans mocked the movement, comparing it to the poisonous snake. But Democrats adopted the name and proudly wore buttons depicting Lady Liberty, which adorned the "copperhead" penny in circulation at the time. After the fall of Atlanta in September 1864, and a Union victory seemingly assured, the movement lost steam. (Cowden, 1983; Weber, 2006).

Monday, September 12th. Have received no letter from home yet. I shall not send this until I get one. Today is a cold windy day. Winter will soon be upon us and we will be in our winter quarters again. We see better times in winter than sumer. After we get settled down in good quarters we then get better living. I will not write any more today. Think I will get a letter tonight.

Wednesday, September 14th. I have received no letter yet. Since you moved back on the old farm how has father done? You have never written anything about him. Is there many apples this year and are the crops good? I have not seen anything in the shape of vegetables growing this summer. There are no people living in this country. They have all left their homes and all of the crops that was planted were trampled down by the army long ago. We are camped in a corn field, but the corn never had a chance of growing. Express boxes come through now and I have a notion of sending for some things this fall.

We expect Genl Grant will make another move for the capture of Petersburg.

September 15th. Last night I received a letter from Sarah but was disappointed in not finding the photographs in it. Last night we expected an attack by the rebels. We got all ready for them but they did not come.

We can buy almost anything here but the prices are enormous. Eggs 60 cents a doz., butter 80 cents a pound, peaches and apples 5 cents a piece, boots from 12 to 20 dollars a pair. It takes money if you buy much.

I did not think you could get the town bounty until this fall. I will not write to Sarah today for I have no news to write. She must write another letter before she can expect an answer although she wrote me a long letter this time.

The other day George Dutcher got hit on the arm with a spent ball. It only made a little black and blue spot. Our battery is in the breast works and fire some every day. I am up there nearly every day.

Love to all from your most affectionate boy

Oney.

Tuesday

A cool, windy day. Everything quiet except picket firing. Business light. No mail for me. Drew clothing. General Meade rode up to the left of the line.

Wednesday

A cool, cloudy day. Wrote to Amy Lady in Rockton, Ill. Everything quiet along the line except cannonading. Received a letter from Sarah. Expected an attack. Received a Times.

Thursday

A very warm, pleasant day. Wrote to mother. A fight expected tomorrow on our left. Battery F 1st Pa. releived from the front by the 11th New York. No mail for me.

Friday

A most beautiful day. No fighting as yet, 9 o'clock. Lake returned to the battery. He was wounded in the wilderness. Received a letter from mother, a express receipt from Kears two Times from New York. The Rebells made a raid into our rear. Captured some cattle. We recaptured them. 2nd Div. went with the cavelery.

Saturday

A most beautiful day. Wrote to mother. Everything quiet along the line. Wrote to S. L. Case. Heard that D. P. Maynard was married. Recd. a letter from Chas. M. Wells.

Sunday, September 18, 1864

Warm, pleasant day. Wrote to Charles M. Wells. Recd. a letter from G. R. Stiles and a paper from Uncle Jos. A shower in the evening.

Monday

A most splendid day. Everything quiet as usual no fighting at all. Wrote to G. R. Stiles. Was up to the 141st Regiment S.V. Heard of the death of poor Guss. He died a good and true soldier to his government. We deeply mourn his loss.

Tuesday

A most beautiful day. Everything quiet. Was down the Prince George C. H. with Lt. Bull. I got no mail. An officer's dispatch from General Sheridan. He has whipped Early.* Captured 6,000 prisoners, five guns, nine Colors and is in full pursuit. <u>Good</u> <u>news</u>.

Wednesday

A cool, cloudy day. At daylight each corps along the line fired one gun in honor of Sheridan's Victory. The artillery firing lasted about thirty minutes and all is quiet. Received a letter from Anna and two papers from Uncle Joseph.

Thursday

Last night it rained. Today it is cool and cloudy. Law. U. Sloat 2nd P.V.R.C. 3rd Brigade 2nd Div. 6th Corps.** Wrote to Anna Barriger. Received a letter and photo from Sarah. Everything quiet along the lines.

Friday

A cool, cloudy, disagreeable day. Made a trip to all the batteries. Capt. Ames, U. S. Mail carrier, got his discharge. Wrote to Sarah and Uncle Joseph. Received a letter from R.F.B. and one from Uncle Jos. Paymaster for the brigade came here.

Saturday

A rainy day. Recd. Marching orders. First V, 2nd Div. marched to the right and relieved the 10th Artillery Corps. I got but very little sleep. No mail for me.

Sunday, September 25, 1864

A most beautiful day. Moved HdQtrs to the deserted house near our camp. Was all along the line with Lt. Bull, Eddy V., Capt. Ed Giles.*** Fixed up the HdQtrs. Was out with Lt. Bull to 3rd Div. Relieved by the 9th Corps. Marched to the right. No mail for me.

---

* Union General Philip Henry Sheridan led the Cavalry Corps of the Army of the Potomac and used a "scorched earth" tactic to weaken the Confederates, but General Jubal Anderson Early never surrendered. He escaped to voluntary exile in Mexico and Canada before being pardoned in 1868 by President Andrew Johnson. He never took the oath and remained an unreconstructed Rebel. (Sheridan, 1988; Jubal Early Trust, 1997)

** Urbane Sloat, private, mustered in July 17, 1861, 6th Pennsylvania Reserves, 35th Regiment Pennsylvania Volunteers, 1861; reenlisted in Company E, 191st Pennsylvania Veteran Volunteers, May 31, 1864. (PRVCHS)

*** "Lt. Bull" possibly Lieutenant William S. Bull, 12th Independent Battery, New York Light Artillery. "Eddy V." possibly Lieutenant Ulysses D. Eddy, 4th Regiment, New York Heavy Artillery. Capt. Ed Giles probably Edward Giles, 4th Independent Battery, New York Light Artillery.

Monday

A warm, pleasant day. Major Hayard returned from furlough. Artillery firing on the right nearly all day. A report that Butler had been attacked. Recd. a letter from Law Root and a Herald from Uncle Joseph.

Tuesday

A most beautiful day. Was over to the company. Got two months' pay — $32. Wrote to Uncle Joseph. Everything quiet along the line. Received a letter from Carrie Edwards; also her "Colh de Visit." Wrote to Law Root.

Wednesday

A most Beautiful day. Wrote to G. C. Jenks and to R.F.B. but did not send it. Everything remains as usual. Quiet. Received marching orders but did not move out all night.

Thursday

A cool, pleasant day. Not a camp in the Army of Potomac. Butler has a fight on the right. He captured 16 guns, 1600 prisoners. Everything remains as usual along the 2nd Corps lines.

Friday

Did not move. A rainy day. Gen'l Meade went to the left and drove the enemy; took the Danville Lane road. Heavy artillery firing at dark on 2nd Corp's line. A very rainy night. Recd. a paper and a letter from Uncle Joseph.

Saturday, October 1, 1864

A very rainy day. Received a letter from Sarah. Heavy fighting on the left. Everything as usual. A letter from Sarah and one from Ann Barriger and her photograph.

Sunday, October 2, 1864

A very rainy, disagreeable day. No change. Wrote to Sarah. Warren holds the South side load. Only one division, 2nd Corps, holding the line in front of Petersburg.

Monday

A rainy day. No fighting of any account. The quietest it has been for many days. Lt. Bull has received a comission as Lt. Col. Received a receipt from the tax collector. George Wells.

Tuesday

Cleared off warm and pleasant. A most delightful day. Some shelling on 2nd corps' line. Everything quiet to the right and left.

Wednesday

A most Beautiful day. Wrote to Anna Berriger. Everything quiet along the line. Recd. a Times. Hear no news from the right or left. Col. Tidball came here to Hd.Qtrs. He does not take command of arty. in this corps.

Thursday

A most splendid day. Very Warm. Wrote to R. F. Ballantine. Sent him $25 by mail. Everything remains quiet. Received a letter and photograph from T. L. Case.

Friday

A very warm day. Very heavy arty. firing on the extreme right. Think it is Butler near Richmond. The artillery firing ceased at noon. Wrote to Carrie Edwards and to T. L. Case. No news from the right.

Saturday

A most beautiful day. Everything quiet. C. V. Snyder got mustered out of the U. S. service.* No letters for me. A very cold night. Slept cold.

Sunday, October 9, 1864

A cool, windy day. Cold night. Everything quiet. Received a Times and a letter from Ella Kendale.

Monday

A most beautiful day. Wrote to Ella Kendale, Rockton, Illinois. Everything quiet along the lines. Wrote to George C. Jenks for him to send paper and envelopes to Sarah. Excused from duty only when called for by the officers. Went out to Ft. Steadman to find out what the firing was.

---

* Charles V. Snyder, private, 1st Pennsylvania Light Artillery.

Tuesday

State Election. A most beautiful warm, pleasant day. Everything quiet as usual. Cast my first vote. Voted the Union ticket. Polls for the election were opened in the battery. Judges were William H. Thurston, S. P. Harder, Carson V. J. Harman and Clark Huges.*

Wednesday

A most splendid day. Everything quiet along the line. Wrote to RFB for him to send me some gloves. Recd. a letter from Law Root. A shower in the evening.

Thursday

A most beautiful morning, but cold and windy. Recd. a Times from New York. Ned Wilson is to be court martialed for using direspectful language to the adjutant.* Everything quiet along the lines.

Friday

A most beautiful day. Took a working party up to Ft. Rice. Camp Clark has a section there. Wrote to Law Root. Everything as usual along the line. Recd. a letter from R. F. Ballantine. He has received the $25. Recd. a letter from Sarah and Charles M. Wells.

Saturday

A most beautiful day. Everything quiet as usual. Wrote to Sarah and Charlie Wells. Was down to the company. Recd. a letter from Anna Berriger.

Sunday, October 16, 1864

A most splendid day. Wrote to Anna Berriger. Everything as usual along the lines. Recd. a New York Times and a letter from G. R. Stiles.

---

* Ned Wilson, possibly L. Kennedy Wilson, private, 3rd Pennsylvania Heavy Artillery.

** Henry J. Carson, private, mustered in July 11, 1861; mustered out with Battery, June 10, 1865.

Jacob M. Harman, private, mustered in March 9, 1864; mustered out with battery, June 10, 1865.

"Clark Huges" possibly Mason B. Hughes, private, mustered in February 27, 1864; mustered out with battery, June 10, 1865.

Monday

A warm, pleasant day. Considerable shelling along the line. Wrote to G. R. Stiles. A band, First Division, came here to HdQtrs. Serenaded General Hancock. Secretary Stanton and Porter were here in the Army. Recd. a Times.

Tuesday

A most beautiful day. Everything quiet along the lines. No letters for me. The 6th Corps is expected back here.

Wednesday

A warm, pleasant day. Everything as usual along the line. A negro shot one of the 4th heavy at City Point. Express boxes came up from City Point.

Thursday

A cloudy, cool day. Looks like rain. Everything quiet along the line. No rain. A dispatch from c that he has gained a victory. Captured 60 guns and many prisoners. Recd. a Times. A salute was fired in honor of Sheridan's victory.*

Friday

A warm, pleasant day. Everything quiet along the line. Was at the battery. Recd. a Times. A cold night. A little rain in the night.

Saturday

A cold, cloudy, windy day. Everything quiet as usual along the lines. No mail for me. Rode the whole length of the line with Lt. Dean.** Was near hit with a piece of shell near Ft. Haskel. A horse race. A shower at dark. Cold and windy.

Sunday, October 23, 1864

A warm, pleasant day. Built a fireplace in my tent. Was not out today. K 4th U.S.F. 1st Penn. as of 1st N.H. were relieved from the front. Recd. a New York Times. Everything quiet along the lines.

---

* Battle of Cedar Creek, October 19, 1864. General Phil Sheridan rallied his troops to launch a crushing counterattack against Jubal Early's Confederates. (Hitchcock, 1868)

** "Lt. Dean" possibly Lieutenant John G. Deane, acting aide-de-camp, First Rhode Island Light Artillery.

Monday

A warm, pleasant day. Wrote to Uncle Joseph. Preparing for a move. A big fight expected. Everything quiet along 2nd Corps lines.

Tuesday

A warm, pleasant day. Everything in readiness for a march. Everything quiet along 2nd Corps line.

Wednesday

A warm, pleasant day. Marched at noon to the yellow house. On to Weldon Railroad. Camped for the night.

Thursday

Marched at one o'clock a.m. Commenced skirmishing with the enemey at daylight. Drove the Rebells all day until noon when we was attacked on all sides and had a very heavy fight. Was surrounded, but cut our way out. Retreated in the night. An awful dark, rainy night.*

Friday

Marched all day. Reached our old camp near dark. Clear and pleasant day. A hundred men charged and took two forts, but could not hold them.

Saturday

A very warm, pleasant day. Received six letters from Sarah, Anna, Carrie, Cutter, Fairbanks and Charlie Wells. Wrote to Anna and Sarah. Everything quiet along the line.

Sunday, October 30, 1864

A warm, pleasant day. Everything quiet. Wrote to Charles M. Wells. Recd. a paper from him. And a Times from Uncle Joseph. The Rebells gobbled up over 3 of our pickets on the Jerusalem plank road.

Monday

A warm, pleasant day. Mustered for four months' pay. Wrote to Carrie

---

* At Burgess Mill, October 27-28, 1864, General Hancock fought his last battle, the Second Corps gaining, then losing the Boydton Plank Road. He went on to head the Department of West Virginia and organized the 1st Veterans' Volunteer Corps. (Jordon, 1988)

Edwards. Recd. N.Y. Times. Wrote to Wm Cutler, Massachusetts, N.H. Everything quiet along the lines.

Tuesday, November 1, 1864

A warm, pleasant day. Mr. Anderson, reporter for N.Y.H. recd. a Captain's commission. A report that Hancock was agoing to be released from this corps. Gen. Humphrey to take his place.*

Wednesday

A cold, cloudy day. McAndrews started home on furlough. Everything quiet along the 2nd Corps line except the Naval Artillery firing. Received a N.Y. Times. Rained all day and night.

Thursday

A cold, rainy morning. Everything quiet along the lines as usual. Recd. a N.Y. Times. A cold, rainy day. Battery F, 1st Pa. moved camp.

Friday

A warm, pleasant day. Recd. a letter from Law Root and a N.Y. Times. Everything quiet along the lines.

Saturday

A warm, delightful day. Wrote to R. Keith, N.Y. Everything quiet along the lines. 2nd Corps building winter quarters, but I don't think we will settle down yet.

Sunday, November 6, 1864

A rainy, stormy day. Everything quiet along the lines through the day. In the evening there was an attack by the enemy in front of Fort Morton. It was repulsed with heavy loss to the enemy. We took 42 prisoners.

Monday

A rainy, stormy day. Everything quiet along the lines as usual. I Was with Lt. Deane along the picket line on the Appomattox River. After dark reported that the enemy were laying a pontoon bridge.

---

* General Andrew Atkinson Humphreys replaced General Hancock as commander of the Second Corps.

Tuesday

Election day. Cloudy with some rain. I voted for Lincoln and Johnson. A hundred and fifteen votes polled in the battery; 23 majority for Lincoln; 5 for Lincoln in Linsgen county, none for McClellan. Recd. a N.Y. Times.

Wednesday

Cloudy in the morning, but cleared off warm and pleasant. Everything quiet along the lines through the day. In the evening there was some firing all along the line. No news of the election.

Thursday

A warm an rainy morning. Battery F, 1st Pa. got two more guns, making six in all. Ridgeway and McFarland sergeants of the new guns.* Wrote to Law Root.

Friday

A warm, pleasant day. Recd. a letter from Sarah, Anna and G. R. Stiles. Business very heavy. A report that the enemy were massing on our left. All quiet.

Saturday

A very cold, cloudy day. Wrote to G.R.S. and to Sarah. Everything quiet along the lines. Recd. a N.Y. Times. Business light. Was not out at all.

Sunday, November 13, 1864

A bitter cold day. Out with Lt. Bull and Gordon up to 9th Corps Hd. quarters.** A very quiet day along the lines. Received a letter from Carrie Edwards and a letter from R. Ruth. The coldest night this fall.

Monday

A cold but pleasant morning. Wrote to Anna Barriger. All quiet along the line. Business light. A report that Sherman is marching on to Charleston passing through George.

Tuesday

A cold, but pleasant day. Wrote to R. Keith, V.Ca, and to Carrie Edwards,

---

* John A. McFarland, sergeant, mustered in June 8, 1861; mustered out with battery, June 10, 1865.

** "Gordon" possibly Lieutenant A.M.E. Gordon, acting assistant adjutant-general to Captain Hazard.

Nellie Clifton, Binghampton, N.Y. Everything quiet along the line. Business very light.

Wednesday

A warm, pleasant day. Received a letter from Ann Foster and paper from Uncle Joseph. Everything quiet along 2nd Corps lines. Was out with Lt. Clark inspecting batterys.

Thursday

A warm, pleasant day. Everything quiet along the lines. Business light. Whiskey plenty in Camp.

Friday

A warm, pleasant day. Off duty. Was at the battery nearly all day. Everything indicates a move of the army. Do not know in what direction.

Saturday

A rainy, cold day. No moving, but think we would move only for the rain. Business light. The mail boat did not come to City Point. No mails. Holley returned to his battery. His time is out. He expects to go home in a few days.

Sunday, November 20, 1864

A cold, rainy day. The movement is all knocked in the head on account of the storm. Everything quiet along the lines.

Monday

A very disagreeable day. Cold and rainy. Everything quiet along the lines. No movement. Considerable business at HdQuarters. No mail for me.

Tuesday

Cleared off pleasant and cold. Aroused up at five o'clock to go to 3rd Jersey Battery. They changed places with 12th N.Y. Battery. Some artillery firing but as quiet as usual.

Wednesday

A cold, but pleasant day. The coldest night this fall. Received a N.Y. Times. Everything quiet along the lines. Recd. a letter from Charley Wells.

Thursday

Thanksgiving. The solders expected a good dinner and did not get one. Recd. a letter from Sarah, Mother, and Nellie E. Clifton. A N.Y. Times. The officers had a big dinner. Express boxes came. A plenty of whiskey in camp.

Friday

A cold, clear day, but very pleasant. Wrote to mother and Nellie Clifton. Everything quiet. A splendid Thanksgiving dinner. Everything a person could wish.

Saturday

A warm and most beautiful day. Everything quiet along the 2nd Corps line. Wrote to Annie Foster. Wrote to Charles M. Wells and Sarah. Recd. a letter from Carrie Edwards. Gen. Hancock left this Corps. Gen. Humphrey takes his place. We lose a good and brave general.

Sunday, November 27, 1864

A little cloudy in the morning, but warm. Recd. a letter from Law Root and Anna Barriger. Wrote to Carrie Edwards and Anna Barriger, Law Root. Looks rain, very much.

Monday

A warm, pleasant day. Got logs to build a house. Business very light. Everything quiet along the lines.

Tuesday

A warm, pleasant day. Commenced to build a house and Lt. Gordon stopped us. Said we would move. First Division and three batterys marched up to 9th Corps. Our Corps agoing to relieve the 9th Corps and the 9th to take our place. Business heavy. Got a new horse.

Wednesday

A warm, pleasant day. Marched at seven o'clock. Had charge of the Hd.Q. Marched to 9th Corps HdQuarters. We are the extreme left of the Army. Only eight batteries marched. Our battery temporarily detached to 9th Corps. The warmest weather I ever saw in this time of year.

We left part of our dead and wounded on the field in the late battle and they fell into the rebel's hands. . . . I thought I would go to Richmond a prisoner at one time.

—Oney F. Sweet

*Hdquarters Artillery Brigade, 2nd Army Corps
Nov. 25th, 1864*

Dear Mother:

I received your letter this morning and was glad to hear you was all well. Yesterday was Thanksgiving but we got no better dinner than any other day. Although some say we will get it today. I doubt it.

We have had several cold nights but not so cold as you are having. I think I can get a furlough this winter but if you are all well I do not know as I will get one. As it will cost considerable to come home and a few days will not be worth while, although I would like to come. Boxes come through direct now but I will wait a week or two before you send one. I want two good woolen shirts and you might make them and have them ready. What is butter worth a pound? I think I will have you send me a tub this winter.

We left part of our dead and wounded on the field in the late battle and they fell into the rebel's hands. Surgeons were left with them. It was as warm a place as I was ever in.* I thought I would go to Richmond a prisoner at one time. We are expecting one more move before we go into winter quarters. We would probably have moved last week but a heavy rain of three days stopped all the moves for a while. George Dutcher is driving team in the train.

Today is a little cold but the sun is shining and in the middle of the day it will be quite warm.

I have no news of any account to write. Will write again soon. Sarah must answer this if you have not time. Love to all. I remain your most affectionate son Oney

---

* "warm" refers to the battle, not the weather.

Thursday, December 1, 1864

A most beautiful day. Warm and pleasant. Did not fix up quarters as we are going to move again. Our battery all near HdQuarters. A report from Thomas. He has whipped Hood, Sherman marching triumphantly through Georgia. Recd a Herald.

Friday

A warm day. Looks like rain. Cloudy. Everything quiet along the lines. Wrote to R. Keith, V company, 15 John St. N.Y. Recd. a Herald from JRS.

Saturday

A warm, pleasant day. Everything quiet. Kearney was killed by a tree falling on him. Recd. a letter from G. R. Stiles.

Sunday, December 4, 1864

A warm, pleasant day. Maj. Ricketts came to Hd.Qtrs. He brought a commission for Wireman and Thurston. Everything quiet. Recd. a letter from Nellie Clifton.

Monday

A warm, pleasant day. Everything quiet. A report that the 6th Corps was at City Point. Wrote to G. R. Stiles and to Nellie Clifton.

Tuesday

A most delightful day. Everything quiet. Recd. a N.Y. Times. The 6th Corps relieved the 5th Corps. Everything indicates a move, but in what direction I do not know.

Wednesday

A rainy, stormy day. Everything quiet. The 5th Corps has gone somewhere. Nobody knows. Recd. a letter from Anna Foster. A part of the 2nd Corps moved.

Thursday

Cleared off warm and pleasant. Just like summer. Saw Lt. Meade. I think there will be a fight within a few days. Business lively Wilson got his sentence. He is returned to duty.

Friday

A very cold day. The 6th Corps has gone South towards Wilmington. A letter from Anna Barriger and one from Sarah. A part of the 2nd Corps gone on a reconnaisance. A snow storm.

Saturday

Most awful cold and snow on the ground. No news from Warren. The 2nd Corps had a fight at Hatches Run. Wrote to Sarah and Anna Barriger.

Sunday, December 11, 1864

A very cold day, but clear and a bright sun. Heard that Warren was near Weldon. Everything quiet along the lines.

Monday

A cold, disagreeable day. Gen. Warren returned with his Corps from Weldon. He ripped up the railroad for many miles and destroyed much property. Received a letter from Carrie Edwards.

Tuesday

A cold day. My birthday. Everything quiet. Commenced to build a house. Worked very hard. Not so cold as yesterday. Received a letter from Law Root.

Wednesday

Worked very hard all day. Everything quiet along the lines. Not very cold. Got no mail.

Thursday

Worked very hard all day. Not very cold. Looks like rain. Received a pocket Album from Law Root and a letter from Nellie. Also a Times. Wrote to Sarah for a box and a letter to Carrier Edwards. Annie Elisa Haman, Atlantic City, N.J.

Friday

A warm, pleasant day. Wrote to Nellie Clifton and Law Root. Received no letters. Everything quiet. Three men hung for desertion. They deserted to the Rebells and then came back into our lines.

Saturday

A warm, pleasant day. Everything quiet. Heard the news of Thomas *gaining a great Victory over Hood. Gen. Sherman is near Savannah. He is in communication with Dalghrum. Wrote to RFB.*

Sunday, December 18, 1864
A cloudy day. Looks like rain. Was over to 1st N.Y. Battery. Saw Cutler. Everything quiet. Received a Times from Uncle Joseph. Wrote to Annie L. Foster, to Minnie Edwards, Binghamton, N.Y.

Monday
A cloudy day. No rain. Everything quiet. Boxes came to the Corps. Wrote to no one. Sherman reported to be in possession of Savannah, Ga.

Tuesday
A pleasant day. Good news from Thomas and Sherman. Thomas whipped and drove Hood eight miles. No letters or papers.*

Wednesday
A rainy, disagreeable day. Sherman has opened communications with Foster and captured Ft. McAllester. Thomas still driving Hood. Received two Times.

Thursday
A very cold, rainy day. Went down to the 9th Corps to the Battery. Drew clothing. Had a gay time. Stayed overnight at the Battery. Received a Times and letter from Charlie Wells, Annie Barriger and Sarah.

Friday
A very cold day. Came up from the 9th Corps. Wrote to Annie L. Barriger. A report in circulation that Jeff Davis is dead.** Wrote to Charles M. Wells.

Saturday
A cool day. Christmas Eve. Aplenty of whiskey in camp. A report that

---

* Battle of Nashville, December 15–16, 1864. Union General George Henry Thomas "completely routed" Confederate General John Bell Hood's entrenched forces. (Hitchcock, 1868)

** A number of rumors circulated during the war alleging the death of Jefferson Davis, president of the Confederate States. However, he died on December 6, 1889, "of a congestive chill, combined with malaria and acute bronchitis" in New Orleans, Louisiana. (Pech, 1900)

Savannah is captured and an attack been made on Wilmington. Wrote to Sarah. Recd. a letter from G. R. Stiles and a Times.

Sunday, December 25, 1864

A warm, pleasant day. A Merry Christmas. Wrote to G. R. Stiles. A report from Rebell sources that Savannah is captured. A plenty of whiskey in camp. Got no papers or letters. Savannah captured with 25,000 bales of cotton, 150 pieces of artillery, locomotives, etc.

Monday

A stormy day. Everything quiet. Many deserters came in. Glorious news from Sherman in Savannah.* Received a number of papers. A darling Jack from Addie.

Tuesday

A cloudy day. Looks like rain. I wrote to Uncle Joseph. Everything quiet. The mail boat did not come to City Point. No mail.

Wednesday

Cleared off warm and pleasant. Everything quiet along the lines. Commenced to rain in the evening. Recd a letter from Sarah and one from Carrie Edwards. A box started the 26th.

Thursday

A cold, cloudy day. Everything quiet along the line. Wrote to Carrie Edwards and to Sarah. No mail. The mail boat delayed by storm.

Friday

A cool, cloudy day. Everything quiet. Recd. a Times. A letter from Anna L. Foster and a letter from Law Root.

Saturday

A rainy, stormy day. The last day of 1864. Wrote to Anna L. Foster and Law Root.

---

* General William Tecumseh Sherman, on December 22, 1864, wired President Lincoln to offer him an early Christmas present after completing his 300-mile "March to the Sea." *The New York Times* published the telegram on its front page on December 26 with the headline: "Savannah Ours, Sherman's Christmas Present." (*The New York Times*, Dec. 26, 1864)

Memorandum

Clothing

> *January 1, jacket, pair of pants*
> *March, drawers &blouse*
> *August, _____ pants*
> *September, socks & 2 drawers*
> *October, 1 blouse*
> *December, 1 pair of pants and blouse*

> | | |
> |---|---|
> | *total paid* | *$42.00* |
> | *billed* | *$32.15* |
> | *due* | *$9.85* |

Letters & Diary, 1865

*Received a letter from Anna L. B. She has taken offense at
something I wrote. I answered it returning to her all of her letters.*
—Oney F. Sweet

[flyleaf notation]

Oney F. Sweet, Headquarters, Artillery Brigade, 2nd Army Corps.

Sunday, January 1, 1865

New Years. A most beautiful day. A Happy New Year to all. Col. Hayard had a big time. Licour in abundance. Everybody gay and festive. Recd. a N.Y. times.

Monday

A clear, pleasant day. Everything quiet as usual. Recd. a N.Y. Times. Wrote to Wm. Roper.

Tuesday

A stormy day. Snowed a little. Col. Hayard's horse, Major, died. Received paper and a letter from A.L.B. Everything quiet in front of P[etersburg].

There are many heavy batteries and eight inch mortar batteries all along the line. Battery 13, 1st New Hampshire; Battery 14, 10th Massachusetts; Fort Morton, G 1st, New York; Battery 20, C 4th New York Mortars, Fort Davis, B New Jersey and 6th Maine; Ft. Alex Hay.

The forts in front of Petersburg are: Ft. McGilvery, Stedman, Haskell, Morton, Meikel, Rice, Sedgwick, Davis, Alexander Hays and Howard. *

Wednesday

Cleared off most beautiful and pleasant. Everything quiet. Wrote to Anna L.B. Mail boat delayed by storm.

Thursday

A splendid day. Express boxes came from City Point. They are all opened by Lt. Charles and all Licours confiscated. Went down to the 9th Corps. Staid over night at the battery.

Friday

Returned to HdQuarters. A most awful disagreeable day. Wind and rain. Business rushing. Recd a letter from Nellie Clifton and one from Sarah. 3 papers.

---

* The siege at Petersburg initiated the construction of a serpentine array of entrenched fortifications and artillery emplacements by both the Confederate army defending the town and the Union army, which had been attempting to capture the town since mid-June 1864. Historians came to view this as a precursor to the static trench warfare of World War I. The "strong points" and redoubts took shape as enclosed forts. At one of the points the opposing lines were barely 130 yards apart. (Terry, 2008; Hess, 2009)

Saturday

A clear, pleasant day. Wrote to Nellie Clifton and to Ella Gilman, Monmouth, Maine.

Sunday, January 8, 1865

A cold, clear day. Everything quiet. Genl. Stoneman made a successful raid into Virginia. Destroyed much property and salt mines.

Monday

A cloudy day. Cold. Everything quiet along the lines. No mail.

Tuesday

Commenced raining last night. A very rainy day. Mud knee deep. My day off duty. Recd. two papers.

Wednesday

A clear, delightful day. Went down to 9th Corps and returned. Took orders to Hq. Recd. a paper, letter from Annie Foster, her photo, a diary, letter from Charlie Wells.

Thursday

A most beautiful day. Everything quiet. Gen. Humphrey reviewed 3rd Division Corps. Recd. a Herald a letter from George Dutcher and wrote Annie LF and to Chs. M.W.

Friday

A most beautiful day. Recd. my anxiously looked for box. Everything good. Recd a letter from Carrie Edwards and some tobacco in a paper from Uncle Jos. Wrote to Sarah stating that I had recd. the box. No news.

Saturday

A warm, pleasant day. Everything quiet. No papers or letters Saw Nell Steanback. Wrote to Gorg. D.

Sunday, January 15, 1865

A most beautiful day. Was with Mjr. Edgele, Gen. Humphrey inspected ambulances, trains and hospitals. Dick Steadford came up here for his box. Wrote to Carrie Edwards.

Monday

A most splendid day. A report that the enemy were marching on our left. Wrote to Geo. G. Jenks. Received a letter from Anna L. B. She has taken offense at something I wrote. I answered it returning to her all of her letters.

Tuesday

A cloudy, cold day. The excitement of the Rebell movements all over. Wrote to G. W. Tomlinson. Wrote to Law Root.

Wednesday

A warm, pleasant day. Everything quiet. Went down to 9th Corps with orderly. Had a gay old time. Lt. Wireman, Rule and Sergt. Mower started home on furlough. Recd. a Herald.

Thursday

A cloudy day. Returned to Hd.Qtrs. Everything quiet. The clerk Hdq. relieved and sent to his battery for drunkeness. Got papers and letters.

Friday

Cold, pleasant day. Everything quiet. Fort Fisher at the entrance of Cape Fear was taken by Porter and Terry. Recd. a letter from Nellie Clifton and answered it.

Saturday

A most awful disagreeable day. Mud and rain. Recd. a box of cigars and two papers from Uncle Jos. A letter from Ella Gilman and one from G.R.S.

Sunday, January 22, 1865

An awful disagreeable day. Wrote to G.R.S., Ella Gilman, Ellen Petterbone, Rockton, Ill. Everything quiet. No mail the boat delayed.

Monday

A very disagreeable day. No mail. A heavy cannonading on our right. Supposed to be between the gunboats on the James River. The Honorable Edward Everett died a few days ago.*

---

* Edward Everett, the featured orator at the dedication ceremony of the Gettysburg National Cemetery in 1863, died on Jan. 15, 1865, at age 70.

Tuesday

Cleared off warm and pleasant. Off duty. Went down to 9th Corps to the Battery. Some firing on the James River. Returned to the Battery late at night. No mail. A report that the Rebels run down the James River 4 gunboats and our boats destroyed them.

Wednesday

A most beautiful day, but very cold. Express boxes came. Everything quiet along the lines. Received a letter from Geo. Dutcher.

Thursday

A cold, pleasant day. Everything quiet. The papers are full of Peace rumors. Blair has gone to Richmond again.

Friday

One of the coldest days this winter. Very windy. Everything quiet. Wrote to Annie Foster. Received a book from Annie. A very cold night. Smithsonian Institute destroyed by fire and such.

Saturday

A most awful cold day. Windy. Everything quiet as usual. Only went out once. Went over to 1st NH Battery to see Bean. No mail. The boat delayed by ice in the Potomac River.

Sunday, January 29, 1865

Warmer than yesterday and quite pleasant. Inspection by Lt. Gordon of horses and equipment. Everything quiet as usual. Received a letter from Sarah and one from Carrie Edwards. Wrote to Sarah.

Monday

A very pleasant day. Quite warm. Received two maps from Boston and

---

* The Hampton Roads Conference, held February 3, 1865, aboard the boat River Queen. President Abraham Lincoln and Secretary of State William H. Seward met with three representatives of the Confederacy: Vice President Alexander H. Stephens, Sen. R.M.T. Hunter of Virginia, and Assistant Secretary of War J.A. Campbell. Lincoln called for a reunion of the nation, emancipation of the slaves, and disbanding of Confederate troops. The Southern representatives had been authorized only to accept independence, so nothing came of it. (*Encyclopædia Britannica*)

two Heralds from Uncle Jose. Everything quiet in the Army of Potomac. Recd.
a note and all of my letters from Annie L.B.

Tuesday

A very warm, pleasant day. A rumor of a movement soon reported.
Arrival of Vice President Stevens and two other distinguished gentlemen from
Rebelldom. From what I hear it is true.

Wednesday, February 1, 1865

A very warm pleasant day. Just like summer. Everything quiet as usual.
Some indication of a move. Many rumors afloat about the men who came from
Rebelldom yesterday.* Recd. a N.Y. times.

Thursday

A warm, delightful day. Wrote to Carrie Edwards and to G. E. Dutcher.
Some indication of an early movement of this army. Received a N.Y. times.

Friday

A warm, pleasant day. Everything quiet. No mail. The boat delayed. Looks
like a storm.

Saturday

A clear, pleasant day. Drew clothing. Recd. orders to be ready to march
tonight. 3 batteries are going along with the 2 V 13 Div. 2nd Corps.

Sunday, February 5, 1865

Aroused up at daylight. Marched towards Hatches Run. A very nice day
for fighting. The Rebells attacked us at 5 o'clock p.m. but they were repulsed.

Monday

A cold, clear day. 2nd Corps had no fighting. 5th Corps and Cavlry had
hard fighting and got worsted. Recd. a Harpers Weekly.

Tuesday

An awful cold, rainy day. Mud knee deep. The troops suffered. No fighting
of any account. Slept on the ground.

Wednesday

Cleared off cold and pleasant. No fighting. Our lines extended several miles to our left. Recd. a letter from Nellie Clifton and Ella Gillman.

Thursday

A clear, cold day. Went back to old Hd.Quarters. Staid all night. Making preparations to move Hd.Qtrs. Recd a Herald. A good deal of fun in camp.

Friday

A very cold day. No fighting. Moved Hd.Quarters to the left. No fighting on our lines. Received a letter from P. S. Harder.

Saturday

A very cold day. No fighting. Our lines established. Commenced to build quarters. Received a letter from Robert Ballantine, Sarah, G. R. Stiles, George Dutcher and Anna L.B.

Sunday, February 12, 1865

A most awful cold day. Nearly finished our house. No letters. A very cold night.

Monday

A most awful cold day. Everything quiet. Note to R.F.B and S.P.H.

Tuesday

A very cold day. Everything quiet. Wrote to Sarah. Wrote to Nellie Clifton & G. R. Stiles.

Wednesday

A rainy day. Not very cold. Everything quiet along the lines. Wilson got drunk and got put in the guard house. Recd. a letter from Anna L. Foster and two papers and some tobacco.

Thursday

A warm, pleasant day. Recd. a Herald. Everything quiet. Heard some artillery firing on our right. Wrote to Ella Gilman and G. E. Dutcher.

Friday

A rainy, disagreeable day. Recd. a valentine. Went down to the battery and returned. Everything quiet. Maj. Edgell and Col. Hayard started home on furlough for twenty days.*

Saturday

Recd. a letter from Carrie Edwards. Answered it. Sent Anna L.B. her picture. Everything quiet. Went with Lt. Eddy and Ball to have some photos taken.

Sunday, February 19, 1865

A most beautiful day. Bensle started home on furlough for 15 days. Recd. a Herald. Everything quiet.

Monday

A warm, pleasant day. Everything quiet. Good news from Sherman, that he has taken Charleston, Branchville and Clommbia.**

Tuesday

A warm, pleasant day. Recd. a Herald and letter from Uncle Joseph. Expected an attack by the enemy.

Wednesday

A most splendid day. Went with Lt. Bull condemning property and inspecting works. Up all night – carrying dispatches. Expected some move of the enemy.

Thursday

Commenced raining. Went to the 4th Heavy after the paymaster to paid Co. F. Rained all day. Everything quiet.

Friday

A warm, pleasant day. Everything quiet. The paymaster came here to pay the Brigade. Recd. a Herald & Times.

---

* Maj. Edgell possibly Frederick M. Edgell, 1st New Hampshire Light Artillery.

** After flanking the Rebels at Branchville, on February 4, 1865, General Sherman went on to capture Columbia, South Carolina, on February 17, and the next day Union forces occupied Charleston. (Hitchcock, 1868)

Saturday

A very rainy day. Received my pay: $108. My horse is sick and will not eat.

Sunday, February 26, 1865

A most delightful day. Took the paymaster over to 5th Corps. My horse played out.

Monday

A warm, pleasant day. Went after express box at the station. Wrote to Willie. Received a letter from Sarah. Wrote to Uncle Jos., sent him $3.00.

Tuesday

A rainy, stormy day. Received a box from RFB. Received a letter from Nellie Clifton. Off duty horse sick.

Wednesday, March 1, 1865

A cloudy day. Wrote to RFB. Everything quiet. Recd. a letter from G.R.S. Recd the official account of the fall of Charleston and Wilmington. Wrote to Tomlinson.

Thursday

A rainy, disagreeable day. Everything quiet. Recd. a letter from Sarah, Carrie and Charley Wells. Wrote to G.R.S.

Friday

A rainy, disagreeable day. Went down to Company F. The boys are going to present Maj. Ricketts with a sword. Everything quiet.

Saturday

A rainy, windy day. Came to headquarters. Recd. a letter from Ella Gillman and her photo. Wrote to Carrie E. and Sarah. Wrote Law Root.

Sunday, March 5, 1865

A most beautiful day. Wrote to Nellie Clifton. Had some pictures taken. Everything quiet. Expressed $50 to C. P. Hawley.

Monday
   A most beautiful day. Everything quiet. No news from Sherman.

Tuesday
   A most splendid day. Wrote to Ella Gillman. Everything quiet. Wrote to Charley Wells.

Wednesday
   A warm, pleasant day. Everything quiet. Recd. a letter from Geo. Dutcher.

Thursday
   A stormy day. Wrote to Sarah. Went down to the battery. Everything quiet.

Friday
   A rainy, disagreable day. Everything quiet. Wrote to S.P. Harder and Geo. E. Dutcher.

Saturday
   A rainy, stormy day. Everything quiet. Recd. a paper. Gen'l Grant and Mead reviewed 2nd Corps. Many Ladies present.

Sunday, March 12, 1865
   A most beautiful day. Everything quiet. The roads dig up very quick.

Monday
   A most splendid day. Everything quiet. Recd. a letter from Sarah. She wrote a long & interesting letter.

Tuesday
   A most beautiful day. Wrote to Sarah and Annie L. Foster. Mr. Cutler came here to see me. Received orders to be ready to march at a moment's notice. Recd. two papers.

Wednesday
   Looks very much like rain. Cloudy, very warm. All Suttlers ordered to City Point. Making preparations for a move.

Got a big mail. About thirty papers from Uncle Joseph and a letter from D. P. M.

—Oney F. Sweet

Post Office at the Army of the Potomac headquarters.
(Timothy H. O'Sullivan, Library of Congress)

Thursday

A warm, pleasant day. Recd no orders to march. The 1st PA and 6th Maine came up here and camped. Recd. a paper.

Friday

A warm, beautiful day. St. Patrick's Day Celebrated a grand time. Horse racing. Two men killed and one Colonel by horses running over them. Recd. a letter from Law R., Charley Wells and Carrie E. Wrote to Law.

Saturday

A most delightful day. Everything quiet. Wrote to Carrie Edwards. Recd. a letter from R. F. Ballantine. Everything quiet.

Sunday, March 19, 1865

A most splendid day. General Humphrey reviewed the Artillery of 2nd Corps. The orderlies had to all turn out. The review passed off very pleasant.

Monday

A very warm, pleasant day. Just like summer. No news. Everything quiet. Wrote to N.Y. Sent a ticket.

Tuesday

A cloudy day, but warm. Wrote to Charley Wells, Ayd, Beach, N.Y. Recd. a letter from Sar. and a letter and photo from Nellie Clifton. Rained very hard in the evening.

Wednesday

A clear, pleasant day. Some wind. Expect to have a review today.

Thursday

A very windy day. Genl. Meade Reviewed 2nd Corps. E. Battery reviewed. While on review the band tents and stables took fire. Three horses burnt. Received a letter from Sar., G.E.D. and Ella Gillman.

---

* Battle of Fort Steadman, one of the fortresses in the Union entrenchment at Petersburg. See diary entry for January 3, 1865.

Friday

A cool, windy day. Wrote to Sarah. Everything quiet. Recd. a letter from Anna Foster and a paper.

Saturday

A cloudy, cool day. The enemy attacked the 9th Corps and took Fort Stedman.* They were driven back and nearly three thousand prisoners were taken. The 2nd and 6th Corps also attacked the enemy and took their picket line with many prisoners. In the afternoon the 2nd Corps had some heavy fighting near dark.

Sunday, March 26, 1865

A most beautiful day. No fighting of any account. Went into our old camp. The President and General Grant visited 2nd Corps.

Monday

A very pleasant day. Everything quiet as usual in 2nd Corps. The enemy attacked the 6th Corps at daylight and retook their picket line with many prisoners.

Tuesday

A very warm, pleasant day. Everything indicates a move tomorrow. Everything quiet as usual.

Wednesday

Marched at daylight. Crosst Hatchers line and skirmished with the enemy. A very bad country to fight in.

Thursday

A rainy, disagreeable day. Some fighting drove the rebells back to their main line of works. Rained some fighting.

Friday

A very rainy, disagreeable day. Roads in very bad condition. Some fighting. HdQuarters battery moved up to the front. Major Mills, Humphreys' A.A.A.G. was killed by a solid shot.* The 5th Corps had a hard fight.

---

* Major Charles J. Mills, Acting Assistant Adjutant-General to General Humphreys, died on March 31, 1865, in a battle near Dinwiddie Court House, Virginia. (Walker, 1886)

Captured 300 wagons, took thousands of prisoners, saw the finest fight I have ever seen. Our men fought like tigers.

—Oney F. Sweet

Saturday, April 1, 1865

Cleared off, but the roads very bad. No very hard fighting. Cavelery and 5th Corps moved to the left. No fighting of any account.

Sunday, April 2, 1865

Clear and pleasant. Some hard fighting. The 6th Corps broke the Rebell's lines and the whole line gave way. We captured many prisoners and guns. A beautiful day. Carried the Rebell works. Camped near Chapel Church, 10 miles from Petersburg. The Rebels hold Petersburg tonight.

Monday

A most beautiful day. Clear and pleasant. Marched all day. 15 miles distance. The cavelery fought the enemy and captured many prisoners. Camped at a strong Rebell's house. He had two sons in the army. The Rebels evacuated Richmond.

Tuesday

A clear, pleasant day. Bad roads. The Rebells destroyed and left many wagons all along the road. We did not march over 7 miles. Camped at a farm house. Army HQtrs near.

Wednesday

A fine day. Marched at 12 o'clock a.m., and marched all day. Marched twenty miles. Overtook the 5th and Cavelery Corps. The cavelery fought the Rebells and captured a wagon train.

Thursday

Beautiful day. Marched at daylight. Saw the enemy and attacked them and drove them over 8 miles. Captured 300 wagons, took thousands of prisoners, saw the finest fight I have ever seen. Our men fought like tigers. Camped at a farm house. Captured many guns.

Battle of Appomattox Court House

April 7-9, 1865

A joyous day in the army. Cheer after cheer rent the air. . . . Everyone in high spirits.

I was all through the Rebell lines. Had $30,000 in Confederate money.

—Oney F. Sweet

Friday

Marched at daybreak. Found the enemy near the Appomattox. They burnt the R.R. bridge. It is a splendid bridge, but very little fighting until near dark and then it was heavy. The whole Rebell Army made a stand. Genl. Smyth wounded.* We drove the enemy from their hill. They abandoned a large train.

Saturday

Commenced following up the enemy at daylight. Took Genl. Lewis prisoner, wounded _____ Minus a flag of truce.** A report that Genl. Lee wishes to surrender. Rode over 40 miles. Was at Farmersville. Saw Genl. Grant, he had his headquarters in town. Marched 'til 12 o'clock at night.

Sunday, April 9, 1865

Commenced advancing early. About noon a flag of truce came in and Genl. Lee surrendered to Grant. A joyous day in the army. Cheer after cheer rent the air. Went into camp. Everyone in high spirits. A rainy night.

Monday

Laid in camp all day. Rained considerable. Genl. Lee & Army to be "paroled," take all their army. Everybody thinks the war at an end, nearly.

Tuesday

A rainy day. 2nd Corps commenced moving back toward Farmersville. I was all through the Rebell lines. Had $30,000 in Confederate money. Overtook HdQtrs at two o'clock a.m. Camped at a Rebell Capts. house.

Wednesday

Marched all day. Very bad roads. Rainy. Marched through Farmersville, camped near the town. A rainy night. Horses give out.

Thursday

A rainy day. Went back to Burks Station to the train after forage. Got a good dinner. Rode back to the Hd. Quarters found _____

---

* General Thomas A. Smyth, mortally wounded at Appomattox on April 7, 1865, the last Union general to be killed during the Civil War. (Dyer, 1908)

** General William Lewis, North Carolina infantry, severly wounded and captured. (Field, 2015)

Appomattox Court House, Virginia, April 1865.
(Timothy H. O'Sullivan, Library of Congress)

Sweet told his children about that day, as noted in letters his daughter Marian wrote to family members later on:

> *Father as you all know was at Appomattox when Lee surrendered and saw General Grant and Lee. His division passed in review at that time.*

> *He served to the end of the war and saw Lee's surrender. The troops passed in review at Appomattox Court House.*

Sweet told the *Long Beach Press-Telegram*, in 1931, that he circulated among the soldiers of the Confederacy at Appomattox at the time of Lee's surrender. (See the diary entry for Tuesday, April 11, 1865.)

Friday

Marched at daylight. Reached Burks Station about 7. Camped in pine woods. Most all our clothese lost.

Saturday

A rainy day. Aplenty of whiskey in camp. A report that President Lincoln had been shot at a theater in Washington.

Sunday, April 16, 1865

A clear, pleasant day. Cleaned up and washed. President Lincoln and Sec. Seward and son were shot in Washington. The President is dead. J. Wilkes Booth was the assassin.* Lt. Wireman and some of the Baty F boys came up from City Point with horses.**

Monday

A clear, pleasant day. Everything indicates another move of this Corps. Recd. a letter from Carrie Edwards.

Tuesday

A most beautiful day. Wrote to Sarah. Everything looks bright for a speedy peace. Abraham Lincoln, President of the United States died April 17th, one o'clock a.m.

Wednesday

A day of mourning in the Army. Flags at halfmast in honor of the President. Wrote to Carrie and Law.

Thursday

A most beautiful day. Wrote to Chas. Wells & Annie L. Foster. Col. Hayard reviewed 2nd Corps Artillery. Raymond and I went out in the country. Recd a paper. The 9th Army Corps gone to City Point.

---

* Actor and Confederate sympathizer John Wilkes Booth shot President Abraham Lincoln on April 14, 1865, at Ford's Theater in Washington, DC. On the same day, would-be assassins attacked Secretary of State William Seward in his home, and severely wounded Seward's son Frederick. Lincoln died the following day, and Vice President Andrew Johnson became president. (Hitchcock, 1868)

Friday

A beautiful day. Everything lovely. President Johnson makes a speech that he will follow the plans of Lincoln. A report that General Johnson has surrendered.

Saturday

A most beautiful day. No news of any account. Went to Army Hd. Quarters with Lt. Gorden.

Sunday, April 23, 1865

A cool, beautiful morning. Papers full of the accounts of the funeral of the President and the capture of his murderer.

Monday

A cool, but pleasant day. Everything quiet. Recd. a Herald. 6th Corps started for Danville. Lt. Brockway and Mower came here.

Tuesday

A most beautiful day. 13 guns were fired at day light and then on a every half hour through the day. Thirty-six guns were fired at sunset. Wrote to R. F. Ballantine. All officers are to wear crepe on their left arms and swords and all flags for six months.

Wednesday

A warm, pleasant day. Everything quiet and no indications of a move. The papers are full of news about Booth and the death of the President.

Thursday

A most beautiful day. Received a dispatch stating that Wilkes Booth's body was in Washington. None of the particulars received.

Friday

A most delightful day. Just like summer. All quiet in camp. Recd. a dispatch that Genl. Johnson had surrendered. Genl. Grant went to Sherman's army a few days ago. The war at an end.*

---

* Confederate General Joseph E. Johnston began negotiating with General Sherman in North Carolina in mid-April; following an ultimatum from General Grant on April 29, Johnston surrendered on terms substantially the same as those agreed upon by General Lee. (*The New York Times*, April 30, 1856)

The surrender effectively ended the war, although President Andrew Johnson did not formally declare the end of the war until August 20, 1866. (Johnson, 1866)

Saturday

A magnificent day. Just like summer. Received a letter from Sarah and answered it. Also wrote to Nellie Clifton. Wrote to S. P. Harder. A shower in the evening.

Sunday, April 30, 1865

A warm, delightful day. Received the account of the capture of Booth near the Rappahanna River, Virginia. Also news of Johnson's surrender. Received a Herald. A shower in the a.m. Battery F brought up their horses for these batterys here. Made preparations to go out on an expedition.

Monday, May 1, 1865

The prospect of a move stoped our expedition, although we went and had a good time with Col. Hayard and Col. Williams. Papers full of account of Johnson and Booth. Recd. orders to be ready to march at a moment's notice. The government's reducing the expenses.

Tuesday

A most delightful day. Received a letter from G.R.S. and answered it. Orders to move at noon. Here we are ready for the start. Marched at 3 o'clock. Marched 10 miles.

Wednesday

Marched at daylight. Passed through Gettysville, Amelia Courthouse. Camped 25 miles from Richmond. Marched 20 miles. Passed through a beautiful country. Camped at a farm house. Recd. a letter from Law Root.

Thursday

Marched at daylight. A beautiful country and a splendid day. Marched 25 miles. Camped three miles from Manchester. Hd.Quarters at a farm house. Received a letter from Chas Wells and Sarah. 8 papers. 15 men died.

Friday

A beautiful day. Pulled out on the road but went into camp again. Camped at a farm house. Went down to Battery A, 1st Pa. saw all the boys. We can see Richmond from our camp.

Saturday

A most pleasant day. Marched at 10 o'clock. Marched through all the principal streets of Richmond. Saw all places of interest. Camped five miles north of Richmond at a farm house.

Sunday, May 7, 1865

A very warm, pleasant day. Marched early. Marched 20 miles. Crosst Presquile River. Hd.Qtrs a Rebells, Col. Bussfleys, A splendid place. *

Monday

A warm, pleasant day. Showers in the evening. Marched 15 miles. Camped at a Rebell Officer's house. Crosst the F&R R.R. at Chesterfield. Passed on the same road we did last summer. Going to Col. H. [Colonel Heights]. Slept in a barn.

Tuesday

A cool, delightful morning. Roads muddy. The artillery on the lead of the Corps. Passed near Spotsylvania Court House. Camped at a brick farm house 5 miles from Fredericksburg. A little rain in the afternoon. Crosst the Nye River.

Wednesday

Marched at daylight. Passed through Fredericksburg. It has been a nice town. Marched through Falmouth. Marched 15 miles. Camped at a farmhouse.

Thursday

Marched at 9 o'clock. Very bad, muddy roads. A heavy rain last night. The worst part of Virginia I was ever in. Camped near Middleburn at a General's house. Got a good supper.

Friday

Marched at five o'clock. Awful roads. Marched 10 miles. Camped near Wolf Run shoals. The river so high it is impossible to cross today. The 5th Corps trains are to cross first.

---

* "Col. Bussfleys" possibly Lieutenant Colonel Hezekiah Bussey, 27th Georgia Infantry, Talbot County, Georgia.

Saturday

Marched at 4 o'clock. Crosst the river. marched through Fairfax C.H. and camped at Baileys Crossroads. We can see Washington.

Sunday, May 14, 1865

Laid in camp all day. A great deal of talk about going home. Received the news of the capture of Jeff Davis. He was captured in Irvinsville, Ga. Recd. a letter from Sarah and Uncle Joseph.

Monday

Moved one mile into camp. Camped in an underbrush. Recd. several papers. Anxious for home.

Tuesday

A most awful warm day. Went down to the battery and Alexandria. The battery has turned everything. Recd. a paper.

Wednesday

A very hot day. Went down to the battery with Ben Van Horn. A good deal of talk about going home. Recd. a paper.

Thursday

A warm day. Heavy shower at dark. Heavy lightning and thunder. Recd. a paper. A good deal of excitement about veterans.

Friday

A rainy, cloudy day. Heard that F 1st Pa. turned in their guns. The grand review to take place next Tuesday. Recd. a Herald.

Saturday

A very rainy, disagreeable day. We have a very muddy camp. The Col. went to Washington.

Sunday, May 21, 1865

A rainy, disagreeable day. A great deal of talk about veterans and going home. Recd. a paper. Wrote to C. Hawley and to Sarah.

Monday

Cleared off warm and pleasant. Making preparations for the review. The band to be mounted on horses.

Tuesday

A cool, delightful day. A better day could not be wished for the review. A grand display. The Ladies welcome the Army. Everything passed off tip top. 2nd Corps made the finest appearance.*

Wednesday

A warm, pleasant day. General Sherman's Army reviewed. I had a pass to go. Had a splendid time. Enjoyed myself bully. Recd. a paper.

Thursday

A cloudy, cool morning. Col. Hayard had some lady friends to see him. Went out after strawberries.

Friday

A very rainy, disagreeable day. Went to army Hd.Quarters. Very muddy. Recd. a letter from Law Root.

Saturday

A rainy, disagreeable day. Wrote to Law Root. The review postponed. Recd. a paper. No news.

Sunday, May 28, 1865

Cleared off warm and pleasant. Recd. a letter from C. P. Hawley containing a $20 greenback. Recd. a paper. No news. Rained in the evening.

Monday

A very warm, pleasant day. Went down to the battery. Sgt. Mulligan under arrest. I am in charge. Wrote to Carrie Edwards and C. P. Hawley.

Tuesday

A most delightful day. Received an order that all artillery would at once be

---

* Nearly 100,000 veterans, led by General Meade, marched down Pennsylvania Avenue in the Grand Review of the Armies in Washington, DC, on May 23, 1865. The following day, General Sherman led his army in a second review. (*The New York Times*, May 24, 1865)

disbanded and report to their respective states. Genl. Hancock reviewed the 2nd Corps. A grand turnout. The artillery all feel gay.

Wednesday

Went down to the battery call in the morning. The boys in fine spirits. Everything gay. Recd. orders to be ready to start for home tomorrow morning.

Thursday, June 1, 1865

Started early in the morning for Washington. Started in one train, ahead of battery. Got to Baltimore and waited. Left B. at 3 o'clock. Young ladies turned out along the road.

Friday

Arrived in Harrisburg at daylight. The battery went to camp. I stopped at Mrs. Eckerts and got breakfast. Went to camp in the afternoon.

Saturday

A very hot day. Board in town at Mrs. Eckerts. Smith French boards with me. Went to camp overnight.

Sunday, June 4, 1865

A very hot day. Staid in town all day. Charley Wells came to camp. Staid in camp.

Monday

Went downtown with Charley. He stopped with me. Went to Sanfords Hall.

Tuesday

T. L. Case came from New York to see the boys. He went to camp. Charley Wells started for home. At noon Smith French and myself took dinner together at the Benlir House.

Wednesday

A cloudy, warm day. Went to camp. The rolls finished. Case started for home.

Thursday

A warm, delightful day. The rolls sent to the mustering officer.

Friday

Expected to be mustered out of service, but was not on account of rolls being wrong. The boys were mad and disappointed.

Saturday, June 10, 1865

A cloudy day. A shower. We was mustered out of service at 10 o'clock a.m. I am once more a free man. 3 years, 9 months and 6 days in active service.

Cash account

Lewis Stiles	*$2.00*
Wm. Statton	*$5.00*
Foster	*$5.00*
Peck	*$1.00*
Bierle	*$1.00*
Richards	*$2.00*

Memorandum

Clothing account
February – 1 jacket $5.00
March 11 – 1 pair pants $5.00

Addresses:
Thomas F. Richardson
McIntire Tavern
Grays Ferry Road
Philadelphia

[entry on last page]

Oney F. Sweet, born in Gibson county, Pennsylvania

Afterword

In the late 1700s and early to mid-1800s, a number of Sweet families began farming in the area known as Gibson Hollow, Susquehanna County, Pennsylvania. In addition to farming, Oney F. Sweet's family operated a store for travelers that grew into a stagecoach stop and hotel in the mid-1800s.

At age 13 or 14, Oney's parents sent him to Newark, New Jersey, to attend a "select school," where he obtained a better education than most of his peers. While there, he lived with his "benefactor," Robert F. Ballantine. (Ballantine, mentioned often in Oney's diaries, belonged to the family that founded and operated the Ballantine breweries in Newark and was related to the Sweets through the DeWitt family in Nyack, New York.)

When Oney completed his schooling, he went to work for a wholesale establishment in New York City. However, the Union blockade of southern ports put Oney's employer out of business. Oney returned to Pennsylvania and enlisted in the recently formed artillery brigade.

Nearly four years after the war ended, in March 1869, Oney followed his sweetheart, Helen Matilda Coon, to Hampton, Iowa. Three months later they married, and their seven children—four daughters and three sons—were born in Hampton.

The *History of Franklin and Cerro Gordo Counties, Iowa* (1883) says this about Oney F. Sweet:

Oney F. Sweet, circa 1869.

> *He has acquired an enviable reputation and has succeeded well in business, but is never happier than when within a circle of old soldier*

boys, recounting the thrilling incidents of his life in the army of the Potomac.

Oney became a partner of Josiah Phelps, who had opened the first grocery store in Hampton, and later Oney bought out Phelps. Oney also operated a candy store.

He applied for and apparently began receiving his veteran pension in 1886, although the record mistakenly states that he served with an Iowa regiment, rather than the 1st Pennsylvania Light Artillery. We don't how much money he received, but it couldn't have been much. At the end of the war, the government paid a maximum of $8 per month, and the amount received depended on the degree of the disability. In 1866, Congress raised the maximum to $20 per month and, in 1872, to $24 per month. (Costa, 1998)

Oney F. Sweet's Civil War pension record.

In 1888, Oney attended a Battery F reunion at the twenty-fifth anniversary ceremony of the Battle of Gettysburg, and later he attended the dedication of the Ricketts' Battery memorial, on September 17, 1889. Afterward, he penned his retrospective on the battle. He also wrote two articles published in *The National Tribune*, one about Ricketts' Battery at Gettysburg, the other about his time as an orderly for General Hancock.

**Ricketts' Battery F, July 3, 1888, on the 25th anniversary of the Battle of Gettysburg;
Oney F. Sweet above the X.** (Courtesy of William J. Ketchum)

His son, Oney Fred Sweet, contributed a poem to *The National Tribune* that described Decoration Day, initiated in 1868 to commemorate Civil War veterans and which is now known as Memorial Day. Oney marched in some of the annual parades. (See page 255.)

In 1912, at the age of 71, Oney moved to Southern California to be closer to his children. His war wound followed him, however, and the complications forced him to walk with a cane. When gan-

grene set in, he had to have the leg amputated below the knee.

In 1931, on the eve of his 90th birthday, the *Long Beach Press-Telegram* ran a story and quoted him as saying:

> *If you want to live long, smile and be happy. Just smile, smile, smile. I have seen all the depressions come and go. There have been hard times before. People weathered them somehow. Anyway, it won't help to be down in the mouth and give up.*

All of his children but one—Oney Fred, who worked as a feature writer for the *Chicago Tribune*—were living in California and on hand to help

Ricketts' Battery memorial at the Gettysburg Battlefield. (William J. Ketchum)

Oney F. Sweet's name on the Ricketts' Battery
memorial, Gettysburg Battlefield. (William J. Ketchum)
Right: Oney F. Sweet, circa 1912.

him celebrate his birthday: Drs. Robert Ballantine Sweet and Will S. Sweet, both of Long Beach, daughters Mrs. Marian Sweet Johnston, Riverside, Mrs. Edna Sweet Atkinson, Ventura, and Mrs. Caroline "Carrie" Sweet Wolfe and Mrs. Helen "Ellen" Sweet Palmer, both of Brawley.

Oney Foster Sweet died the following year in Long Beach at 90 years of age.

His eldest child, Marian, strived to preserve her father's letters and diaries, and wrote in a letter to her grandson, William J. Ketchum:

> *I sent [these letters] to my family to have them see the difference in the life of a service man then and now. . . . They told me much of what it meant for a boy of 19 to meet hardship. I was brought up on war stories, and I only wish I had those stories in written form now. . . . I appreciate the interest the present generation may have for them.*

Marian wrote a children's book, *The Snow House*, published by Dutton in 1940. She also wrote *Trumpets of the Morning*, a fictionalized account of the loneliness, anxiety, and difficulties she believed families endured during the Civil War. Three of her grandchildren—William J. Ketchum, Joan Ketchum Reamer, and James Grant—published her book posthumously in 2014. It serves as a companion to this book and may be purchased online.

Marian Julia Sweet, circa 1890.

William J. Ketchum has privately published several books, including *Snow House Island*, a memoir, and *Ulithi and Saipain, 1944-45*, the war-time diary of his father, William K. Ketchum.

Genealogical data

Oney Foster Sweet, b: December 13, 1841, Gibson, Susquehanna County, Pennsylvania; d: September 19, 1932, Long Beach, Los Angeles County, California; m: Helen Matilda Coon (1850-1921), June 13, 1869, Hampton, Iowa; parents: Almon[d] Sweet (1817-1900), Caroline Foster (1821-1909); children: Marian Julia Sweet (1872-1959, m: John E. Johnston, 30 Dec 1903), Edna Foster Sweet (1874-1950, m: Arthur W. Atkinson), Robert Ballantine Sweet (1876-1956), William Spencer Sweet (1878-1951), Oney Fred Sweet (7 Feb 1882-1965), Caroline "Carrie" Sweet (22 Oct 1883-21 Jul 1952, m: Abner Wolfe), Helen "Ellen" Louise Sweet (1886-1978, m: Palmer).

Appendix

Battery F
1st Pennsylvania Light Artillery
43rd Volunteers (14th Reserves)

Battery F formed on August 5, 1861, under the command of Capt. Ezra W. Matthews and Lieutenants Robert Bruce Ricketts, Elbridge McConkey, and Henry L. Godbald. In September, the battery marched to Washington, DC, to join General Banks' Division of the Army of the Potomac in the defense of the nation's capitol.

Pennsylvania historian Samuel P. Bates (1869) chronicled the early months of the section's service:

> On the 8th of October [1861], the battery was enlarged by the addition of two Parrott rifled, ten-pounder guns. . . . Soon afterwards Sergeant Charles B. Brockway was elected Second Lieutenant and placed in command of the detached section, and was sent to oppose the enemy making demonstrations at Hancock, Maryland. A slight skirmish ensued, in which the great accuracy of the rifled pieces was demonstrated, several [enemy] men and horses being killed and wounded by the first shell discharged.
>
> A few days later it was reported that the enemy were destroying the railroad in that vicinity, and Lieutenant Brockway was ordered to mask one of his pieces and open upon the party. The first shot struck the engine employed, and the second burst among the men, killing five and wounding twelve others.

The battery engaged in its first major action on December 20, 1861, where it had one gun disabled while attempting to destroy Dam No. 5 on the Upper Potomac, near Dranesville, Maryland.

Bates describes the battery's following engagements as:

Early in January, 1862, [Lieutenant] Ricketts, with his section, after a wearysome night march, joined General [Frederick W.] Lander, near Hancock, in time to participate in the engagement with [General Thomas J. "Stonewall"] Jackson in his attack upon the town, and in effecting his complete repulse. . . . Jackson's pieces were of smooth bore and short range, whereas Ricketts' section consisted of two rifled, ten-pounder, Parrott guns. He could therefore take position out of range of the enemy, and easily reach him with his missiles. Jackson was consequently forced to withdraw.

Until February, 1862, the guns were kept in motion singly and in sections between Edwards' Ferry and Hancock, occasionally engaging detachments of the enemy. On the 20th, the sections were united at Hagerstown, where new equipments were received, and the guns furnished by the State were exchanged for six regulation, three-inch, rifled guns, together with new carriages and Sibley tents. The morning report of the 1st of March showed its effective strength to be one hundred and nineteen officers and men, with one hundred and five horses.

That set the stage for rest of the war, which, other than when in winter quarters, required frequent moves, at times through cold rain and axle-deep mud—and traveling all night—to counter the movements of the Confederate forces, sometimes marching as much as 30 miles in a single day.

The battery—first known as Matthews' Battery, then Ricketts' Battery for most of the war, and finally Campbell's Battery in the final days of the war—participated in most of the major battles in Virginia, Maryland, and Pennsylvania, most notably Gettysburg.*

The battery also took part in the Grand Review held in Washington, DC, following the end of the war. From there, Battery F returned to Harrisburg, Pennsylvania, where it disbanded and the soldiers were mustered out on June 10, 1865.**

---

* Lt. John F. Campbell received a promotion to captain on April 17, 1865. (Miscellaneous Documents)

** See the footnote at the end of the Battery F Service Record.

Battery F Service Record, as detailed in *A Compendium of the War of the Rebellion* (Dyer, 1908):

Attached to:
- Banks' Division, Army of the Potomac, October, 1861, to March, 1862.
- 1st Division, Banks' 5th Army Corps and 1st Division, Dept. of the Shenandoah, to May, 1862.
- Artillery, 2nd Division, Dept. of the Rappahannock, to June, 1862.
- Artillery, 2nd Division, 3rd Corps, Army of Virginia, to September, 1862.
- Artillery, 2nd Division, 1st Army Corps, Army of the Potomac, to January, 1863.
- Artillery, 3rd Division, 1st Army Corps, to May, 1863.
- 3rd Volunteer Brigade, Artillery Reserve, Army of the Potomac, to July, 1863.
- Artillery Brigade, 2nd Army Corps, Army of the Potomac, to September, 1864.
- Artillery Reserve, Army of the Potomac, to June, 1865.

Service:
- Duty in the Defences of Washington till October, 1861, and on the Upper Potomac, between Edwards' Ferry and Hancock, Md., till February, 1862.
- Advance on Winchester, March 1-12, 1862.
- Reconnoissance toward Strasburg and action near Winchester, March 7.
- Ordered to join Abercrombie's Brigade, March 21, and moved to Warrenton Junction.
- Pursuit of Jackson up the Shenandoah Valley, March 24-April 27.
- Rappahannock Crossing, April 18.
- Pope's Campaign in Northern Virginia, August 1-September 2.
- Battle of Cedar Mountain, August 9.
- Fords of the Rappahannock, August 21-23.
- Thoroughfare Gap, August 28.
- Battles of Groveton, August 29.
- Second Battle of Bull Run (Manassas), August 30.
- Chantilly, September 1.

- Maryland Campaign, September 6-24.
- Battle of Antietam, Md., September 16-17.
- Duty at Sharpsburg, Md., till October 30.
- Movement to Falmouth, Va., October 30-November 19.
- Battle of Fredericksburg, December 12-15.
- "Mud March," January 20-24, 1863.
- At Falmouth and Belle Plain till April.
- Chancellorsville Campaign, April 27-May 6.
- Operations at Pollock's Mill Creek, April 29-May 2.
- Fitzhugh's Crossing, April 29-30.
- Chancellorsville, May 2-5.
- Gettysburg (Pa.) Campaign, June 11-July 24.
- Battle of Gettysburg, Pa., July 2-4.
- Advance to line of the Rapidan, September 13-17.
- Bristoe Campaign, October 9-22.
- Auburn and Bristoe, October 14.
- Advance to line of the Rappahannock, November 7-8.
- Mine Run Campaign, November 26-December 2.
- Demonstration on the Rapidan, February 6-7, 1864.
- Morton's Ford, February 6-7.
- Camp near Stevensburg, Va., till May.
- Rapidan Campaign, May 4-June 12.
- Battle of the Wilderness, May 5-7;
- Spotsylvania, May 8-12;
- Spotsylvania Court House, May 12-21.
- Assault on the Salient (Bloody Angle), May 12.
- North Anna River, May 23-26.
- Line of the Pamunkey, May 26-28.
- Totopotomoy, May 28-31.
- Cold Harbor, June 1-12.
- Before Petersburg, June 16-18.
- Siege of Petersburg, June 16, 1864, to April 2, 1865.
- Jerusalem Plank Road, June 21-22, 1864.
- Demonstration north of the James River at Deep Bottom, July 27-29.
- Deep Bottom, July 27-29.
- Demonstration north of the James at Deep Bottom, August 13-20.
- Strawberry Plains, August 14-18.
- Fall of Petersburg, April 2.

- Moved to Washington, D.C., May.
- Grand Review May 23.
- Mustered out July [10], 1865.**

Lost 1 Officer and 17 Enlisted men killed and 13 Enlisted men by disease. Total 31.

** Dyer's *Compendium* and the compiled military service record (Moodey, 1890) both state that the men were mustered out on June 9. However, according to Oney F. Sweet's diary entries for June 9-10, 1865, the proceeding was postponed due to errors in the paperwork, so he and his comrades were not actually mustered out until the following day, June 10, at 10 a.m.

Decoration Day

A poem written by Oney Fred Sweet, son of Civil War veteran Oney Foster Sweet, for The National Tribune and published on May 24, 1906.

Decoration Day.

There's the chirp of birds in the pinetree tops
    And there's morning dew in the grass.
The streets lined with those who've come
    To watch the procession pass.
There's the grand old Flag that floats ahead,
    There's children with flowers of May
There's daddy hobbling with the "boys"—
    'Tis Decoration Day.

No wonder that garden and field and wood
    Have given their fairest blooms;
No wonder the petals and leaves leap high
    Beside the soldiers' tombs.
No wonder the village band plays sweet
    As they wind along their way;
No wonder the skies are blue above—
    'Tis Decoration Day.

But there's sort of a look in daddy's face
    And the "boys" that go halting by,
As though their thoughts were drifting on
    To another earth and sky.
For their minds are back to the youthful time
    When they marched as boys away,
And they're pondering 'bout where they'll all be
    Next Decoration Day.

Memorial Day

On May 5, 1868, Major General John A. Logan, the head of the Grand Army of the Republic, an organization of Union veterans, declared Decoration Day as a time for the nation to honor the Civil War dead by decorating their graves with flowers, and that it should be observed on May 30. The first observance was held at Arlington National Cemetery and presided over by various Washington officials, including General and Mrs. Ulysses S. Grant.

By the end of the 19th century, communities throughout the country staged Decoration Day festivities. Following World War I, the day became known as Memorial Day in honor of those who had died in all U.S. wars. In 1971, Congress declared Memorial Day as a national holiday, which is now celebrated on the last Monday in May.

(U.S. Department of Veterans Affairs)

References

"12th Vermont Infantry, Knapsacks," Vermont in the Civil War, http://vermontcivilwar.org/units/12/knapsacks.php.

"Admiral Farragut's Operations at Mobile: The Capture of Fort Morgan," *The New York Times*, August 29, 1864, http://www.nytimes.com/1864/08/29/news/admiral-farragut-s-operations-mobile-capture-fort-morgan-grant-s-movements.html.

Armistead, Gene C., *Horses and Mules in the Civil War: A Complete History with a Roster of More Than 700 War Horses* (Jefferson: McFarland & Co., 2013), 3.

Artillery in the Civil War, in U.S. Army Ordnance Corps, http://www.goordnance.army.mil.

Atkinson, Norman, *Sir Joseph Whitworth 'The World's Best Mechanician'* (Gloucestershire, United Kingdom: Sutton Publishing Limited, 1996).

"Attack upon a Train at Catlett's Station by Moseby's Guerrillas," *The New York Times*, June 1, 1863, http://www.nytimes.com/1863/06/01/news/fight-virginia-attack-upon-train-catlett-s-station-moseby-s-guerrillas.html.

Bates, Samuel Penniman, *History of Pennsylvania Volunteers, 1861-5: Prepared in Compliance with Acts of the Legislature* (Harrisburg: B. Singerly, State Printer, 1869), 958-967, 999, http://catalog.hathitrust.org/Record/000454271.*

Bates, Samuel Penniman, *Martial Deeds of Pennsylvania* (Philadelphia: T.H. Davis & Co., 1875), 284, http://catalog.hathitrust.org/Record/009535515.

"Battery F muster roll," The Pennsylvania Reserve Volunteer Corps Historical Society (PRVCHS), http://www.pareserves.com/?q=node/2678.

---

* Bates states on page 961 that the Battle of Fredericksburg took place in September 1862; it actually took place in mid-December. On the same page, Colonel Charles S. Wainwright's name is spelled as "Wainright." On page 999, Oney F. Sweet's first name is spelled in the muster roll as "Only." Sweet's date of enlistment is given as "Jan. 1, 1864"; however, Sweet enlisted on Sept. 4, 1861, and reenlisted December 21, 1863. The muster-out date is given as June 9, 1865, but according to Sweet's diary entries for June 9-10, 1865, the proceeding was postponed due to errors in the paperwork, so he and his comrades were not mustered out until the following day, June 10, at 10 a.m.

"Battle of Antietam," Library of Congress, http://www.loc.gov/exhibits/lincoln/lincoln-as-commander-in-chief.html.

Bergeron, Arthur W., "John Randolph Chambliss, Jr." in *The Confederate General*, Volume 1, edited by William C. Davis and Julie Hoffman (Harrisburg, PA: National Historical Society, 1991).

"Bucktails," 42nd Pennsylvania Volunteer Infantry Regiment, 1st Pennsylvania Rifles, http://www.pabucktail.com/oldbuck.htm.

Cannan, John, *The Spotsylvania Campaign: May 7-21, 1864* (Cambridge: De Capo Press, 2007), 174, https://books.google.com/books?id=D_ZEMEIOZLYC.

"Captain Robert B. Ricketts, Battery F, 1st Pennsylvania Light Artillery," The Pennsylvania Reserve Volunteer Corps Historical Society, http://pareserves.com/?q=node/1813.

"Civil War By the Numbers," Public Broadcasting Service (PBS), http://www.pbs.org/wgbh/americanexperience/features/general-article/death-numbers/.

Civil War Soldiers and Sailors Database (Compiled Military Service Records), National Park Service, http://www.nps.gov/civilwar/soldiers-and-sailors-database.htm.

"Civil War Casualties: The Cost of War: Killed, Wounded, Captured, and Missing," Civil War Trust, http://www.civilwar.org/education/civil-war-casualties.html.

Compton, Lt. M.H., "The Post Exchange," *Co-operation*, Volume 5 (New York: Co-operative League of America, 1919), 69, https://books.google.com/books?id=_ppUAAAAYAAJ.

Costa, Dora L., The Evolution of Retirement: An American Economic History, 1880-1990 (Chicago: University of Chicago Press, 1998), 198-9, in National Bureau of Economic Research, http://www.nber.org/chapters/c6116.pdf.

Cowden, Joanna D., "The Politics of Dissent: Civil War Democrats in Connecticut," *The New England Quarterly*, Vol. 56, No. 4 (Dec. 1983), 538–55, http://www.jstor.org/discover/10.2307/365104?uid=3739560.

Crawford, Richard, The Civil War Songbook: Complete Original Sheet Music for 37 Songs (New York: Dover Publications, Inc., 1977).

Curry, W.L., ed., Four Years in the Saddle: History of the First Regiment, Ohio Volunteer Cavalry. War of the Rebellion, 1861-1865 (Columbus: Champlin Printing Company, 1898), 318, https://books.google.com/books?id=_UQ-AAAAYAAJ.

Collins English Dictionary (online edition), http://www.collinsdictionary.com.

Dyer, Frederick H., A Compendium of the War of the Rebellion, Volume I, (Des Moines: Dyer Publishing Company, 1908), 1573, https://archive.org/details/08697590.3359.emory.edu.*

"Emancipation Proclamation," National Archives, http://www.archives.gov/exhibits/featured_documents/emancipation_proclamation/.

"Fauquier County in the Civil War," Fauquier County, Va., http://www.fauquiercounty.gov/documents/departments/commdev/pdf/EditNoVa02.pdf.

Field, Ron, *Appomattox 1865: Lee's Last Campaign* (Newbury: Osprey Publishing, 2015), 77, https://books.google.com/books?id= ExS3BgAAQBAJ.

Foreman, T.E., "Civil War Soldiers Griped and Fought Much Like GI's of Today," Riverside *Press-Enterprise*, March 19, 1961, A-6.

Fox, William F., *Regimental Losses in the American Civil War, 1861-1865* (Albany: Albany Pub. Co., 1889), 68, https://archive.org/details/reglossescivilwar00foxwrich.

French, William H. Bvt. Major, Capt. 1st. Artillery, William F. Barry, Capt. 2nd. Artillery, Henry J. Hunt, Bt. Major, Capt. 2nd. Artillery, *Instruction for Field Artillery* (Philadelphia: J.B. Lippincott, 1860), 290, http://books.google.com/books/about/Instruction_for_Field_Artillery.html?id=sr6CHiD2TEsC.

"General Burnside's Second Attempt to Cross the Rappanahock," *The New York Times*, in *The Rebellion Record: A Diary of American Events, with Documents, Narratives Illustrative Incidents, Poetry, Etc.*, Volume 6, Doc. 110, ed. Frank Moore, (New York: G.P. Putnam, 1863), 396-400, https://books.google.com/books?id=3mwPAAAAYAAJ.

"General Jubal Anderson Early, 1816–1894, 'Lee's Bad Old Man,' " Jubal A. Early Preservation Trust, Inc., http://www.jubalearly.org/jubal.html

Gordon, John Steele, "How the Civil War United Our Money," Baron's January 19, 2013, http://online.barrons.com/articles/SB50001424052748703596604578235552788285428.

Grant, Ulysses S., *Personal Memoirs of U.S. Grant*, 2 vols. (New York: Charles L. Webster & Co., 1885-1886), II, 177-78, 344, http://www.gutenberg.org/ebooks/1068.

Guerin, T. M., *General Orders Affecting the Volunteer Force*, Volume 4, Adjutant General's Office, United States War Dept (Washington: Government Printing Office, 1865), 171, https://books.google.com/books?id=0sy4AAAAIAAJ.

---

* Oney F. Sweet's first name is spelled in the muster roll as "Orly."

"Hampton Roads Conference," *Encyclopædia Britannica* (online edition), http://www.britannica.com/EBchecked/topic/253803/Hampton-Roads-Conference.

Heaps, Willard, and Porter W. Heaps, *The Singing Sixties: The Spirit of the Civil War Days Drawn from the Music of the Times*. (Norman: University of Oklahoma Press, 1960), 133, 235-236.

Hess, Earl J., *In the Trenches at Petersburg: Field Fortifications and Confederate Defeat: Field Fortifications & Confederate Defeat* (Chapel Hill: University of North Carolina Press, 2009), 143, https://books.google.com/books?id=dI4MOLZnruAC.

History of Franklin and Cerro Gordo Counties, Iowa, (Cerro Gordo County: Union Publishing Company, 1883), 398-399, https://books.google.com/books?id=jklEAQAAMAAJ.

Hitchcock, Benjamin W., (New York: B. W. Hitchcock, 1868), 85, http://catalog.hathitrust.org/Record/009604645.

Holsinger, M. Paul, *War and American Popular Culture: A Historical Encyclopedia*. (Westport: Greenwood Press, 1999), 117-8, https://books.google.com/books?id=Oe4AOVHkJ9oC.

"Hooker Appointed Commander," Library of Congress, http://www.loc.gov/exhibits/lincoln/lincoln-as-commander-in-chief.html.

"How to spot a collodion positive," National Media Museum, Bradford, UK, http://blog.nationalmediamuseum.org.uk/2013/04/24/find-out-when-a-photo-was-taken-identify-collodion-positive-ambrotype/.

James, Edgar, *The Lives and Battles of the Champions of England: From the Year 1700 to the Present Time* (New York: Edgar James, 1879), 66, https://books.google.com/books?id=elICAAAAYAAJ

Johnson, Andrew, President of the United States, Proclamation 157 - Declaring that Peace, Order, Tranquility, and Civil Authority Now Exists in and Throughout the Whole of the United States of America, August 20, 1866, http://www.presidency.ucsb.edu/ws/?pid=71992.

Johnson, Robert Underwood ed., *Battles and Leaders of the Civil War*, Volume 2, Part 2 (New York: The Century co., 1888), 598, https://books.google.com/books?id=uD06AQAAMAAJ.

"Johnston's Surrender," *The New-York Times*, April 30, 1865, 1, http://www.nytimes.com/1865/04/30/news/johnston-s-surrender-return-general-grant-washington-his-notice-illegality.html.

Jordan, David M., *Winfield Scott Hancock: A Soldier's Life* (Bloomington: Indiana University Press, 1988), 169-171, https://books.google.com/books?id= ubSem4UEn9AC.

Keenan, Bethany, and Colby Blanchette, "Civil War: Northern Draft Riots" in Wentworth Institute of Technology (2012), http://blogs.wit.edu/hist-415/northern-draft-riots/.

LaFantasie, Glenn W., "Civil War Soldiers: Decimated by Disease," Military History Quarterly, Spring 2004, Vol. 16, No. 3, in HistoryNet, http://www.historynet.com/civil-war-soldiers.

Lee, Francis Bazley, Genealogical and Memorial History of the State of New Jersey (New Jersey: Lewis Historical Publishing Company, 1910) 1067, https://books.google.com/books?id=S5E-AAAAYAAJ.

"Lincoln Fires McClellan," Library of Congress, http://www.loc.gov/ exhibits/lincoln/lincoln-as-commander-in-chief.html.

Lord, Francis A., *They Fought For the Union* (New York: Bonanza Books, 1960), 4-7, 12-13, 63-64.

Luebke, P. "Kilpatrick-Dahlgren Raid," in Encyclopedia Virginia (online edition), Virginia Foundation for the Humanities, April 5, 2011, http://www.encyclopediavirginia.org/Kilpatrick-Dahlgren Raid.

Martin, James, "Civil War Conscription Laws," November 15, 2012, blog in Library of Congress, http://blogs.loc.gov/law/2012/11/civil-war-conscription-laws/.

McDowell, Irvin, Brigadier General, Report of, to Headquarters Department Northeastern Virginia, August 4, 1861, http://www.civil-war.net/ searchofficialrecords.asp?searchofficialrecords=McDowell_1st_Bull_Run.

McNeil, Keith, and Rusty McNeil. *Civil War Songbook with Historical Narration* (Riverside: WEM Records, 1999).

McPherson, J.M., *Battle Cry of Freedom: The Civil War Era* (New York: Oxford University Press, 1988), 445-447, http://books.google.com/books?id= GXfGuNAvm7AC.

"Memorial Day History," U.S. Department of Veterans Affairs, http://www.va.gov/opa/speceven/memday/history.asp.

Merriam-Webster Dictionary, http://www.merriam-webster.com.

"Minie Ball," in Smithsonian Institution, http://www.civilwar.si.edu/ weapons_minieball.html.

Miscellaneous Documents of the House of Representatives for the Second Session of the Fifty-third Congress, 1893-'94, in Forty Volumes Congressional Edition, Volume 3261(Washington: Government Printing Office, 1895), 660, https://books.google.com/books?id=pSxHAQAAIAAJ.

Mitchell, Wesley Clair, *A History of the Greenbacks: With Special Reference to the Economic Consequences of Their Issue, 1862-65* (Chicago: The University of Chicago Press. 1903), 44-81, https://archive.org/details/ahistorygreenba00mitcgoog.

Modern Pocket Hoyle, The (New York: Dick & Fitzgerald, 1868), 78-94.

Moodey, John Sheldon, et al., United States War Dept., *The War of the Rebellion: A Compilation of the Official Records of the Union and Confederate Armies* (Washington: Gov't. Printing Office, 1890), 229, 259, 285, 305-7, 319-20, 350-1, 354, 367, 507-8, 510-1, 531-2, 676-8, 855, 873, 877, 1357, http://ebooks.library.cornell.edu/m/moawar/waro_fulltext.html.

Moore, Frank, *Emancipation Proclamation: The Rebellion Record: A Diary of American Events*, Volume 6 (New York: Putnam, 1863) 207-8, https://books.google.com/books?id=3mwPAAAAYAAJ.

"Moseby's Guerrillas," *New York Times*, Nov. 28, 1863, http://www.nytimes.com/1863/11/28/news/moseby-s-guerrillas.html.

"Moseby's Guerrillas at Catlett's Station," *New York Times*, May 31, 1863, http://www.nytimes.com/1863/05/31/news/washington-moseby-s-guerrillas-catlett-s-station-destruction-railroad-train.html.

Pech, Harry Thurston and Selim Hobart Peabody, Charles Francis Richardson, *The International Cyclopædia: A Compendium of Human Knowledge*, Volume 4 (New York: Dodd, Mead, 1900), 630b, https://books.google.com/books?id=ZQUoAAAAYAAJ.

"Private Sloat, Urbane, Company K," The Pennsylvania Reserve Volunteer Corps Historical Society, http://www.pareserves.com/?q=node/1855.

Public Laws of the State of Rhode Island and Providence Plantations Passed at the General Assembly, 1861-3 (Providence: Alfred Anthony, 1868), 220, https://books.google.com/books?id=-X5CAQAAMAAJ.

Quarstein, John V., *A History of Ironclads: The Power of Iron Over Wood* (Mount Pleasant, SC: The History Press, 2006), 171-2.

"Review of the Armies; Propitious Weather and a Splendid Spectacle," *The New York Times*, May 24, 1865, http://www.nytimes.com/1865/05/24/news/review-armies-propitious-weather-splendid-spectacle-nearly-hundred-thousand.html.

Ricketts, James B., Brig. Gen., U.S. Army, Report to Headquarters Second Division, Third Corps, September 21, 1862, *The War of the Rebellion: A Compilation of the Official Records of the Union and Confederate Armies* (Washington: Gov't. Printing Office, 1890), 258-9, https://books.google.com/books?id=iJktAAAAIAAJ.

Ricketts, Robert B., Captain, Battery F, 1st Pennsylvania Light Artillery, August 30, 1863, *Congressional Serial Set* (Washington: U.S. Government Printing Office, 1891), 894-5, https://books.google.com/books?id= wRAZAAAAYAAJ.

"Savannah Ours, Sherman's Christmas Present, " *The New York Times*, December 26, 1864, 1.

Sears, Stephen W., *Chancellorsville* (New York: Houghton Mifflin, 1996), 440.

Shankman, Arnold, "Draft Resistance in Civil War Pennsylvania," *The Pennsylvania Magazine of History and Biography*, Vol. 101, No. 2 (April, 1977), 190-204, published by The Historical Society of Pennsylvania, http://www.jstor.org/stable/10.2307/i20091143.

Sherburne, Lt. John H. Jr., *Battery A: Field Artillery, M. V. M.: 1895-1905*, (Boston: Published by the Battery by Subscription, 1908), 21-22, https://books.google.com/books?id=8oHUEhuYdwgC.

Sheridan, General Philip Henry, *The* Memoirs of General *P. H.* Sheridan, (New York: Chester L. Webster & Co., 1988), Vol. II, Part 5, Chap. VII, http://www.gutenberg.org/files/4362/4362-h/4362-h.htm.

"Shrapnel, Semantics and Such," *Combat Forces Journal*, March 1952.

Sweet, Oney Foster, "With Hancock During and After a Battle," *The National Tribune*, October 3, 1907, 6.

Sweet, Oney Foster, "Ricketts' Battery: It Was One of Those at Gettysburg Which Came to Stay," *The National Tribune*, April 29, 1909, 7.

Sweet, Oney Fred, "Decoration Day," *The National Tribune*, May 24, 1906, 6.

Terry, Mark R., "The Federal Forts at Petersburg," November 15, 2008, in *The Siege of Petersburg*, http://www.petersburgsiege.org/fedforts.htm.

"The Fall of Atlanta; The Official Report of Maj.Gen. Sherman," War Department dispatch dated Sept. 4, 1864, *The New York Times*, September 5, 1864, 1.

Towne, Stephen E.. "Rising Up Against the Civil War," September 10, 2013, in *The New York Times* Opinionator blog, http://opinionator.blogs. nytimes.com/2013/09/10/rising-up-against-the-civil-war/.

"Veteran About to Celebrate 90th Birthday," *Long Beach Press-Telegram*, Dec. 12, 1931.

Walker, Francis Amasa, *History of the Second Army Corps in the Army of the Potomac* (New York: C. Scribner's Sons, 1886), 664, https://books.google.com/books?id=59BaLZv7JUQC.

Weber, Jennifer L., *Copperheads: The Rise and Fall of Lincoln's Opponents in the North* (New York: Oxford University Press, 2006), 3, http://books.google.com/books?id=lsdKFM2aoLQC.

Wert, Jeffry D. "Girardey, Victor Jean Baptiste" in *Historical Times Illustrated History of the Civil War*, edited by Patricia L. Faust (New York: Harper & Row, 1986).

"Who Killed General John Sedgwick?"in Sedgwick Genealogy North America, October 20, 2013, http://www.sedgwick.org/na/families/robert1613/B/2/9/2/powell-benjaminm1841.html.

Wolf, Hazel C., ed., "Campaigning with the First Minnesota: A Civil War Diary," Minnesota History, Vol. 25, No. 3, 225, http://collections.mnhs.org/MNHistoryMagazine/articles/25/v25i03p224-257.pdf.

Wright, John D., *The Routledge Encyclopedia of Civil War Era Biographies*, (New York: Routledge, 2013), 258-9, https://books.google.com/books?id=V_wpKWzSmvUC.

Reading & Resources

"1st Pennsylvania Light Artillery, 43rd Volunteers," PA-Roots, http://www.pa-roots.com/pacw/artillery/1startillery/1stltartillary.html.

Armistead, Gene C., "California's Confederate Militia: The Los Angeles Mounted Rifles," *Confederate Veteran*, Volume 3 (1997).

Armistead, Gene C., *Horses and Mules in the Civil War: A Complete History with a Roster of More Than 700 War Horses* (Jefferson: McFarland & Co., 2013).

Artillery Reserve, Inc., http://www.artilleryreserve.org.

Bates, Samuel Penniman, *The Battle of Chancellorsville* (Meadville: Ron R. Van Sickle Military Books, 1882), http://books.google.com/books?id=oWE9AQAAMAAJ.

Bates, Samuel Penniman, *The Battle of Gettysburg* (Philadelphia: T. H. Davis & Company, 1875), http://books.google.com/books?id=rPOCXCUyIrwC.

Bates, Samuel Penniman, *History of Pennsylvania Volunteers, 1861-5: Prepared In Compliance With Acts of the Legislature* (Harrisburg: B. Singerly, State Printer, 1869-71), http://catalog.hathitrust.org/Record/000454271.

Bates, Samuel Penniman, *Martial Deeds of Pennsylvania* (Philadelphia: T.H. Davis & Company, 1876), https://books.google.com/books?id=ro4dAQAAMAAJ.

"Battle of Fredericksburg," National Park Service, http://www.nps.gov/frsp/fredhist.htm.

Civil War Reenactors, http://www.cwreenactors.com.

Civil War Trust: Saving America's Civil War Battlefields, http://www.civilwar.org.

Civil War Soldiers and Sailors Database, National Park Service; http://www.nps.gov/civilwar/soldiers-and-sailors-database.htm.

Confederate Veteran Magazine, http://confederateveteran.blogspot.com.

Davis, William C., *Jefferson Davis: The Man and His Hour* (Louisiana State University Press, 1996).

Garcia, Pedro, *Port Hudson: Last Bastion on the Mississippi*, (Paragon Agency, 2005).

Garcia, Pedro, *Raising the Northern Blockade: Submarine Warfare in the Civil War*, (Paragon Agency, 2009).

Gottfried, Bradley M., *The Artillery of Gettysburg* (Nashville: Cumberland House Publishing, 2008).

National Archives, Archives Library Information Center, Reference Books on the Civil War, http://www.archives.gov/research/alic/reference/military/civil-war-reference-books.html.

Nevins, Allan, ed., *A Diary of Battle: the Personal Journals of Colonel Charles S. Wainwright, 1861-1865*, (New York: Harcourt, Brace & World, 1962).

Pennsylvania Civil War Volunteer Soldiers, Forty-third Regiment, First Artillery, Battery F; http://www.pacivilwar.com/cwpa43f.html.

Pennsylvania Reserve Volunteer Corps Historical Society, http://www.pareserves.com.

"Regimental Index," Civil War Archive, http://www.civilwararchive.com/regim.htm.

Sauers, Richard A., and Peter Tomasak, *Ricketts' Battery: A History of Battery F, 1st Pennsylvania Light Artillery* (Luzerne: Luzerne National Bank, 2001).

"Susquehanna County 1858 Landowner Map," Warrantee Maps from Pennsylvania Archives, http://ancestortracks.com/ Susquehanna_Resources.html.

Susquehanna County (Pennsylvania) 1872—Historic Map Works, http://www.historicmapworks.com/Atlas/US/7083/Susquehanna+County+1872/.

Susquehanna County, Pennsylvania, ancestry, family history genealogy, https://familysearch.org/learn/wiki/en/Susquehanna_County,_Pennsylvania.

Tucker, Spencer C., *American Civil War: The Definitive Encyclopedia and Document Collection* [6 volumes] (Santa Barbara: ABC-CLIO, 2013), https://books.google.com/books?id=9dvYAQAAQBAJ.

U.S. Civil War in Government Documents, University of Missouri Libraries, http://libraryguides.missouri.edu/civilwargov.

Index

C

Acknowledgements

Oney F. Sweet great-grandchildren William J. Ketchum, Joan Ketchum Reamer, and James Grant, for their contributions, encouragement, and support, without which this book would not have been possible.

Marian Julia Sweet Johnston (1872-1959) for initiating the process of preserving and reproducing the letters and diaries for her children and grandchildren.

George Olney Sweet (1912-2010) for completing his aunt's project.

Gene Armistead, author and Civil War buff, for his kind words, advice, and encouragement.

August Marchetti & Justin Sanders, The Pennsylvania Reserve Volunteer Corps Historical Society, for their support, contributions, and providing a great resource.

Colonel Rick Dennis, Civil War reenactor, Chief of Artillery, Artillery Reserve Brigade, for his support and contributions.

Pedro Garcia, author and Civil War buff, for pointing me toward additional historical resources.

The La Jolla Writers' Group, whose members provided insightful feedback and for suggesting the title for this book—Kathy Foley, Lynn Gahman, Mike Irbi, Pennie James, Walter Karshat, Laurie Richards, and Jane Williams.

Tim Brittain for turning the cover into a work of art and his eternal patience with my fussing over miniscule details.

The Library of Congress for digitizing historical photographs and publishing historical information online, and the many academic institutions that have made historical documents available online.

Google, for its lightning-fast search tool and for digitizing out-of-print books and historical records, now accessible online.

My loving wife, Janis Cadwallader, for putting up with my publication of yet another book.

Other Books by Wigeon Publishing

Beyond the Spotlight: On the Road With Phyllis Diller, Robin Skone-Palmer

Dare I Call It Murder?: A Memoir of Violent Loss, Larry M. Edwards

Home From The Banks, poems from Arthur William Raybold

Murder Survivor's Handbook: Real-Life Stories, Tips & Resources, Connie Saindon

Coming from Wigeon

The Journey: Learning to Live with Violent Death, Connie Saindon (2015)

The Greatest Cattle Drive: California to Oregon, 1837 — a dramatization of the diary of Philip L. Edwards (2016)

www.WigeonPublishing.com